SRI Internet Information Series

Franklin F. Kuo, Series Editor

INTERNET:

GETTING STARTED

Edited by

April Marine
Susan Kirkpatrick
Vivian Neou
Carol Ward

D1088798

Englewood Cliffs, New Jersey 07632

Library of Congress Cataloging-in-Publication Data

Acquisitions Editor: Mary Franz
Buyer: Mary McCartney
Cover Design: Bruce Kenselaar
Editorial/production Supervision: Lisa Iarkowski

ISBN   0-13-289596-X

Prentice-Hall International (UK) Limited, London
Prentice-Hall of Australia Pty. Limited, Sydney
Prentice-Hall of Canada, Inc., Toronto
Prentice-Hall Hispanoamericana S.A., Mexico
Prentice-Hall of India Private Limited, New Delhi
Prentice-Hall of Japan, Inc., Tokyo
Simon & Schuster Asia Pte. Ltd., Singapore
Editora Prentice-Hall do Brasil, Ltd., Rio de Janeiro
SRI Internet Information Series
Franklin F. Kuo, Series Editor

Updated 1993 Edition

Table of Contents

Chapter 1

Introduction to the Internet

Chapter 2

How to Join the Internet

Chapter 7   *139*

**The Internet—
More Information**

Chapter 9   *211*

Applications

BIBLIOGRAPHY AND REFERENCES

LIST OF FIGURES

LIST OF TABLES

THE INTERNET INFORMATION SERIES

Electronic networks are a modern phenomenon; prior to the 19th century nothing existed that could even approximate the world wide networks which seem so commonplace today. Telephone and fax services are now so expected, even banal, that few can imagine a world without them. The collection of computer networks known as the Internet, which has developed in the last twenty-five years, has not yet achieved that level of ubiquity, but it is rapidly approaching it.

An internet, loosely defined, is an interconnection of two or more networks. When we refer to *The Internet* in this series we refer to a specific collaboration of networks that allows users at disparate, heterogeneous computer networks to communicate with each other across organizational and geographical boundaries.

According to Dr. Vinton Cerf, the President of the Internet Society,

The Internet is a global network of networks linked by means of the TCP/IP and other protocols. The system incorporates thousands of networks, hundreds of thousands of computers, and millions of users in several dozen countries of the world. It is a grand collaboration involving private nets, public nets, and government and industry sponsored nets whose operators cooperate to maintain the infrastructure.

The Internet system is now poised for a rapid period of expansion during and beyond the final decade of the 20th Century. As networking, personal computing, workstations, mobile communication, and distributed computing become more widespread and as information in digital form becomes a norm, the utility of systems like the Internet will rise dramatically.

The Internet is a dynamic system; its technology and protocol base are undergoing continuous change. A large community of network designers, users, and implementors are contributing to the knowledge-base of the Internet. Growth in network usage occurs so quickly as to be almost impossible to quantify, but indications are that usage has grown by at least 2000 percent just since the beginning of this decade. The users of more than a million host machines now have some sort of access to interconnected electronic networks. For them, computer use no longer stops with their machine's capabilities or even with their organization's internal resources; their horizon is a vast, interconnected electronic world.

One of the biggest surprises to the creators of computer-based electronic networks has been the extent to which their creations have been used to connect people to people. Many networks were originally built to give people access to machine-based resources unavailable to them at their local sites, but increasingly networks have been used for access to information and human resources. Powerful mechanisms for enabling computers to share resources have become even more powerful methods for the users of those machines to share insights.

The books in SRI International's *Internet Information Series* are intended as reference sources for users, implementors, designers, and students of the Internet and the protocols it uses. The *Internet Information Series* is meant to be a guide both to understanding how to use certain networks for particular purposes and to understanding what our world will be like when these new resources have become as commonplace as the telephone is now.

OVERVIEW

Many millions of people all over the world use the Internet every day. Anybody can become a part of it—from the hobbyist with a PC at home, to a state-of-the-art super-computer center at a university, to a multinational corporation with offices around the globe. This book tells you how to do it.

What is this book about?

Internet: Getting Started tells you what the Internet is, what access choices you have, how much it typically costs to join, and who you can call to get connected.

The book provides the background material that will help you understand the new world of the Internet. Topics such as domain naming, IP addressing, and network protocols are introduced so that you have the basic foundation that will enable you to start working now and to learn more when you're ready.

Plus, we introduce Internet resources and applications. Learn how to send electronic mail, transfer files, and log on to remote databases. Find out how to discover the wealth of information the Internet offers!

Who should read this book?

If you're a local area network administrator and one day the boss comes into your office and says, "You're in charge of getting us hooked up to the Internet," you should read this book.

If you used to have Internet access at work or at school, but don't have it now, and miss it, and have been wondering if maybe you could hook up that computer you have at home, you should read this book.

If you've got an office in Virginia and one in San Francisco and one in Tokyo and a couple in between and have been wondering about ways to get all these people working together, you should read this book.

If you find yourself in possession of an account on the Internet, but haven't a clue as to what that means or how to use it, you should read this book.

If you're a sometime user of the Internet, but suspect you haven't even begun to tap its full potential, you should read this book.

If you've never heard of the Internet, you should definitely read this book because it's the best place to Get Started!

An idea about the contents

The first part of the book concentrates on giving you details about what you need to do to gain Internet access. Sections in this part of the book:

➤ Define the Internet.

➤ Discuss types of network access.

➤ Provide an overview of the steps to initiate network access.

➤ Discuss the costs of connecting.

➤ List extensive information regarding service providers, including both commercial and research providers in the U.S. and providers outside of the U.S.

➤ Present the NSFNET backbone Acceptable Use Policy.

The latter half of the book introduces the Internet itself. This part is aimed at explaining the Internet and its concepts to people who have only a vague idea of what it all is. These chapters help people take their first steps in the Internet world.

Sections in this part of the book discuss such general topics as:

➤ Internet "concepts", such as RFCs, Protocols, Internet Protocol (IP) Addressing, the Domain Name System, and network security.

➤ Internet applications, such as electronic mail, file transfer, and remote login.

➤ Internet organizations, both national and international.

➤ Resources available on the Internet and how to find more information.

A set of appendices contains more extensive information on certain topics. The first appendix presents a list of acronyms used in this document.

Help us keep current

The Internet is such a dynamic environment that it is really impossible to capture it completely in any one place, and this book is no exception. Not only will some information noted here become out of date soon, but new information will appear the minute the book arrives in bookstores. Recognizing this fact of life, we provide here our contact information so that helpful readers can forward us corrections and additions to the book, which we would greatly appreciate!

SRI International
Network Information Systems Center
333 Ravenswood Avenue, Room EJ290
Menlo Park, CA 94015
+1 415 859 6387
+1 415 859 3695
FAX: +1 415 859 6028
nisc@nisc.sri.com

ACKNOWLEDGEMENTS

SRI would like to extend our thanks to a great number of people who provided us with information included in this book. In addition to the many people we explicitly note in the next paragraphs, we would like to acknowledge our debt to those who wrote information provided online for public file transfer. SRI gained a lot of information from such files and, although we cite the files in the text where appropriate, often the writers of such information remain anonymous, their efforts becoming part of the tradition of Internet cooperation and information sharing. We salute both these people and that Internet tradition.

In addition, however, there are numerous people to thank specifically, people who responded to our queries, who pointed us to information, who wrote text we included in the book, and who read our drafts and provided valuable feedback.

We would especially like to thank our readers: Ole J. Jacobsen, Editor and Publisher of *ConneXions—The*

Interoperability Report, and John C. Klensin, PhD., Principal Research Scientist, Department of Architecture, Massachusetts Institute of Technology. To them goes the credit of immensely improving the quality of this document. Of course, any weaknesses remaining rest solely on the shoulders of the authors.

Tremendous thanks are also offered to our many information contributors, those who kindly took the time to enlighten us.

George Abe (Infolan)
Jorge Marcelo Amodio (Argentina)
Farhad Anklesaria (Gopher)
Susie Arnold (CERFnet)
Alessandro Berni (Italy)
Borka Jerman-Blazic (YUNAC)
Antonio Blasco Bonito (Italy)
Laura Breeden (FARNET)
Corinne Carroll (NNSC)
Vint Cerf (Internet Society)
Robert Collet (Sprint)
Yannis Corovesis (ARIADNE)
Stephen Coya (IETF Exec Dir)
John Curran (NEARnet)
Bob Day (JANET/JIPS)
Peter Kokosky Deforchaux (SURFnet)
Esra Delen (TUVAKA)
John Demco (CA*net)
Peter Deutsch (Bunyip Information Systems)
Dominique Dumas (EARN-France)
Susan Eldred (ANS)
Alan Emtage (Bunyip Information Systems)
Jill Foster (RARE WG3)
Donnalyn Frey (UUNET Technologies, Inc.)
Peter Flynn (HEANET)
Andrea Galleni (USENIX)

Geoff Goodfellow (Anterior Technology)
Nadine Grange (EARN)
Andy Green (RISCnet)
Jack Hahn (SURAnet)
Anders Halldin (TIPnet)
Geoff Huston (Australia)
Alan Jay (CONNECT)
Daniel Kalchev (Bulgaria)
Daniel Karrenburg (RIPE NCC)
Sam Lanfranco (Bolivia)
Thomas Lenggenhager (SWITCH)
Gary Malkin (Xylogics)
Balazs Martos (Hungary)
Owen Scott Medd (MSen)
Jun Murai (Japan)
Sam Neely (CompuServe)
Torben Nielsen (PACCOM)
Seppo Noppari (DataNet)
Hank Nussbacher (Israel)
Richard Nuttall (PIPEX)
Petri Ojala (FUNET)
Marius Olafsson (ISnet)
Teresa Ortega (Nicaragua)
Florin Paunescu (Romania)
Allison Pihl (JvNCnet)
Daniel Pimienta (REDID)
Tim Pozar (FidoNet)
John Quarterman (Matrix)
Annie Renard (Fnet)

Joyce Reynolds (ISI)
Alexis Rosen (Panix)
Charlie Rosenberg (PeaceNet/IGC)
Pavel Rosendorf (Czechoslovakia)
Diana Scotti (ANS)
Vic Shaw (South Africa)
Eugene Siciunas (CA*net)
Patricia Smith (Merit)
Jan P. Sorensen (DENet)
Art St. George (University of New Mexico)
Milan Sterba (Eastern Europe)
Bernhard Stockman (NORDUnet)
Marianne Swanson (NIST)
Jerry Sweet (Anterior Technology)
Igor Sviridov (Ukraine)
Guy de Teramond (Costa Rica)
Ing. Hugo E. Garcia Torres (Mexico)
Knut L. Vik (UNINETT)
Ruediger Volk (DIGI)
Dimitry (Dima) Volodin (Russia)
Hans Wallberg (SUNET)
Martin Wilhelm (DFN)
Ants Work (Baltic countries)
Lui Zi-Di (TANet)

And from SRI:
Jose J. Garcia-Luna
Franklin Kuo
Edward T. L. Hardie
Ruth Lang
Mark Lottor
Chan Wilson
Angela Jones

1

INTRODUCTION TO THE INTERNET

This chapter provides a general introduction to what the Internet is and what it is not. For a more detailed discussion of the Internet and its architecture, history, and growth, please see Chapter 7. The purpose of this brief chapter is to give you the basic knowledge that will be helpful before you contact a network service provider with the goal of initiating Internet access. The first steps to joining the Internet are described in Chapter 2.

1.1. What Is the Internet?

 The packet-switched network that is the focus of this book is the network of networks called the Internet. The Internet is a unique collection of networks, mainly in the U.S., but also throughout the world, most of which are built using the Transmission Control Protocol/Internet Protocol (TCP/IP) protocol suite and all of which share a common name and address space. What does that mean? Basically, that means that the computers on the Internet use compatible communications standards and share the ability to contact each other and exchange data. Users of the Internet communicate mainly via electronic mail (e-mail), via Telnet, a process that allows them to login to a remote host, and via implementations of the File Transfer Protocol (FTP), a protocol that allows them to transfer information on a remote host to their local site.

Currently, there are more than 100 countries that have some access to the Internet, at least 39,000 networks assigned unique IP network numbers, more than one million hosts known to the domain name system, and at least 5,000,000 users worldwide.[1]

The Internet exists to facilitate the sharing of resources among participating organizations, which include government agencies, educational institutions, and private corporations; to promote collaboration among researchers; and to provide a testbed for new developments in networking.

Today the Internet includes research sites, such as universities and research laboratories; government sites, such as the Environmental Protection Agency and the U.S. Geological Survey; military sites, such as naval air stations and the U.S. Army Corps of Engineers; commercial sites, such as Xerox, Citibank, and Walt Disney Imagineering; hospitals, libraries, schools; and individuals like you!

1.2. Who Is in Charge of the Internet?

 No one is in charge of the Internet. The Internet is a cooperating group of independently administered networks. Each component network on the Internet has its own administrative body, its own policies, and its own procedures

---

[1] Numbers were taken respectively from Landwebber's *International Connectivity* file (see Appendix VIII); the Internet Monthly Report (see Section 12.3); SRI's October 1992 Internet Domain (ZONE) Survey [31]; and an assumption of an average of 5 users per host.

and rules. There is no central, overseeing authority for the whole of the Internet.

However, certain government agencies have traditionally been prominent in setting policy that is followed throughout the Internet. Today important policy decisions come from the National Science Foundation (NSF), administrator of the National Science Foundation Network (NSFNET).

Although government agencies have traditionally controlled the Internet and still have enormous influence, today there is a large and growing "private" or "commercial" component of the Internet. This component is spearheaded by organizations whose common goal is to establish a part of the Internet that is open to everyone and supports a wider range of traffic, not traffic dedicated only to the support of research or education. This component particularly would like to see the Internet available to meet the full span of everyday business needs.

In addition to influential government agencies, a strong, mostly voluntary, coalition of technically knowledgeable individuals guide the development of the Internet. Innovations that upgrade the technical quality of the Internet are usually worked out cooperatively by the technical community working together under the auspices of a group called the Internet Architecture Board (IAB). The IAB has recently been included as part of the structure of the Internet Society (ISOC) (at which time the IAB changed its name from the Internet Activities Board). There is a hierarchy of Task Forces, Areas, and Working Groups under the IAB that address technical problems and develop solutions. Eventually, solutions are agreed upon by the Internet community and the IAB recommends they be implemented. In this way, new additions to the TCP/IP suite of protocol standards are developed, tested, recommended, and implemented. Implementation of such new

standards, however, depends on the cooperation and resources of each Internet site. There is no mechanism for
requiring a site to implement a new standard. The IAB
and its main task forces are discussed further in Section
10.3.1.

1.3. What Is Part of the Internet?

 It is often confusing trying to distinguish so-called "Internet
networks" from other networks accessible to the Internet
via electronic mail.

Why does it matter if a site is on the Internet or not? If you
just want to send an electronic mail (e-mail) message, it
probably doesn't matter to you. However, if you wish to
search a database, transfer a file, or use a remote application, it may matter a great deal. Doing all of these things
and more is possible on the Internet because Internet computers (or "hosts") accommodate a set of protocols specifically designed to allow resource sharing across networks. Section 8.3 discusses the Transmission Control Protocol and Internet Protocol (TCP/IP) family of protocols
further, along with other networking protocols.

One generally agreed upon test of whether a site is an
Internet site or not is whether it has "IP connectivity." In
fact, you might hear the term "the IP Internet" to refer to
hosts reachable in these ways.

One way of testing IP connectivity is to "ping" the host.
Ping is a program that uses a required feature of the
Internet Control Message Protocol (ICMP) to elicit a response from a specified host or gateway. If you ping a
host and it responds, it is on the Internet.

Another common test is to see if a host will open a *Telnet*
connection. Some Internet hosts do not implement the
Telnet Protocol, however, so if this test fails, you cannot

necessarily conclude that the host is not part of the Internet. A Telnet connection allows you to connect to a remote host. That is, given site *A* that is on the Internet, can site *B* Telnet to it? If so, then site *B* is also on the Internet. It is quite easy to get people to agree on several possible sites *A* to begin such an experiment. While a site *B* may implement Telnet, Telnet implementations usually require you to log in once you have made a connection to a remote host. If you do not have an account on the host, disconnect as soon as possible. Hosts do not always welcome random Telnet connections!

1.4. What Is Not Part of the Internet?

 For the purposes of this document, we agree with the IP connectivity criterion discussed in the last section as the test of what is and is not part of the Internet. By this test, then, what is considered *not* part of the Internet?

The Internet does not include:

> ➤ networks, even very large ones, that do use the TCP/IP protocols, but do not have a connection to the Internet that allows IP connectivity.

> ➤ sites that are accessible only via e-mail.

> ➤ networks built on suites of protocols other than TCP/IP if all they provide is limited access (such as e-mail) to and from the Internet.

For example, there are major wide area networks, such as BITNET, that allow only e-mail interaction with the Internet and are therefore not considered part of the Internet. Universal mail delivery is possible because of mail gateways that serve as "translators" between the different network protocols.

This distinction of Internet vs. non-Internet sites is made only for the purposes of definition, however. We recog–

nize that for many in search of access to the Internet, e-mail connectivity may be totally satisfactory. Therefore, Chapter 4 includes many references to dialup e-mail access providers, and Chapter 2 includes such access in its discussion.

1.5. Some Major Networks

 This section provides brief descriptions of some of the major Internet and non-Internet networks. All the non-Internet networks discussed have electronic mail access to the Internet. These descriptions are included to provide some idea of the types of networks that exist, to illustrate the diversity of the networking environment, and to clarify some references you are likely to hear and wonder about. Some of the information in the following descriptions was taken from *!%@:: A Directory of Electronic Mail Addressing and Networks* by Donnalyn Frey and Rick Adams [1], and *The Matrix* by John Quarterman [2].

1.5.1. ARPANET

The ARPANET does not exist any more, but we include its description because you will sometimes hear the term ARPANET used interchangeably with the term Internet. The ARPANET was the predecessor of today's Internet.

The ARPANET was the first packet-switched network to connect heterogeneous computers. That is, computers of different types could exchange information for the first time because of the network protocols developed for the ARPANET. There is more information about the ARPANET in Chapter 7. The ARPANET was not initially an Internet because it connected hosts rather than networks. The ARPANET underwent many changes as it reflected developments in networking and, eventually, in inter-networking. In 1984, the ARPANET was split into two networks: the ARPANET for research oriented activities, and the Defense Data Network (DDN) for military operational activities. The DDN still exists as one of the Internet networks; its MILNET network provides unclassified operational support to military users. The ARPANET itself was phased out in 1990 in favor of the more advanced NSFNET backbone.

1.5.2. NSFNET

The National Science Foundation (NSF) sponsors the main research and education backbone of the Internet today. This network is called the NSFNET. The history of the Internet is discussed is more depth in Section 7.1, but it may help some readers now to know that the NSFNET is probably the most direct descendant of the original ARPANET in terms of its research mission.

Some people today think of the Internet as equivalent to the NSFNET Internet. The NSFNET is certainly a very major component of the Internet, so we will introduce it here.

The NSFNET is a hierarchical network of networks. At the highest level is the backbone. At first, the NSFNET backbone connected supercomputer centers, but the NSFNET evolved to interconnect a group of networks originally referred to as "regional" networks because each was focused on serving a different area of the U.S. Eventually the term "regional" became misleading as the missions of several of these networks became either broader or narrower than that of connecting sites within a geographic area; therefore, today, the networks at this level are commonly called "mid-level" networks. Many regions of the U.S. share more than one mid-level network. At the bottom of the hierarchy are the many campus networks. Currently most of these represent colleges and universities; however, there is a new emphasis on connecting K-12 grade schools in the U.S. Many commercial companies are also connected to the Internet via NSFNET mid-level networks and would be considered on the same hierarchical level as the campus networks.

1.5.3. MILNET

The MILNET was established as a separate network in 1984 when it was partitioned off of the ARPANET. This network is supported by the Defense Information Systems Agency (DISA) of the Department of Defense. The MILNET is the unclassified component of the Defense Data Network (DDN). There are currently six gateways, called "mailbridges," that link the MILNET with the NSFNET/Internet. When the MILNET and the ARPANET split, the Network Information Center became the DDN Network Information Center. The MILNET was important to the rest of the Internet because the DDN NIC formerly performed many central Internet functions, such as administering the root domain of the Domain Name System and registering IP addresses.

1.5.4. BITNET

BITNET is a worldwide network; a user can send mail to another user across the world just as easily as sending a message to a colleague down the hall. However, some parts of it are referred to by different names, which reflect administrative differences rather than technological ones. In Canada, the network using the NJE protocols and interconnected with BITNET is called NetNorth. In Europe, it is called the European Academic Research Network (EARN). BITNET supports mail, mailing lists, and a type of file transfer. It provides the LISTSERV mailing list function. It does not support remote login or general file transfer. It is administered in the U.S. by the Corporation for Research and Education Networking (CREN).

Information about the BITNET Information Center (BITNIC) can be found in Section 10.5.5. Information about EARN can be found in Section 6.1.1.2.

1.5.5. USENET

U.S.ENET is a worldwide network that provides the news broadcast service, which is rather like informational bulletin boards. U.S.ENET uses the UUCP (UNIX to UNIX Copy Program) protocol and the NNTP (Network News Transport Protocol). The UUCP protocol was developed for UNIX computers, but most other types of computers can access the services via special software packages. There is no central administrative organization for U.S.ENET; normally sites wishing to join must find and attach to a site already connected. However, several service providers provide access to U.S.ENET news.

1.5.6. NASA Science Internet

The NASA Science Internet (NSI) combines the Space Physics Analysis Network (SPAN) with the NASA Science Network (NSN), and other NASA networks, into one worldwide internet. The SPAN portion of NSI was built using the DECnet protocols, while the NSN component was supported by TCP/IP. This is a very large internet which has connections to several NSFNET mid-level networks.

1.5.7. ESnet

ESnet is the Energy Sciences Network. It is a U.S. Department of Energy network with access to the Internet. The ESnet backbone was designed to support the High Energy Physics Network (HEPnet) and the Magnetic Fusion Energy Network (MFEnet), among other efforts. HEPnet has an extensive European component and was one of the first pan-European networks. The use of these networks is restricted to projects supported by DoE, but they are included here because, due to their size, you may hear references to them.

1.5.8. FidoNet

FidoNet is a network connecting personal computers. It is a cooperative, worldwide network administered by volunteers. FidoNet is open to anyone able to meet the technical requirements, but like other networks, also requires that users adhere to network etiquette and usage policies.

FidoNet does not use TCP/IP protocols, but relies on a special dialup protocol. Hosts are arranged in a hierarchical structure of zones, nets, nodes, and points, each indicated by a number. For example, the address of a FidoNet node (host) looks like 1:105/302.0. Usually, when the zone is 1 and the point is 0, they are left off this form of the node address because they are the defaults. In that case, the address would be 105/302. That address is read as "Zone 1, Net 105, FidoNode 302, Point 0" and can be translated to a dotted format as p0.f302.n105.z1. (In Europe, the zone is 2; in the Pacific Basin, it is 3.)

FidoNet has established an Internet domain of fidonet.org. It is possible to send mail from the Internet to FidoNet by translating the FidoNet address into its dotted form and adding the domain name. The Internet address for the host used in the example above would be: f302.n105.z1.fidonet.org. (Note that the default "p0" has been eliminated.) The node 1:105/4.3 would be written as p3.f4.n105.z1.fidonet.org (since there is a point number other than 0, it is specified). So, if you wanted to send mail from the Internet to Lily Michael at the node 1:105/4.3, you would address it as Lily.Michael @p3.f4.n105.z1.fidonet.org (note that the user's first and last names are used, separated by a period or "dot").

HOW TO JOIN THE INTERNET

This chapter discusses the factors to assess when considering connecting to the Internet. Chapter 4 is a list of network service providers who can help you join the Internet. The information in this chapter and in Chapter 1 should help you define your requirements in a service provider and narrow your selection from the list in the next chapter.

Chapter 3 discusses the range of costs for various types of access; however, this document does not list costs for each service available from each provider. Such a list would probably be quickly out of date and perhaps more misleading than helpful. It is expected that you will obtain such information, as well as in-depth details regarding services offered, directly from your prospective service providers.

Types of Internet Access

Access to the Internet falls into two broad categories: access for individuals and access for sites supporting local area networks. You can also classify Internet access into the broad categories of dedicated access and dialup access. It seems to be most often the case that *individuals* who have no network access in their workplace or school tend to opt for dialup access, while most *sites* on the Internet access via dedicated lines. The type of access you choose is determined more by what you need to do and your budget than by the size of your site.

This chapter will first focus on the factors an individual should consider, then will discuss network access for sites. For the purposes of simplicity, dialup access concerns have greater focus in the discussion of individual access, and dedicated connections are discussed more fully in the section addressing access for sites, but there are dialup options for sites and dedicated options for individuals. First, however, let's say a brief word about two fairly recent means of access.

2.1. MX and Dialup IP Access

Traditionally, Internet access has consisted of a site connecting its big mainframe computer or its local area network to the backbone of the Internet. Alternatively, if someone didn't work at a big site like this, he could have a dialup account for electronic mail access. In the past, Internet access was largely limited only to those two choices.

Now there are a few more flavors of Internet access. Two of the most commonly used are MX access and dialup IP.

MX Access

An MX record is a special type of record in the Domain Name System. The Domain Name System (DNS), which is discussed more fully in Section 8.5, is the basis for keeping track of the names and addresses of all the computers on the Internet. It is possible to have your own fully qualified Internet domain name even though you are not an Internet site. This is done by listing an MX record for your site in the DNS. MX stands for Mail Exchange record. An MX record points not to your site—because your site is not directly connected to the Internet—but to a host that acts as an intermediary between you and the Internet. This host computer agrees to hold your mail for you until you dial up to get it, or forwards it to you on a private, non-Internet connection. The advantage of using MX records is that users on the Internet can send mail in one standard format (user@host—see Section 9.1 for more discussion), even to sites not directly connected to the Internet.

This type of Internet access supports only electronic mail. This is the type of access some of the larger "commercial e-mail" companies, such as CompuServe and MCIMail, initially had, and is the option many smaller sites choose as well. To set up this type of access for your site, you need to arrange an agreement with an Internet host to handle your mail, and you need to register a domain name, either with the InterNIC Registration Service, or another domain administrator. Some service providers interact with the proper domain administrator on your behalf. Information on registering your domain name is provided in Section 2.3.2. It is possible to set up an agreement privately with some host that will act as a mail intermediary for you. In addition, some service providers make this service available as well.

Dialup IP

Dialup networking can refer to several types of access. The most basic refers to using a modem to connect a terminal to a host, thus affording that terminal dialup access to the host. A terminal in this case can be just a dumb terminal or a more sophisticated computer emulating a terminal. This type of dialup access is referred to in this book as ***dialup e-mail*** access because it is one method users have traditionally used for such access.

UUCP mail uses a variation of this method. UUCP is used for exchanging e-mail between computers over phone lines. A user sends one or several mail messages on his local computer, and they are queued up on his disk. Then, once in a while his machine dials up another machine, and, using the UUCP protocol, sends whatever mail has accumulated and receives any incoming mail. It is possible for UUCP mail users and Internet mail users to communicate because some of the machines running the UUCP protocol are also on the Internet and can act as gateways between the two systems.

Dialup IP is distinct from these other dialup methods. Dialup IP applications are built on the Serial Line IP (SLIP) or the Point-to-Point Protocol (PPP). In general, PPP obsoletes SLIP, but services built on both are available.

These protocols allow two machines to communicate using TCP/IP protocols, but over a standard dialup phone line instead of a permanent network medium such as ethernet. By using SLIP, for example, a machine that has no permanent connection to the Internet (and it would have to be a computer running the network protocols, not a dumb terminal) would dialup another machine that is a terminal server or a gateway with SLIP capabilities or perhaps just an Internet host. The SLIP program would login to that remote machine, then issue a command that would cause the phone line to become a TCP/IP network connection, from which time only IP packets would go back and forth across that line. Once this connection is established, everything works for the user as if his personal machine were directly on the Internet. He has access to all Internet protocols and services. When he's finished, he simply hangs up, severing his Internet connection. This last type of dialup service is referred to in this book as **dialup IP**. If you are interested in obtaining dialup service, be sure to ask service providers which of these types of service they offer.

2.2. Individual Access

Individual access to the Internet is defined as a person having an account on, that is, the permission to use, a host that can at least send electronic mail to the Internet. An e-mail account is certainly "access" to the Internet, but it would not provide access to the full range of Internet capabilities in the way an account on an Internet host would, with "Internet host" defined as in Section 1.3.

In general, individuals access the Internet in one of the following ways:

➤ by obtaining an account where they work or go to school.

➤ by arranging with a friend or colleague for an account.

➤ by paying for an account, which they usually access by telephone using a modem.

If your company or campus has access to the Internet, you are probably already aware of it and don't need to read this section. However, if you think it's possible that you are unaware of such access, the first thing to do is to check with the facilities or computer center of your company, or the computer science department of your college, or some other likely department, to determine if such access exists and the prerequisites to getting an account.

Many people are introduced to the Internet while in college or at work. Often when they leave that position and find they no longer have Internet access, they wish to obtain it again. Sometimes they can do so by taking advantage of their contacts and arranging privately for an account. Chances are that if this were possible for you, you've already thought of it as well.

Probably the greatest number of people who need access for themselves obtain it by paying for an account. There are a variety of types of accounts and a variety of costs associated with them. Some accounts, as mentioned, allow only electronic mail access to the Internet. Others allow use of the full range of Internet protocols, such as file transfer (FTP) and remote login (Telnet). Some accounts that offer only e-mail access to the Internet include other services on other types of networks, such as the ability to read newsgroups, play games, or consult databases of specialized information.

2.2.1. General access procedures

Usually these types of Internet accounts are called *dialup* accounts because the user accesses them via the telephone. **Before you can establish a dialup e-mail connection, you will need:**

① a terminal or a personal computer with terminal emulation software.

② a modem capable of the appropriate baud rate for your connection.

③ access to a phone line.

Once you have the equipment, an account, and a list of phone numbers from your access provider that you can use for access, you follow these general procedures:

① Dial one of the phone numbers and use your modem to connect your terminal to the host, terminal switch, or terminal server.

② Login to the host with your unique account name and password.

③ Choose whatever services you need from those the host makes available, such as electronic mail.

Your service provider will supply you with the exact, step-by-step procedures that apply to its service.

Different service providers, while usually similar in the constant of providing at least electronic mail access to the Internet, offer different types and ranges of services at different costs. Most electronic mail providers also provide access to network mailing lists, network news, or bulletin boards. Costs for dialup connections often take into consideration the speed (modem baud rate) at which you access your account, the amount of time you are connected, and the range of services available. Sometimes there are membership fees, initial administrative fees, or additional fees for certain transactions or services. Some providers offer services at a flat fee rate. See Chapter 3 for more information.

2.2.2. Factors to consider

Choosing a service provider means weighing the services they offer against the prices charged for those services, how those services will match your needs, and your options. For example, how much competition do you have to choose from in your area? Perhaps you will find a provider that meets all your needs at a reasonable price. Perhaps, however, your final choice will involve a trade-off between services desired and costs you can afford.

Before deciding on a specific provider, it is probably prudent to evaluate:

> What services do you need? Are you primarily interested in e-mail access to the Internet, or would you prefer more extensive capabilities? Which providers offer the services you want?

> With whom do you want to communicate? Does a provider you're considering offer access to your audience?

> Does a service provider you are considering have a local or toll free phone number you can call?

> What type of electronic mail protocol does a provider you're considering use? Are you comfortable with that software?

> Will you be accessing the network often, or only occasionally?

> Does a provider you're considering have different fees for occasional use?

> At what times of day would you usually be using the network?

> Does a service provider you are considering offer peak (daytime) and non-peak rates?

> Does a local service provider offer information and support services?

2.3. Connecting a Network to the Internet

 According to RFC 1296 [3], more than 350,000 hosts were added to the Internet between January 1991 and January 1992. Networks are added to the Internet daily. If you wish to connect a site to the Internet, take the following steps:

① If you have not already done so, obtain a unique IP network number from InterNIC Registration Services or other authorized registration site, and configure the hosts on the network to use that network number. (If you are not sure where to get an IP network number, contact InterNIC Registration Services. Contact information can be found in Section 2.3.1.)

② Establish a domain.

③ Determine if you need an Internet connection primarily for commercial or research activities. Then, locate a site for your physical connection.

④ Make sure that the appropriate hardware (e.g., gateway) has been installed and is configured correctly.

⑤ Make sure that the proper software (e.g., TCP/IP protocols) is installed on the hosts on the LAN.

⑥ Make sure your gateway has the proper routing protocols installed (e.g., EGP/BGP).

⑦ Order the appropriate circuits from the telephone company to connect your gateway to the Internet access point you're using, or arrange some other connection medium.

Most of these steps can be taken in parallel. Some service providers take responsibility for completing some of these steps as part of their service. For example, a provider may coordinate with the InterNIC Registration Services provider in the administrative process of obtaining an IP network

number for you. Or a provider may acquire a router machine to act as a gateway for you. They may make sure
you have the proper networking protocols running correctly. They may coordinate leasing a circuit for you with
the phone company. On the other hand, they may do none
or only some of these things. At any rate, it is to your
advantage to have a general knowledge of these steps regardless of who ends up doing them, so let's look at each
in a little more detail.

2.3.1. Obtain a unique IP network number

All sites wishing to connect to the Internet must obtain an
official IP network number. It is also strongly recommended that *everyone* implementing an IP network obtain
a unique network number as well, even if they will not
immediately connect to the Internet. By obtaining an official IP network number when first setting up a TCP/IP
network, a site is assured of having unique addresses, and
is spared the expensive necessity of reconfiguring their
address space to a new, unique number if they later join
the Internet. Many companies that do not at first envision
joining the Internet do indeed connect eventually. A
unique network number is necessary for every network
connected to the Internet in order to avoid very unpleas-
ant routing problems.

The central IP registration service provider is the InterNIC
Registration Services provider, located at Network Solutions, Inc., in Herndon, Virginia. This central registration
site has the authority to choose delegate registries which
have the responsibility of performing registrations for certain regions. For example, the RIPE Network Coordination Center (see Section 6.1.1.6) coordinates IP network
number registrations for Europe, and has the authority to
further delegate that responsibility for its region. If you do
not know whether there is a registration authority in your

area, contact the InterNIC; they can refer you to the correct authority.

A registration authority assigns only the network portion of the address. The responsibility of assigning host addresses falls to the requesting organization. (See Section 8.4 for background information on IP addressing.)

In order to obtain a unique IP network number, you will need to provide the registration authority with some information about your network and who will be acting as a Point of Contact for it. Once you return this information, they will process your application and assign you a unique address.

Contact InterNIC Registration Services to get the most current application for an IP network number.

Section 8.4.4 contains an explanation of the concept of a network "sponsor," which relates to one of the questions on the current version of the IP network number registration template. That discussion will probably make more sense in the context of the background information provided in Section 8.4. This question may not appear on the most current application forms; always make sure you have the most current form before submitting it to a registration authority.

To contact InterNIC Registration Services:

> Network Solutions, Inc.
> InterNIC Registration Services
> 505 Huntmar Park Drive
> Herndon, VA 22070
> 800 444 4345
> +1 703 742 4777
> hostmaster@rs.internic.net

2.3.2. Establish a domain

Establishing a domain means adding an entry for your site into the distributed database the Internet uses for name to address resolution. What *that* means is that other hosts on the network will be able to send traffic to you if they know your host name, and users can specify your host name easily because it will follow the logical pattern of the Domain Name System (DNS). Please refer to Section 8.5 for an explanation of what a domain is and how the DNS works. This section will touch generally on some DNS concepts, but will concentrate mainly on explaining how to establish a domain.

Think of the DNS as a hierarchy containing the names of every site on the Internet. At the top of the hierarchy is the root domain, that entity responsible for maintaining the DNS at the topmost level. Today, InterNIC Registration Services acts as the root domain. All top-level, many second-level, and some third-level domains are registered through the InterNIC.

If you are going to establish a domain under the top-level domains COM, NET, MIL, ORG, EDU, or GOV, or if you wish to have a top-level country domain delegated to you, contact the InterNIC.

Section 8.5 provides background information about the Domain Name System, including an explanation of the top-level domains and answers to common questions.

Network Solutions, Inc.
InterNIC Registration Services
505 Huntmar Park Drive
Herndon, VA 22070
800 444 4345
+1 703 742 4777
hostmaster@rs.internic.net

The InterNIC will ask you to fill out a form that requests information about the name of your domain, the names and addresses of at least two hosts that will act as name servers, and Points of Contact for administrative and technical matters.

A name server refers to a host that acts as a repository for a portion of the domain database. A name server runs software that allows it to answer queries for DNS data. On the Internet, the most commonly used name server software is BIND, which stands for *Berkeley Internet Name Domain* software. The BIND software was written for UNIX systems, but is now available for other platforms. The DNS name server-resolver concept is discussed further in Section 8.5.7.

You may control your own name servers for your domain. All you need are two hosts, preferably configured so their contact with the Internet cannot be severed easily at the same time, that run domain name server software. When registering for both an IP network number and a domain, you would register the domain after the IP network number so you can inform the InterNIC of the addresses of the domain name servers that will reside within your local network.

If you are not able to maintain your own name servers, you must gain the cooperation of two other sites on the Internet willing to provide name service for you. There is no central "public" name service clearinghouse, so you will have to negotiate such an arrangement yourself. Some network service providers will provide name service for a fee. Some network service providers also coordinate the establishment of your domain with InterNIC Registration Services for you.

If you are going to establish a domain under any top-level domain other than COM, MIL, GOV, EDU, NET, or ORG, you must coordinate with the administrator of the top-level domain under which you wish to join. For example, sites in countries other than the U.S. join under top-level domains that correspond to the name of their country. Some sites in the U.S. join under the top-level domain "US" (see Section 8.5.10 for more information).

You may wish to join at the third level rather than the second level. For example, your company may already have a domain established. In this case, you would probably join under that domain. You need to contact the administrator for the domain under which you wish to join. InterNIC Registration Services can help you identify the contacts you'll need to work with to establish a domain if it turns out that the InterNIC itself cannot serve as your contact.

It is possible to establish a domain although you are not connected to the Internet. Sometimes a site without a direct Internet connection will have a host that is connected to the Internet hold or forward mail for them. For ease of electronic mail correspondence, such a site will be said to establish a domain, even though they are not connected to the Internet. While it is true that they then have a fully qualified domain name, technically what they've done is had a special type of record, called an MX record, entered into the domain database for them. This is discussed in Section 2.1.

2.3.3. Locate a connection point

In the past, the entire Internet was devoted to research, educational, or military pursuits, mainly because it was funded by research or defense agencies of the U.S. Government. Therefore, any site that joined the Internet, including commercial companies, agreed to send only traffic that complied with this research-oriented climate. A fairly recent development, however, has been the emergence of commercial backbones, meaning components of the Internet that allow commercial traffic. What is the difference between commercial and research traffic? This line has always been somewhat fuzzy. Clearly, however, billing activities and advertising are considered commercial.

When considering a network provider, you should always ask to see their "Acceptable Usage Policy." This policy defines what types of traffic are acceptable on that particular network. Network providers will explain any restrictions they have. In some cases, they will explain restrictions on traffic you might send to other networks that have different acceptable use policies. See Chapter 5 for an example of an acceptable use policy.

Of course, joining a network that allows you to send commercial traffic does not mean that you must send commercial traffic. Often, any type of organization may join any network it wishes as long as it agrees to abide by the usage policy of that network. So commercial companies may join NSFNET mid-level networks, and universities can join commercial backbones. This rule of thumb obviously does not apply to networks with missions to serve only specific communities, such as the MILNET.

There are two avenues for commercial traffic in the U.S. One is to contract with a service provider that supports commercial traffic. The other is to join a network with access to the NSFNET backbone that is a member of the Commercial Internet Exchange Association (CIX—see section 10.1.2). CIX members route commercial traffic differently than research traffic. Some commercial network providers are also members of CIX. In general, the service providers handle the details and headaches about what traffic routes to where. Although the subject is complicated, it's not necessarily a problem average first-time Internet users have to solve beyond determining what type of traffic they are most likely to be sending, as that may well influence their choice of network provider.

2.3.4. Install a router

You will need a machine to act as a gateway between your local network and the Internet. The terms *gateway* and *router* are often heard for these machines. There are many companies that manufacture Internet routers. Your service provider may provide a router or tell you which router to buy. The router vendor and the service provider will give you support when initially configuring your gateway. In many cases, the service provider will actually own the gateway, and may take care of all the details of acquiring and installing one for you. The cost of doing so will, of course, be passed on to you as part of their service.

Rather than buying a special system to act as the gateway between your network and the Internet, you may be able to use a host already on your network as a router. The system must have two or more network interfaces. Each interface would be connected to one of the networks between which packets will be exchanged. You will need to check with your vendor to see if the network software on your system can provide this type of functionality. If it can, you will then need to configure your system so that it knows how packets should be routed.

2.3.5. Obtain proper software

If you are connecting a TCP/IP network to the Internet, you are already running compatible protocols and will need only to add the routing protocols necessary as described in the previous section.

If you are connecting a network that is based on protocols other than TCP/IP, you will need to make sure that your gateway can understand the TCP/IP-based traffic it receives from the Internet, and is able to convert it to a form understandable by the rest of the hosts on your network.

Your service provider, gateway vendor, or LAN vendor can probably guide you.

2.3.6. Order circuits

Most sites connecting to the Internet in the U.S. connect via dedicated lines leased from a phone company. Sites at greater distances, such as those overseas, often connect in other ways, such as via satellites, fiber optic cables, or microwave dishes.

You can lease lines of different speeds; the faster lines are more expensive. You may also need to estimate the amount of traffic you'll be sending at peak times so that you make sure you order lines that are able to handle your expected capacity. Again, your service provider will guide you in knowing what to ask for with the telephone company. In fact, some service providers will arrange this for you.

If you are arranging your own circuits, be sure to contact your telephone company as early as possible so that you allow enough lead time for their installation.

2.3.7. Factors to consider

When evaluating service providers for network connections, here are some factors to consider.

➤ What sort of traffic do you want to support?

➤ Do you understand the Acceptable Use Policy of your prospective provider?

➤ Does the provider offer the level of service and support you wish?

➤ Will the provider connect you with everyone with whom you need to communicate?

➤ Does the provider offer support services, such as help during initial configuration, user information, assistance with security matters, or operations and monitoring?

➤ Do you have a choice of providers in your area? If so, will being responsible yourself for some of the connection steps save you money with one provider but not with another? If you don't have the time to arrange the details, is there a provider willing to oversee everything for you?

3

COSTS

This chapter gives a very brief idea of what different types of Internet connection services cost, plus some of the factors that often are involved in determining such costs. In no way should any service provider or vendor be held to these prices! They are meant only to give you an idea of the current costs of internetworking. Costs can vary widely depending on network service provider and often on the area of the country in which you're located. More remote areas generally are more expensive and there is usually less competition nearby to help bring prices down.

When considering the costs of access, you should also consider the distance between you and your connection point (sometimes referred to as a provider's nearest "point of presence") because that distance will probably influence the fee your phone company charges for leased lines or long distance phone calls.

These prices focus only on the U.S., although the factors that influence costs may be relevant elsewhere.

3.1. Cost of Connecting a LAN

 When connecting a LAN to the Internet, the biggest costs will be the cost of the hardware (routers) and the costs of the circuits you lease to use for the physical connection from your site to the provider's site. Most providers also charge either a start-up or an annual fee towards the cost of their backbone, support services, and administrative costs. Such an annual charge may also include a fee towards the line costs incurred for the operation of the whole network.

Some providers may take into consideration the amount of line capacity a site will use, offering incentives to connect via a faster line if a site will not need its full bandwidth.

Some access providers recognize a mission to connect primarily or solely certain types of sites, such as schools or supercomputer center researchers. Such providers may not connect your site if it does not fit within their constituency parameters (which may be determined by an outside funding source). Or such providers may have different pricing structures for sites that fit within their primary mission and those that do not. Such cost differentiations may be made by considering the type of site seeking access (most commonly distinguishing between a commercial company and a research or education site); whether a company is for-profit or non-profit; and the annual budget or revenue of a site.

Examples: The following prices were taken from marketing information provided by various service providers. In the examples cited, much of the detail of exactly what services the costs cover is summarized. This section aims only to give you a rough idea of the range of prices for different types of services.

Remember, costs can vary widely depending on service provider and the area of the country in which you're located.

One research-oriented provider's prices for a 64 kbps or faster connection range from approximately $900 per year to $3,200 per year for non-profit members. There are five levels of pricing within that range determined by the annual budget of the organization. The same service for a corporate member ranges from $1,800 per year to $6,500 per year. Again, there are five levels of pricing within that range determined by the annual revenue of the corporation.

Added to those fees are installation and activation fees that cover the cost of hardware and the services to install, configure, and activate the hardware. In this example, these range from $13,000 to $30,000, depending on the type of equipment and the speed of the connection. These are one-time fees.

In addition, the site must pay for the data circuits from their site to the network access point determined by the service provider.

One commercial service provider differentiates its fees solely on the speed of the connection. This provider's annual fees range from approximately $10,000 per year to $100,000. The prices include all hardware and software, line ordering, maintenance, and operations. Line costs (data circuit costs) are additional.

A third provider offers connection options from 9.6 kbps to T1, with a total of five graduated options. The initial hardware and start-up costs for the slower connection total $8,000; for the fastest connection, the total is about $14,000. These prices cover the cost of equipment for the local site as well as some of the cost of the equipment on the backbone. In addition, there are monthly recurring fees for the backbone and local line costs that total from approximately $650 to approximately $3,000, depending on the speed of the connection.

3.2. Cost of Dialup Connections

 For the sake of this book, dialup connections are classified as either simple e-mail access or dialup IP (as explained in Chapter 2). Dialup IP is more sophisticated and will cost more. In general, the cost of dialup access of both types can take into account the speed of the connection and the length of your dialup session. Some providers offer a flat rate alternative to the need to track session length (also sometimes called *connect time*). Some providers combine a flat monthly rate with an hourly charge. The monthly rate may cover the costs of providing the access equipment, line costs, and administrative fees. Most providers also have an initial fee.

Some dialup providers may also have specific constituencies they wish to serve, so may consider the suitability of a prospective site in those terms. As with LAN connections, then, factors such as whether a site is a commercial company or a university or research site, whether a company is for-profit or non-profit, and the annual budget or revenue of a site may be considered when setting costs.

Examples: Here are several examples of rates charged by dialup providers. You will see that charges vary greatly and are broken down in different ways. It is important to evaluate the full range of services a provider offers when making a decision, as well as to remember that the cost of the phone call to the provider's access number is additional in most cases.

> One dialup e-mail provider charges $25 to $40 per month, depending on the frequency of billing, or $75—$100 per month for mail plus news. The cost of the phone call is extra.
>
> Another dialup e-mail provider charges $2 per minute for connect time, plus the cost of your phone call to their network, plus a $35 per month administrative charge for the account. This provider also offers alternatives to this

plan, including a $5 per hour connection handshake through another network, and a low volume yearly flat rate.

A third dialup e-mail provider charges $20 per month or $45 for 3 months or $72 dollars for 6 months. As you can see, with this plan, if you pay a higher amount in advance, you save money. Many other providers also use some version of this pricing strategy.

A fourth dialup e-mail provider charges $15 per month, plus $2 per hour.

A provider of dialup services that includes SLIP (a dialup IP) charges $1 per off-peak hour, $2 per peak hour up to a maximum of $250 per month, with an additional $20 sign-up fee.

Another provider charges dialup IP services at the rate of $10 per hour plus $20 per month. Weekend rates are $8 per hour.

Yet another dialup IP provider charges a flat $250 per month.

And a fourth SLIP provider charges $30 per month with a $50 initial administrative fee.

4

SERVICE PROVIDERS

This chapter provides information regarding Internet access providers, the general types of services they provide, and how to contact them. Although some of these providers can help with international connections, Chapter 6 contains more information about many non-U.S. networks and whom to contact for more information about gaining access to them.

This chapter first lists national providers of network connections, then lists dialup providers, then lists the providers by state.

The information contained here was current as of the publication of this book, and contains information as complete and accurate as we were able to find. We would appreciate corrections and additions to this chapter. They can be sent online to nisc@nisc.sri.com or in hardcopy to SRI International at the address in the Overview.

Format

Each provider is listed in the following format:

> **Provider name**
> Contact name (if any)
> Phone number
> Internet e-mail address
> Services:

Those items in italics are listed without an identifier pre-pended (e.g., CERFnet rather than Provider name: CERFnet).

The services item is used to indicate the general type of service a provider offers. It will usually contain either:

➤ Network connections

➤ Dialup e-mail

➤ Dialup IP

One provider may offer any or all of these services.

These types of access methods are each described in Chapter 2. Sometimes other services may be noted as well. For further details about any service, contact the access provider. This chapter lists only phone numbers and electronic mail addresses. Complete postal addresses can be found in the alphabetical access provider listing contained in **Appendix II**.

Important: Providers often offer services in addition to those noted! This book is concerned mainly with high-lighting types of Internet access. Most often, providers offer a range of value-added services in addition to initial access options. For example, most providers also offer access to USENET news.

If a provider is in your area, but seems from this list not to offer the service you desire, definitely contact them to ascertain their current range of services. Providers expand services often, and it is possible that we were unaware of a service.

Many access providers in the U.S. began with support from the National Science Foundation (NSF) with the mission of connecting research and education sites to the NSFNET backbone, or with funding from state agencies to fulfill a similar purpose. Some providers retain this as their primary goal and do not provide access to commercial sites. Other such providers have expanded their missions to include more commercial services, so now serve a wider community. All providers charge fees for their services, which has helped blur the distinction between "commercial" and "research" providers. With a few exceptions, it is generally true that any organization may join any network as long as it agrees to abide by that network's Acceptable Use Policy. However, it may be the case that a provider listed in this chapter as serving a particular area may have some restrictions regarding the type of community it wishes to serve.

Access for Individuals

Individuals usually access the Internet via some dialup means. Therefore, if you are looking for access for yourself, start with the section listing Providers of Dialup Services, but also check listings under your state for other providers that may offer dialup services.

4.1. National Providers of Network Connections

This section lists providers that offer network connections throughout the United States. Network connections means that they will coordinate with you to establish a dedicated connection between your host or your local area network to the Internet.

In most cases, these providers are not repeated in Section 4.3, **Providers by State**. When shopping for an access provider in the United States, therefore, using this section

in tandem with the **Providers by State** section will give
you the maximum information from which to make your
selection.

Advanced Network and Services, Inc. (ANS) and ANS CO+RE
   800 456 8267
   +1 313 663 2482
   info@ans.net
   Services: Network connections. ANS CO+RE is a wholly owned,
    taxable subsidiary of ANS. ANS is a not-for-profit organization.

AlterNet
   800 488 6384
   +1 703 204 8000
   alternet-info@uunet.uu.net
   Services: Network connections; a product of UUNET Technologies.

Infolan
   George Abe
   +1 310 335 2600
   abe@infonet.com
   Services: Network connections.

MSEN, Inc.
   Owen Scott Medd
   +1 313 998 4562
   info@msen.com
   Services: Network connections, dialup IP, dialup e-mail.

NSFNET
   Referrals available from:
   InterNIC Registration Services
   800 444 4345
   +1 619 455 4600
   info@internic.net

Performance Systems International, Inc. (PSI)
   800 827 7482
   +1 703 620 6651
   info@psi.com
   Services: Network connections; dialup IP; dialup e-mail.

SprintLink
   Bob Doyle
   +1 703 904 2167
   rdoyle@icm1.icp.net
   Services: Network connections.

4.2. Providers of Dialup Services

This section lists providers that offer dialup connections.
This list includes only national dialup access providers and
providers that specialize in dialup e-mail services for specific geographic areas. Those providers that offer both
network connections and dialup access to a specific region are listed in Section 4.3 rather than here. This is only

for the sake of simplicity. This section is provided mainly for easy reference by individuals seeking dialup access to the Internet. If you are such a person, also look in the section that lists providers by area to see if the mid-level or regional network in your area also provides dialup services.

Even though some providers seem to serve smaller, perhaps municipal areas, their services can be accessed via a long distance phone call, or sometimes via a public data network. It is worth contacting them to see how you might use their services.

All of these providers are listed elsewhere in this chapter as well as here. Many national access providers also offer dialup services, so they are listed here and in the previous section. Those dialup e-mail providers that serve specific areas are listed again in Section 4.3 under the state they serve.

Although this section emphasizes dialup access, it is important to recall that most of these providers offer other services as well.

If no Area Served information is listed for the dialup providers, they serve all of the U.S. and probably provide international dialup connections as well. Contact the provider directly for more information.

---

a2i communications
info@rahul.net
Area Served: San Jose, CA (408 area code)
Services: Dialup e-mail, SunOS software development environment.

America Online, Inc.
800 827 6364
+1 703 8933 6288
info@aol.com
Area Served: US and Canada
Services: Dialup e-mail.

Anterior Technology
+1 415 328 5615
info@radiomail.net
Area Served: San Francisco Bay area
Services: Dialup e-mail; RadioMail.

Big Sky Telegraph
800 982 6668 (in Montana only)
+1 406 683 7338
jrobin@csn.org
Area Served: Montana
Services: Dialup e-mail.

The Black Box
+1 713 480-2684
mknewman@blkbox.com
Area Served: Houston, TX
Services: Dialup e-mail.

BIX
800 695 4775
+1 617 354 4137
TJL@mhis.bix.com
Area Served: Area code 617; local
dialup connections outside 617
available through TYMNET.
Services: Dialup e-mail.

CAPCON Connect
+1 202 466 7057
jhagermn@capcon.net
Area Served: Area code 202
Services: Dialup e-mail, dialup IP.

CERFnet
800 876 2373
+1 619 455 3900
help@cerf.net
Services: Network connections,
national dialup IP, dialup e-mail.

Channel 1
+1 617 864 0100
whitehrn@channel1.com
Area Served: Massachusetts
Services: Dialup e-mail.

CLASS
Cooperative Agency for Library
Systems and Services
800 488 4559
class@class.org
Area Served: US
Services: Dialup access for libraries in
the US.

Community News Service
800 748 1200
+1 719 592 1200
info@cscns.com
Area Served: US
Services: Dialup e-mail.

CompuServe Information System
800 848 8990
+1 614 457 0802
postmaster@csi.compuserve.com
Services: Dialup e-mail.

The Cyberspace Station
+1 619 944 9498 ext. 626
help@cyber.net
Area Served: San Diego, CA
Services: Dialup e-mail.

DELPHI
800 695 4005
+1 617 491 3393
walthowe@delphi.com
Area Served: Boston, MA Services:
Dialup e-mail.

Express Access Online Communications Service
+1 301 220 2020
info@digex.com
Services: Dialup e-mail in the
northern VA;
Baltimore, MD;
Washington, DC areas
(area codes 202, 310, 410, 703).

EZ-E-Mail
+1 603 672 0736
info@lemuria.sai.com
Area Served: US and Canada
Services: Dialup e-mail.

Halcyon
+1 206 426 9298
info@remote.halcyon.com
Area Served: Seattle, WA
Services: Dialup e-mail.

HoloNet
+1 510 704 0160
info@holonet.net
Area Served: Berkeley, CA
(area code 510)
Services: Dialup e-mail.

Institute for Global Communications (IGC)
+1 415 442 0220
support@igc.apc.org
Services: Dialup e-mail; affiliated with
PeaceNet, EcoNet, and
ConflictNet; member of the Association for Progressive Communications
(APC).

IDS World Network
+1 401 884 7856
sysadmin@ids.net
Area Served: East Greenwich, RI;
northern RI
Services: Dialup e-mail.

JvNCnet
Sergio F. Heker
Allison Pihl
800 358 4437
+1 609 258 2400
market@jvnc.net
Services: Network connections,
national dialup IP, dialup e-mail.

MCI Mail Engineering
  800 444 6245
  +1 202 833 8484
  2671163@mcimail.com
  3248333@mcimail.com
  Services: Dialup e-mail.

MindVox
  +1 212 989 2418
  +1 212 989 4141
  info@phantom.com
  Area Served: New York City (area
  codes 212, 718)
  Services: Dialup e-mail.

MSEN, Inc.
  Owen Scott Medd
  +1 313 998 4562
  info@msen.com
  Area Served: US
  Services: Network connections,
  dialup IP, dialup e-mail.

New Mexico Technet
  +1 505 345 6555
  reynolds@technet.nm.org
  Area Served: New Mexico
  Services: Dialup e-mail.

Old Colorado City Communications
  +1 719 632 4848
  dave@oldcolo.com
  Area Served: Colorado
  Services: Dialup e-mail.

Seattle Online
  +1 206 328 2412
  bruceki@online.com
  Area Served: Seattle, WA
  Services: Dialup e-mail.

Panix Public Access Unix
  Alexis Rosen
  alexis@panix.com
  +1 212 877 4854
  or
  Jim Baumbach
  jsb@panix.com
  +1 718 965 3768
  Area Served:New York City, NY
   (area codes 212, 718)
  Services: Dialup e-mail.

**Performance Systems International,
  Inc. (PSI)**
  800 827 7482
  +1 703 620 6651
  info@psi.com
  Services: Network connections, dialup
  IP, dialup e-mail.

Portal Communications, Inc.
  +1 408 973 9111
  cs@cup.portal.com
  info@portal.com
  Area Served: Northern California
  (area codes 408, 415)
  Services: Dialup e-mail.

Sugar Land Unix
  +1 713 438 4964
  info@NeoSoft.com
  Area Served: Texas
  (Houston metro area)
  Services: Dialup e-mail.

UUNET Technologies, Inc.
  800 488 6384
  +1 703 204 8000
  info@uunet.uu.net
  Services: Network connections,
  dialup e-mail; Alternet is
  a product of UUNET Technologies.

Village of Cambridge
  +1 617 494 5226 (voice)
  +1 617 252 0009 (modem)
  service@village.com
  Area Served: Massachusetts
  Services: Dialup e-mail.

Whole Earth 'Lectronic Link (WELL)
  +1 415 332 4335
  info@well.sf.ca.us
  area Served: San Francisco Bay Area
  (area code 415)
  Services: Dialup e-mail.

The World–Public Access UNIX
  +1 617 739 0202
  office@world.std.com
  Area Served: Boston, MA
  (area code 617)
  Services: Dialup e-mail.

4.3. Providers by State

This section lists Providers by State. Many providers serve more than one state, so are listed more than once. Dialup e-mail providers are listed again here for the areas they serve. National access providers are not listed here; see Section 4.1 for more information. It is a good idea to contact both national providers and more regional providers when considering an Internet connection in order to have enough information to make the best selection.

Alabama
SURAnet
Deborah J. Nunn
+1 301 982 4600
marketing@sura.net
Services: Network connections.

Alaska
NorthWestNet
Eric Hood
+1 206 562 3000
ehood@nwnet.net
Services: Network connections.

Arizona
Westnet
Pat Burns
+1 303 491 7260
pburns@yuma.acns.colostate.edu
Services: Network connections.

Arkansas
MIDnet
Dale Finkelson
+1 402 472 5032
dmf@westie.unl.edu
Services: Network connections.

California
BARRNet
William Yundt
+1 415 723 7520
info@nic.barrnet.net
Services: Network connections, dialup IP, dialup e-mail.

CERFnet
800 876 2373
+1 619 455 3900
help@cerf.net
Services: Network connections, national dialup IP,
dialup e-mail.

Los Nettos
Ann Westine Cooper
+1 310 822 1511
los-nettos-request@isi.edu
Services: Network connections.

SDSCnet
Paul Love
+1 619 534 5043
loveep@sds.sdsc.edu
Services: Network connections.

a2i communications
info@rahul.net
Services: Dialup e-mail to San Jose area; SunOS software development environment.

Anterior Technology
+1 415 328 5615
info@radiomail.net
Services: Dialup e-mail; RadioMail to San Francisco Bay area.

Cyberspace Station
help@cyber.net
+1 619 944 9498 ext. 626
Services: Dialup e-mail to San Diego area; UNIX systems facilities for programming.

HoloNet
info@holonet.net
+1 510 704 0160
Services: Dialup e-mail to Berkeley area.

Portal Communications, Inc.
+1 408 973 9111
cs@cup.portal.com
Services: Dialup e-mail.

Whole Earth 'Lectronic Link (WELL)
+1 415 332 4335
info@well.sf.ca.us
Services: Dialup e-mail in the San
Francisco Bay area.

**Netcom Online Communication
Services**
+1 408 554 8649
info@netcom.com
Services: Dialup e-mail, dialup IP in the
San Jose, San Francisco area.

DASNET
+1 408 559 7434
postmaster@das.net
Services: Dialup e-mail in California.

Colorado
Colorado SuperNet
Ken Harmon
+1 303 273 3471
info@csn.org
Services: Network connections, dialup IP.

Community News Service
800 748 1200
+1 719 592 1200
info@cscns.com
Services: Dialup e-mail.

Westnet
Pat Burns
+1 303 491 7260
pburns@yuma.acns.colostate.edu
Services: Network connections.

**Old Colorado City
 Communications**
Dave Hughes
+1 719 632 4848
dave@oldcolo.com
Services: Dialup e-mail.

Connecticut
NEARnet
John Curran
+1 617 873 8730
nearnet-join@nic.near.net
Services: Network connections, dialup IP.

Delaware
SURAnet
Deborah J. Nunn
+1 301 982 4600
marketing@sura.net
Services: Network connections.

JvNCnet
Sergio F. Heker
Allison Pihl
+1 609 258 2400
800 358 4437
market@jvnc.net
Services: Network connections, dialup IP.

District of Columbia
SURAnet
Deborah J. Nunn
+1 301 982 4600
marketing@sura.net
Services: Network connections.

JvNCnet
Sergio F. Heker
Allison Pihl
+1 609 258 2400
800 358 4437
market@jvnc.net
Services: Network connections, dialup IP.

**Express Access Online Communica-
tions Service**
+1 301 220 2020
info@digex.com
Services: Dialup e-mail in the northern
VA; Baltimore, MD;
Washington, DC areas (area codes 202,
310, 410, 703).

Florida
SURAnet
Deborah J. Nunn
+1 301 982 4600
marketing@sura.net
Services: Network connections.

Georgia
SURAnet
Deborah J. Nunn
+1 301 982 4600
marketing@sura.net
Services: Network connections.

Hawaii
PACCOM
Torben Nielsen
+1 808 956-3499
torben@hawaii.edu
Services: Network connections.

Idaho
NorthWestNet
Eric Hood
+1 206 562 3000
ehood@nwnet.net
Services: Network connections.

Westnet
Pat Burns
+1 303 491 7260
pburns@yuma.acns.colostate.edu
Services: Network connections.

World dot Net
Internetworks, Inc.
+1 206 576 7147
info@world.net
Services: Network connections.

Illinois
CICNet
John Hankins
+1 313 998 6102
hankins@cic.net
Services: Network connections.

netILLINOIS
Joel L. Hartmann
+1 309 677 3100
joel@bradley.bradley.edu
Services: Network connections.

Indiana
CICNet
John Hankins
+1 313 998 6102
hankins@cic.net
Services: Network connections.

INet
Dick Ellis
+1 812 855 4240
ellis@ucs.indiana.edu
Services: Network connections.

Iowa
CICNet
John Hankins
+1 313 998 6102
hankins@cic.net
Services: Network connections.

MIDnet
Dale Finkelson
+1 402 472 5032
dmf@westie.unl.edu
Services: Network connections.

Kansas
MIDnet
Dale Finkelson
+1 402 472 5032
dmf@westie.unl.edu
Services: Network connections.

Kentucky
SURAnet
Deborah J. Nunn
+1 301 982 4600
marketing@sura.net
Services: Network connections.

Louisiana
SURAnet
Deborah J. Nunn
+1 301 982 4600
marketing@sura.net
Services: Network connections.

Maine
NEARnet
John Curran
+1 617 873 8730
nearnet-join@nic.near.net
Services: Network connections, dialup IP.

Maryland
SURAnet
Deborah J. Nunn
+1 301 982 4600
marketing@sura.net
Services: Network connections.

JvNCnet
Sergio F. Heker
Allison Pihl
+1 609 258 2400
800 358 4437
market@jvnc.net
Services: Network connections, dialup IP.

Express Access Online Communications Service
+1 301 220 2020
info@digex.com
Services: Dialup e-mail in the northern
VA, Baltimore, MD;
 Washington, DC areas (area codes 202,
310, 410, 703).

CAPCON Connect
+1 202 466 7057
jhagermn@capcon.net
Services: Dialup e-mail, dialup IP.

Massachusetts
NEARnet
John Curran
+1 617 873 8730
nearnet-join@nic.near.net
Services: Network connections, dialup IP.

BIX
+1 617 354 4137
800 695 4775
tjl@mhis.bix.com
Services: Dialup e-mail (local dialup
connections
outside 617 area available through
TYMNET).

Channel 1
+1 617 864 0100
whitehrn@channel1.com
Services: Dialup e-mail.

DELPHI
800 695 4005
+1 617 491 3393
walthowe@delphi.com
Services: Dialup e-mail.

Village of Cambridge
+1 617 494 5226 (voice)
+1 617 252 0009 (modem)
service@village.com
Services: Dialup e-mail.

The World - Public Access UNIX
+1 617 739 0202
office@world.std.com
Services: Dialup e-mail.

Michigan
CICNet
John Hankins
+1 313 998 6102
hankins@cic.net
Services: Network connections.

MichNet
Jeff Ogden
+1 313 764 9430
jogden@merit.edu
Services: Network connections, dialup IP.

Minnesota
CICNet
John Hankins
+1 313 998 6102
hankins@cic.net
Services: Network connections.

MRnet
Dennis Fazio
+1 612 342 2570
dfazio@mr.net
Services: Network connections.

Mississippi
SURAnet
Deborah J. Nunn

+1 301 982 4600
marketing@sura.net
Services: Network connections.

Missouri
MIDnet
Dale Finkelson
+1 402 472 5032
dmf@westie.unl.edu
Services: Network connections.

Montana
NorthWestNet
Eric Hood
+1 206 562 3000
ehood@nwnet.net
Services: Network connections.

Big Sky Telegraph
Jon Robinson
800 982 6668
+1 406 683 7338
jrobin@csn.org
Services: Dialup e-mail.

Nebraska
MIDnet
Dale Finkelson
+1 402 472 5032
dmf@westie.unl.edu
Services: Network connections.

Nevada
NevadaNet
Don Zitter
+1 702 784 6133
zitter@nevada.edu
Services: Network connections.

New Hampshire
NEARnet
John Curran
+1 617 873 8730
nearnet-join@nic.near.net
Services: Network connections, dialup IP.

EZ-E-Mail
+1 603 672 0736
info@lemuria.sai.com
Services: Dialup e-mail to Nashua area.

New Jersey
JvNCnet
Sergio F. Heker
Allison Pihl
800 358 4437
+1 609 258 2400
market@jvnc.net
Services: Network connections, dialup IP.

New Mexico
Westnet
Pat Burns
+1 303 491 7260
pburns@yuma.acns.colostate.edu
Services: Network connections.

New Mexico Technet
Lee Reynolds
+1 505 345 6555
reynolds@technet.nm.org
Services: Dialup e-mail.

New York
NYSERnet
Jim Luckett
+1 315 443 4120
info@nysernet.org
Services: Network connections, dialup e-mail, dialup IP.

Mindvox
+1 212 989-2418
info@phantom.com
Services: Dialup e-mail to New York City area.

Panix Public Access Unix
Alexis Rosen
alexis@panix.com
+1 212 877 4854
or
Jim Baumbach
jsb@panix.com
+1 718 965 3768
Services: Dialup e-mail to New York City area.

North Carolina
CONCERT
Joe Ragland
+1 919 248 1404
jrr@concert.net
Services: Network connections, dialup e-mail, dialup IP.

SURAnet
Deborah J. Nunn
+1 301 982 4600
marketing@sura.net
Services: Network connections.

North Dakota
NorthWestNet
Eric Hood
+1 206 562 3000
ehood@nwnet.net
Services: Network connections.

Ohio
CICNet
John Hankins
+1 313 998 6102
hankins@cic.net
Services: Network connections.

OARnet
Alison Brown
+1 614 292 8100
nic@oar.net
Services: Network connections, dialup IP.

PSCNET
Eugene Hastings
+1 412 268 4960
pscnet-admin@psc.edu
Services: Network connections.

Oklahoma
MIDnet
Dale Finkelson
+1 402 472 5032
dmf@westie.unl.edu
Services: Network connections.

Oregon
NorthWestNet
Eric Hood
+1 206 562 3000
ehood@nwnet.net
Services: Network connections.

World dot Net
Internetworks, Inc.
+1 206 576 7147
info@world.net
Services: Network connections.

Pennsylvania
PREPnet
Thomas W. Bajzek
+1 412 268 7870
twb+@andrew.cmu.edu
Services: Network connections, dialup IP.

PSCNET
Eugene Hastings
+1 412 268 4960
pscnet-admin@psc.edu
Services: Network connections.

Puerto Rico
SURAnet
Deborah J. Nunn
+1 301 982 4600
marketing@sura.net
Services: Network connections.

Rhode Island
NEARnet
John Curran
+1 617 873 8730
nearnet-join@nic.near.net
Services: Network connections, dialup IP.

RISCnet
Andy Green
+1 401 885 6855
info@nic.risc.net
Services: Network connections, dialup IP.

The IDS World Network
+1 401 884 7856
sysadmin@ids.net
Services: Dialup e-mail, SLIP.

South Carolina
SURAnet
Deborah J. Nunn
+1 301 982 4600
marketing@sura.net
Services: Network connections.

South Dakota
MIDnet
Dale Finkelson
+1 402 472 5032
dmf@westie.unl.edu
Services: Network connections.

Tennessee
SURAnet
Deborah J. Nunn
+1 301 982 4600
marketing@sura.net
Services: Network connections.

Texas
SESQUINET
Farrell Gerbode
+1 713 527 4988
farrell@rice.edu
Services: Network connections, dialup IP.

The Black Box
Marc Newman
+1 713 480-2684
mknewman@blkbox.com
Services: Dialup e-mail

THEnet
William Green
+1 512 471 3241
green@utexas.edu
Services: Network connections.

Sugar Land Unix
+1 713 438 4964
info@NeoSoft.com
Services: Dialup e-mail.

Utah
Westnet
Pat Burns
+1 303 491 7260
pburns@yuma.acns.colostate.edu
Services: Network connections.

Vermont
NEARnet
John Curran
+1 617 873 8730
nearnet-join@nic.near.net
Services: Network connections, dialup IP.

Virginia
SURAnet
Deborah J. Nunn
+1 301 982 4600
marketing@sura.net
Services: Network connections.

VERnet
James Jokl
+1 804 924 0616
jaj@virginia.edu
Services: Network connections.

CAPCON Connect
+1 202 466 7057
jhagermn@capcon.net
Services: Dialup e-mail, dialup IP.

Express Access Online Communications Service
+1 301 220 2020
info@digex.com
Services: Dialup e-mail in the northern
VA; Baltimore, MD;
Washington, DC areas (area codes 202,
310, 410, 703).

Washington
NorthWestNet
Eric Hood
+1 206 562 3000
ehood@nwnet.net
Services: Network connections.

World dot Net
Internetworks, Inc.
+1 206 576 7147
info@world.net
Services: Network connections.

Halcyon
+1 206 426 9298
info@remote.halcyon.com
Services: Dialup e-mail to Seattle area.

Seattle Online
Bruce King
+1 206 328 2412
bruceki@online.com
Services: Dialup e-mail to Seattle area.

West Virginia
PSCNET
Eugene Hastings
+1 412 268 4960
pscnet-admin@psc.edu
Services: Network connections.

SURAnet
Deborah J. Nunn
+1 301 982 4600
marketing@sura.net
Services: Network connections.

WVNET
Harper Grimm
+1 304 293 5192
cc011041@wvnvms.wvnet.edu
Services: Network connections, dialup IP.

Wisconsin
CICNet
John Hankins
+1 313 998 6102
hankins@cic.net
Services: Network connections.

WiscNet
Tad Pinkerton
+1 608 262 8874
tad@cs.wisc.edu
Services: Network connections.

Milwaukee Internet X
+1 414 962 8172
sysop@mixcom.com
Services: Dialup e-mail to the Milwaukee
area.

Wyoming
NorthWestNet
Eric Hood
+1 206 562 3000
ehood@nwnet.net
Services: Network connections.

Westnet
Pat Burns
+1 303 491 7260
pburns@yuma.acns.colostate.edu
Services: Network connections.

5

Nsfnet Acceptable Use Policy

For networks that expect to pass only research or educational information, connection to one of the NSFNET mid-level networks is a possibility. The NSFNET and many of its mid-levels have acceptable usage policies which offer guidelines as to what acceptable use of their network is and what the traffic policies are for those interested in sending traffic through these networks. Reprinted here is the Acceptable Use Policy for the NSFNET backbone. Many of the policies of the mid-level networks resemble this one. However, always ask explicitly what a network provider's acceptable use policy is. For example, those mid-level networks that are also members of the CIX will have different sorts of policies from those that are not CIX members. Networks that are members of the CIX Association have no restrictions on the types of traffic sent as long as traffic conforms to legal practices.

The NSFNET Backbone Services Acceptable Use Policy

General Principle:

(1) NSFNET backbone services are provided to support open research and education in and among U.S. research and instructional institutions, plus research arms of for-profit firms when engaged in open scholarly communication and research. Use for other purposes is not acceptable.

Specifically Acceptable Uses:

(2) Communication with foreign researchers and educators in connection with research or instruction, as long as any network that the foreign user employs for such communication provides reciprocal access to U.S. researchers and educators.

(3) Communication and exchange for professional development, to maintain currency, or to debate issues in a field or subfield of knowledge.

(4) Use for disciplinary-society, university-association, government-advisory, or standards activities related to the user's research and instructional activities.

(5) Use in applying for or administering grants or contracts for research or instruction, but not for other fundraising or public relations activities.

(6) Any other administrative communications or activities in direct support of research and instruction.

(7) Announcements of new products or services for use in research or instruction, but not advertising of any kind.

(8) Any traffic originating from a network of another member agency of the Federal Networking Council if the traffic meets the acceptable use policy of that agency.

(9) Communication incidental to otherwise acceptable use, except for illegal or specifically unacceptable use.

Unacceptable Uses:

(10) Use for for-profit activities (consulting for pay, sales or administration of campus stores, sale of tickets to sports events, and so on) or use by for-profit institutions unless covered by the General Principle or as a specifically acceptable use.

(11) Extensive use for private or personal business.

This statement applies to use of the the NSFNET backbone only. NSF expects that connecting networks will formulate their own use policies. The NSF Division of Networking and Communications Research and Infrastructure will resolve any questions about this policy or its interpretation.

6

NON-U.S. SITES

The Internet, having originated in the United States, is not surprisingly strongest and most diverse in that country. However, the Internet is a worldwide enterprise and there are many networks in many countries that are full and active Internet participants. Larry Landweber of the University of Wisconsin maintains a file describing international connectivity that covers not only IP connectivity, but BITNET, UUCP, FidoNet, and OSI connectivity as well. According to the April 15, 1993, version of this file, there are 127 entities (mostly countries) with international connectivity. A slightly earlier version of this file is included in Appendix VIII.

This chapter describes some of these networks. These descriptions are provided so that if you are in one of these countries and would like to connect to the Internet, you can contact the resource listed for your country and get started.

However, what if you are in a country that is not listed here? How would you go about joining the Internet? This can be a challenge if there is currently no Internet presence in your country, but here are some ideas about how to get started.

First, determine whether the top-level domain for your country has been delegated by the InterNIC Registration Service. That is, does InterNIC Registration Services list an administrative contact for that domain? You can find this out by contacting InterNIC:

> Network Solutions, Inc.
> InterNIC Registration Services
> 505 Huntmar Park Drive
> Herndon, VA 22070
> 800 444 4345
> +1 703 742 4777
> +1 619 455 4600
> hostmaster@rs.internic.net

If the InterNIC does list someone, contact that person. He or she is probably knowledgeable about networking in your country and can help you get started. You will need to register your domain name with him as well.

If your country's domain has not been delegated, there is probably no connection to the Internet based on the TCP/IP protocols. However, there may be at least electronic mail access based on other protocols. You may wish to check books that have lists of networks. For example, *!%@:: A Directory of Electronic Mail Addressing and Networks* by Donnalyn Frey and Rick Adams [1], *The Matrix* by John Quarterman [2], and *Users' Directory of Computer Networks* by Tracy LaQuey [4] have network listings that are much more extensive than those provided here. In addition, there are a couple of newsletters that often discuss the international aspects of networking. One is the *Internet Society News* [5], whose first volume was issued in January 1992; another is *Matrix News* [6], offered by Matrix

Information and Directory Services, Inc. More information about each of these newsletters can be found in Chapter 12.

If you can find no established networking presence in your country, you will have to start from scratch by contacting possible providers and seeing what they can do for you. Some good places to start are:

➤ The commercial service providers listed in Chapter 4. As they are in the business of providing Internet connections, they are very motivated to help. Some of them already have connections from the U.S. to other countries. These particular providers are repeated in Section 6.39. However, some of their non-U.S. connections may be due to special project affiliations or some other arrangement that might make it difficult for these sites to help some other organization, even within the same country, join the Internet.

➤ InterNIC Information Services. The InterNIC is very knowledgeable about connections to the Internet from other countries and can be helpful in suggesting contacts or strategies.

➤ The BITNET Network Information Center (BITNIC) (see Section 10.5.5). Although BITNET access is not full Internet access, it can be used for electronic mail. BITNET has a strong sister network in Europe called EARN (see Section 6.1.1.2).

➤ In Europe, the RIPE Network Coordination Center (NCC) supports the network providers in the member countries. They may know of some activity in IP networking in your area and be able to refer you to a local contact (see Section 6.1.1.6).

The following sections provide information about specific countries or areas. We are grateful to the contacts in these countries who have supplied this information for us. If you are a provider of Internet access in your country and do not see your information reflected in the following sections, please feel free to send it to us at SRI via the contact information provided in the Overview. Most notably we regret the comparative lack of information regarding networking activities in South America and Africa. The newsletters mentioned above are a good source of current information for networking in these, as well as other, areas.

6.1. Europe

Internetworking in Europe is quite strong in many countries—in many more countries, in fact, than we include here. As mentioned in the introduction to this chapter, there are several books whose purpose it is to list networks, but that is not the primary purpose of this book. If you cannot gain access to any of the books mentioned, a network information center (such as the InterNIC) can provide information for you about what they contain.

Europe is the home of the OSI protocols, so networking based on these protocols is much more extensive there than in the U.S. Networking based on TCP/IP, however, is also strong, as shown by the influence of the RIPE group (see Section 10.1.6). In addition, the goal of communicating between networks based on each of these suites of protocols is given very high priority in Europe.

However, in some individual countries, there is some conflict between which suite of protocols should be used for national networking. There may also be some uncertainty regarding which agency or site will coordinate a national networking effort. This makes it more confusing both for those trying to gain access to the network world and for those trying to ascertain service provider referrals.

This section provides two general types of information. First, several groups are working in Europe at coordinating networking efforts in individual countries into Internets that serve larger areas. These groups are introduced in the following subsections. Second, thanks to input from the RARE Information Services and User Support Working Group (ISUS), we list contacts in Section 6.1.2 for many European networks taken from the first RARE Technical Report. This section includes contacts for some networks about which we have more extensive information elsewhere in this chapter, as well as contacts for some networks for which we have yet not gathered further descriptions.

6.1.1. Pan-European cooperation

There are several efforts being made toward uniting networking efforts in individual countries into a pan-European cooperation. EUnet currently provides a framework for uniting many national networks. The EBONE project is a new effort at a pan-European, multi-protocol backbone. In addition, the EARN and HEPnet networks have existed across Europe for some time. The RIPE Network Coordination Center is a relatively new group tasked to provide support to the RIPE member networks. Each of these widespread European efforts is described briefly in this subsection. However, as yet, there is no one organization we can point to if you are in a country not listed here and wish to join the Internet.

6.1.1.1. EUnet

SRI thanks Alessandro Berni for forwarding this information about EUnet.

EUnet is the largest subscription-funded research-oriented network in Europe, serving users from Iceland to Russia, and as far south as Tunisia. Operating since 1982, EUnet connects over four thousand sites and networks, with gateways to major research networks around the world including NSFNET and the Internet.

EUnet is constituted as a service by and for the members of EurOpen, the European Forum for Open Systems. Founded in 1977, EurOpen is a non-profit association of Open Systems users, organized into National User Groups in Europe and beyond. At present EurOpen has more than 6,000 members. The close association of EUnet with EurOpen provides a continuing source of user input.

EUnet is a pan-European cooperative network made up of national networks located across Europe. Each EUnet National Network (or NalNet) operates in conjunction with their respective national EurOpen User Group. Each NalNet operates its own National Network Operations Center (National NOC), which provides user support in the local languages. Technical problems and requests for services at the national level should be addressed to postmaster@<country>.eu.net. Many NalNets provide unique services. Please contact your NalNet for additional information.

Each EUnet NalNet connects to the European Network Operations Center (or NOC) in Amsterdam. From Amsterdam, EUnet connects to every major R & D network in Europe, and, via a 128kb leased line, to UUNET and the

NSFNET in the United States. Technical problems at the European level should be addressed to postmaster@eu.net. Users interested in information on how to obtain an EUnet subscription should contact glenn@eu.net or their National EUnet Network.

EUnet services include electronic mail, network news, InterEUnet (TCP/IP based networking services), UUCP, the EUnet Archive, and user support services.

EUnet connects to every major research network in Europe, and most research networks around the world. Peer international networks include EARN, HEPnet, NORDUnet, NSFNET. EUnet is also a member of EBONE (European Backbone), and the Commercial Internet Exchange (CIX) Association. Several EUnet NalNets are users of IXI, the X.25 service.

EUnet has a social-technical mission to provide services to a wide range of users, from the one-person software development organizations to research centers of large, multinational corporations. EUnet has a special focus on helping to make networking available to as many members of the R & D community, in as many countries, as is possible. Accordingly, should EUnet develop a budgetary surplus, it is to be used for grants to networks in developing countries.

For more information about EUnet, contact:

```
EUnet
c/o NIKHEF
Postbus 41882
1009 DB Amsterdam
NETHERLANDS
glenn@eu.net
+31 20 592 5109
FAX: +31 20 592 5155
```

6.1.1.2. EARN

We would like to acknowledge and thank Nadine Grange of the EARN office in France for the following information.

EARN, the European Academic Research Network, is the first general purpose computer network dedicated to universities and research institutions throughout Europe, the Middle East, and Africa.

The network is widely used for scientific, educational, academic, and research purposes. Commercial and political use is not allowed, either directly or indirectly.

EARN is made up of nearly 500 institutions including universities, European research centers (e.g., CERN, the European Space Agency, and the European Molecular Biology Laboratory), and national research centers and laboratories such as CNRS (France); Rutherford Appleton Laboratory (U.K.); CNR, INFN, and CINECA (Italy); DESY, GSI, DFLVR, and the Max Planck Institute (Germany).

EARN also has links to 27 countries including Yugoslavia, Turkey, Algeria, Morocco, Tunisia, Egypt, Iceland, and Luxembourg, to name a few.

EARN is an integral part of BITNET (see Section 1.5.4), in that it is based on the same protocols and shares the same name space. Through BITNET, EARN members have access to equivalent facilities in Argentina, Brazil, Canada, Chile, Japan, South Korea, Mexico, Singapore, Taiwan, and the United States.

Most of the academic networks in the world can be accessed through EARN including EUnet, HEPnet, NSFNET, national European networks such as DFN in Germany and JANET in the U.K., as well as a regional European network such as NORDUnet, which links all the Nordic countries (see Section 6.28).

One of EARN's major objectives is to stimulate cooperative research, support the day-to-day exchange of research information, and execute joint projects and publications. Like BITNET, EARN supports mail, mailing lists, and a type of file transfer. It provides the LISTSERV mailing list function. Its facilities also allow users access to remote applications, databases, and libraries.

EARN is also an international member of RARE (Reseaux Associes pour la Recherche Europeenne) and cooperates actively with RARE and COSINE (Cooperation for Open Systems Interconnection Networking in Europe) on OSI for the research community. RARE and COSINE are more fully described in Sections 10.1.5 and 10.1.7.

For information about access to EARN, how to become a member organization or member country, or any other general information, contact your country's EARN representative or:

European Academic Research Network
BP 167
F-91403 Orsay CEDEX
FRANCE
BITNET/EARN/NetNorth: grange@frors12
Internet: grange%frors12.bitnet@mitvma.mit.edu
+33 1 69 82 39 73
FAX: +33 1 69 28 52 73

6.1.1.3. HEPnet

HEPnet is a worldwide network used by researchers in the field of High Energy Physics; however, the European portion of the network is very prominent. It is mentioned here because HEPnet was one of the first pan-European internets. In Europe, HEPnet is coordinated by a committee chaired by a CERN (Organisation Europeenne pour la Recherche Nuclearie) representative.

For information about HEPnet, contact:

> Denise Heagerty
> DD Division
> CERN
> CH-1211 Geneve 23
> SWITZERLAND
> denise@priam.cern
> denise%priam.cern@cwl.nl
> +41 022 83 49 75
> TELEX: 419000 CER CH

6.1.1.4. EBONE

EBONE (E1 Backbone) is an effort aimed at filling the need for a well-managed, pan-European multi-protocol backbone service in Europe. An initial meeting to delineate the technical and operational aspects of such a backbone was held in September 1991, so this effort is very new. An EBONE task force has recommended a two-step approach to implementing this backbone:

1. During 1992, create a kernel backbone by combining and enhancing existing facilities.

2. In 1993, merge the 92 backbone into the planned RARE Operational Unit.

The target group for EBONE is all the national and international networks and international research institutions that provide network services for users at higher education and research sites. In principal, the EBONE will have no restrictions on traffic. It will be up to participating networks to restrict traffic according to their own norms.

In September 1992, it was announced that the the final link of the initially defined EBONE, the London-Montpellier link, was put in place. The EBONE is now complete as a resilient pan-European IP backbone.

The RARE Secretariat has the responsibility for maintaining information regarding EBONE. They are the contact

point for organizations planning to contribute and/or connect to the EBONE.

```
RARE Secretariat
Singel 466-468
NL-1017 AW
AMSTERDAM
+31 20 639 1131
FAX: +31 20 639 3289
raresec@rare.nl
```

6.1.1.5. RARE

RARE, the Reseaux Associes pour la Recherche Europeenne, is described more fully in Section 10.1.5, but briefly
it is an association of European networking organizations.
Its purpose is to promote network services for the European research community, and especially to promote international interconnections of such services. Please also
refer to Section 10.1.6 for information regarding the RARE-
sponsored organization RIPE (see Section 10.1.6).

For more information, contact:

```
RARE Secretariat
Singel 466-468
NL-1017 AW
AMSTERDAM
+31 20 639 1131
FAX: +31 20 639 3289
raresec@rare.nl
```

6.1.1.6. The RIPE Network Coordination Center (NCC)

The RIPE NCC began operation on April 1, 1992, with the
mission of supporting the networking organizations that
cooperate in RIPE (see Section 10.1.6 for information
about RIPE). The RIPE Network Coordination Center
(NCC) supports all those RIPE activities that cannot be effectively performed by volunteers from the participating
organizations. Besides supporting RIPE activities in general, the NCC provides the following services to network
operators:

> Network Management Database containing information about IP networks, DNS domains, IP routing policies, and contact information

> Delegated Internet registry, a clearing house distributing IP network numbers

> Coordinated network statistics gathering

> Domain Name System (DNS) coordination

> Graphical maps of IP networks (planned)

> Repository for network operations software

> RIPE document store

> Interactive information service

The RIPE NCC provides services to the networking organizations that cooperate in RIPE. It does not provide direct services to end users.

The RIPE NCC currently has three permanent staff members. The RARE association provides the formal framework for the NCC. Funding for the first year of operation of the NCC is provided by the national members of RARE and EARN.

The RIPE NCC will function as a "Delegated Registry" for IP addresses in Europe, as anticipated and defined in RFC 1174. The NCC keeps the registry of IP (Internet Protocol) numbers and AS (Autonomous System) numbers for the RIPE member organizations. This will mean that the NCC allocates blocks of numbers to local registrars in Europe. It remains the responsibility of the NCC to collect information regarding how the local registrars allocate IP addresses and make such information available globally. The local registries are set up by RIPE member organizations as appropriate. Particular requests that cannot be handled by local registries will be handled by the NCC.

To contact the RIPE NCC:

RIPE NCC
c/o NIKHEF
Kruislaan 409
NL-1098 SJ Amsterdam
THE NETHERLANDS
+31 20 592 5065
FAX: +31 20 592 5155
ncc@ripe.net

6.1.2. European Network Contacts List

We are indebted to the RARE Information Services and
User Support Working Group for the information contained in this section. It is taken from RARE Technical
Report 1, *User Support and Information Services in Europe:
A Status Report* [32]. This report aims to provide guidance
regarding the numerous networks and the information
found on them, specifically focusing on the answers to
the questions "Who should I ask about a network?" and
"Where can I find the 'signposts' to this information?" It is
an excellent introduction to networking efforts in Europe,
from which we have extracted only contact information to
help you get started. The document also contains information about what services each network offers and how
they may be accessed, as well as information about how
the survey was conducted and background information
about RARE, the Information Services and User Support
working group, and various network servers from which
information can be obtained online.

To obtain this document, send a message to the Mailbase
server. The address is mailbase@mailbase.ac.uk. In X.400
format, the address is C=gb; ADMD= ; PRMD=uk.ac;
O=mailbase; S=mailbase. In the text of your message, type
send rare-wg3-usis rtr-usis-92.

Some of these contacts are repeated in information elsewhere in this chapter, with more extensive descriptions of
their networks. They are included again for completeness

in representing the RARE information. The other contacts are included as a starting point for people in their countries, even though we have not yet collected more extensive descriptions of their networks.

Contacts for the networks reported in the RARE WG3 Technical Report are listed next. For each network listed, entries follow this format:

```
Network Name
Contact person(s)
Postal address
Telephone number
E-Mail address in RFC 822 format
E-Mail address in X.400 format
```

Austria
ACONET
  Austrian Scientific Data Network
  Florian Schnabel
  ACONET-Verein
  Gusshausstrasse 25
  A-1040 Wien
  AUSTRIA
  +43 222 58801 3605
  schnabel@edvz.tu-graz.ada.at
  schnabel@fstgss01.tu-graz.ac.at
  C=at; ADMD=ada; PRMD=tu-graz;
  O=edvz; S=schnabel

Belgium
Future Belgian National Academic Network
  P. Van Binst
  R. Vandenbroucke
  ULB
  CP 230, Bd du Triomphe
  1050 Bruxelles
  BELGIUM
  +32 2 641 32 11
  vanbinst@helios.iihe.rtt.be
  C=be; ADMD=rtt; PRMD=iihe; O=helios;
  S=vanbinst

Denmark
DENet
  Jan.P.Sorensen
  Jan.P.Sorensen@uni-c.dk
  Building 305, DTH, DK-2800, Lyngby
  DENMARK
  +45 45 93 83 55
  C=dk; ADMD=DENET; O=UNI-C;
  OU=NET; S=SORENSEN

France (EARN)
EARN-France
  Dominique Dumas
  950 re de St. Priest
  F-34000 Montpellier
  FRANCE
  +33 67 14 14 14
  BITNET: bruch@frmop11
  Internet: bruch@frmop53.cnusc.fr
RED400
  Serge Aumont
  CICB
  Campus de Beaulieu
  35042 Rennes
  FRANCE
  or
  Paul-Andre Pays
  INRIA
  Domaine De Voluceau
  Rocquencourt
  BP 105
  78150 Le Chesnay Cedex
  FRANCE
  +33 1 39 63 54 58
  contact-red@cicb.fr
  C=FR; ADMD=atlas; PRMD=cicb;
  S=contact-red

Germany
DFN/WIN
  DFN-Verein
  Pariser Str. 44
  D-1000 Berlin 15
  GERMANY
  +49 30 88 42 99 20
  dfn-verein@dfn.dbp.de
  C=de; ADMD=dbp; PRMD=dfn; S=dfn-
  verein

Greece
ARIADNE
> Yannis Corovesis
> NRCPS Demokritos, 153 10 Athens
> GREECE
> +30 1 6513392
> ycor@isosun.ariadne-t.gr
> C=gr; ADMD= ; PRMD=ariadne-t;
> OU=iosun; S=corovesis; G=yannis

Hungary
HUNGARNET
> Istvan Tetenyi
> Computer and Automation Institute
> H-1132 Budapest
> 18-22 Victory Hugo
> HUNGARY
> +36 11497352
> postmaster@ella.hu

Iceland
ISnet
> Marius Olafsson
> c/o SURIS
> University of Iceland
> Dunhaga 5
> 107 Reykjavik
> ICELAND
> +354 1 694747
> marius@rhi.hi.is
> C=is; ADMD=0; PRMD=isaneet; O=hi;
> OU=rhi; S=marius

Ireland
HEANET
> Higher Education Authority Network
> Peter Flynn
> Computer Centre, University College,
> Cork IRELAND
> +353 21 276871 x2609
> cbts8001@iruccvax.ucc.ie

Italy
GARR
> Gianfranco Turso
> Tecnoplois CSATA Novus Ortus
> SP. Casamassima Km. 3
> I-70010 Valenzano (BA)
> ITALY
> +39 80 877011 Gianfranco Turso
> turso@vm.csata.it

Luxembourg
RESTENA
> Antoine Barthel
> 6 Rue Coudenhove Kalergi
> L-1359 Luxembourg
> +352 424409
> admin@restena.lu
> C=lu; ADMD=pt; PRMD=restena;
> O=restena; S=admin

The Netherlands
SURFnet
> Maria Heijne
> P.O.Box 19035
> 3501 DA Utrecht,
> THE NETHERLANDS
> +31 30310290
> info@surfnet.nl
> C=nl; ADMD=400net; PRMD=surf;
> O=surfnet; S=info

Norway
UNINETT
> Petter Kongshaug
> SINTEF DELAB
> 7034 Trondheim
> NORWAY
> +47 7 592980
> Petter.Kongshaug@delab.sintef.no
> C=no; ADMD= ; PRMD=uninett; O=sintef;
> OU=delab;
> S=kongshaug; G=petter

Portugal
RCCN
> Vasco Freitas
> Dr. Vasco Freitas
> CCES
> Universidade do Minho
> Largo do Paco
> P-4719 Braga Codex
> PORTUGAL
> +351 53 612257
> vf@ce.fccn.pt
> C=pt; ADMD= ; PRMD=fccn; O=ce;
> S=Freitas; G=Vasco

Slovenia
ARNES
> Marko Bonac
> ARNES Network
> Jamova 39, Ljubljana
> SLOVENIA
> +38 61 159199
> bonac@ijs.si
> C=si; ADMD=mail; PRMD=ac; O=ijs;
> S=bonac

Spain
RedIRIS
> Fundesco/RedIRIS
> Alcala, 61
> E-28014 Madrid
> SPAIN
> +34 1 4351214
> info@iris-dcp.es
> C=ES; ADMD=mensatex; PRMD=iris;
> O=iris-dcp; S=info

Sweden
SUNET
> Anders Gillner
> KTH,100 44, Stockholm
> SWEDEN
> +46 8 7906502
> postmaster@sunic.sunet.se

Switzerland
SWITCH
> Thomas Lenggenhager
> SWITCH Head Office
> Limmatquai 138
> CH-8001 Zuerich
> SWITZERLAND
> +41 1 261 8178
> postmaster@switch.ch
> C=CH; ADMD=arCom; PRMD=SWITCH;
> O=SWITCH; S=postmaster

Turkey
TUVAKA
> Esra Delen
> Ege Universitesi
> Bilgisayar Arastirma ve Uygulama
> Merkezi
> Bornova, Izmir 35100
> TURKEY
> +90 51 887228
> Esra@ege.edu.tr
> Esra@trearn.bitnet

United Kingdom
JANET
> Joint Academic Network
> JANET Liaison Desk
> c/o Rutherford Appleton Laboratory
> Chilton
> Didcot
> Oxon
> OX11 OQX
> UNITED KINGDOM
> +44 235 5517
> JANET-LIAISON-DESK@jnt.ac.uk
> O=GB; ADMD= ; PRMD=uk.ac; O=jnt;
> G=JANET-LIAISON-DESK

Regional Networks

Both NORDUnet and YUNAC are discussed
more fully elsewhere in this
chapter.

NORDUnet
> Peter Villemoes
> UNI-C,
> Build. 305, DTH
> DK-2800 Lyngby
> DENMARK
> +45 45 938355
> Peter.Villemoes@uni-c.dk

YUNAC
> Avgust Jauk
> Jozef Stefan Institute
> Jamova 39, Ljubljana,
> SLOVENIA
> +38 61 159199
> postmaster@ijs.ac.mail.yu
> C=yu; ADMD=mail; PRMD=ac;
> O=ijs; S=postmaster

6.1.3. Eastern and Central Europe

The following information is taken from a report by Milan Sterba published as Ripe 74, Version 5, November 1992 [33]. At the time of this writing, it was available from host ftp.ripe.net as ripe/docs/ripe-drafts/ripe-draft-ece.v5.txt. The report is more complete than the information we include here. Again, we are primarily concerned with providing contacts from whom you can gain more detailed information. Some of the countries mentioned in this section may be listed elsewhere in the chapter as well.

The report begins by noting that "considerable progress has been made during the last year in IP connectivity of ECE [Eastern and Central European] countries." He notes that all connected countries have rapidly challenged the initial capacity of their international lines and are seeking to upgrade the existing lines and establish fallback solutions.

"All the countries considered have at the present time some (often more than one) connection to international networks. Certain countries have only a dialup e-mail connectivity, others have low- or medium-speed leased lines."

In this section, for each country discussed, we reproduce the points of contact given in the report.

Albania

Maksim Raco
maksi@dinf.uniti.al
University of Tirana

Francesco Gennai
francesco.gennai@cnuce.cnr.it
CNUCE, Pisa, Italy

Estonia

Ants Work
ants@ioc.ew.su
Institute of Cybernetics, Tallinn

Latvia

Guntis Barzdins
gbarzdin@cs.lu.riga.lv

Ugis Berzins
ugis@fidogate.riga.lv

BaltNet

Sergei Rotanov
rotanov@lumii.lat.su
Institute of Electronics

Sergey Dmitrijev
dmit@lynx.riga.lv
JET (RELCOM Riga)

Lithuania

Laimutis Telksnys
telksnys@ma-mii.lt.su
Institute for Mathematics, Vilnius

Algirdas Pakstas
Algirdas.Pakstas@idt.unit.no
Institute for Mathematics, Vilnius

Bulgaria

Daniel Kalchev
daniel@danbo.bg
EUnet backbone manager BG and
contact for top-level domain BG

Anton Velichkov
vam@bgearn.bitnet
EARN president for Bulgaria

Alexander Simeonov
sasho@bgearn.bitnet
Center for Informatics, Sofia

Commonwealth of Independent States

Valery Bardin
fox@ussr.eu.net
EUnet - RELCOM

Misha Popov
popov@hq.demos.su
EUnet - RELCOM Demos

Andrej Mendkovich
mend@suearn2.bitnet
CIS EARN director

Nickolay M.Saukh
nms@ussr.eu.net
EUnet - RELCOM

Igor Sviridov
sia%lot.cs.kiev.ua@relay.ussr.eu.net
EUnet - Ukraine contact

Oleg Tabarovsky
olg@ussr.eu.net
EUnet - RELCOM

Dima Volodin
dvv@hq.demos.su
EUnet - RELCOM Demos

Czechoslovakia

Jaroslav Bobovsky
bobovsky @csearn.bitnet
SANET

Gejza Buechler
gejza@mff.uniba.cs
EUnet backbone manager CS

Karol Fabian
Karol.Fabian@uakom.cs
SANET

Jan Gruntorad
tkjg@csearn.bitnet
EARN director for Czechoslovakia
and CESNET coordinator

Vladimir Kassa
kassa@iaccs.cs
SANET

Jiri Orsag
ors@vscht.cs
CS NIC and EUnet Prague

Peter Pronay
peter@mff.uniba.cs
President of EUnet Czechoslovakia

Pavel Rosendorf
prf@csearn.bitnet
Contact for .CS top-level domain

Ivo Smejkal
ivo@vse.cs
CESNET - user services

Milan Sterba
Milan.Sterba@vse.cs
Author of this report, CESNET

Hungary

Peter Bakonyi
h25bak@ella.hu
President of IIF Exec Com.

Laszlo Csaba
ib006csa@huearn.bitnet
EARN director for Hungary

Piroska Giese
giese@rmk530.rmki.kfki.hu
HEPnet

Nandor Horvath
horvath@sztaki.hu
EUnet backbone manager,
domain contact for HU

Balazs Martos
martos@sztaki.hu
HBONE project manager

Ferenc Telbisz
telbisz@iif.kfki.hu
HEPnet

Istvan Tetenyi
ib006tet@huearn.bitnet
EARN deputy director

Geza Turchanyi
h2064tur@ella.hu
HUNGARNET CRIP

Laszlo Zombory
h340zom@ella.hu
EARN president, chairman of HUNINET

Poland

Daniel J.Bem
bem@plwrtu11.bitnet
Polish academic network (NASK)

Jerzy Gorazinski
Gorazi@plearn.bitnet
Polish State Committee for
Scientific Research

Krzystof Heller
uiheller@plkrcy11.bitnet
Contact for PL domain

Tomasz Hofmokl
fdl50@plearn.bitnet
EARN director for Poland

Rafal Pietrak
rafal@fuw.edu.pl
IP within NASK

Jerzy Zenkiewicz
jezenk@pltumk.bitnet
Polish academic network (NASK)

Andrzej Zienkiewicz
osk03@plearn.bitnet
Polish academic network (NASK)

Romania

Florin Paunescu
florin@imag.fr
National Council for Informatics

Paul Dan Cristea
pdcristea@pi-bucuresti.th-
darmstadt.de
Polytechnic Institute of Bucharest

Slovenia

Leon Mlakar
leon@ninurta.fer.si
EUnet backbone manager YU

Borka Jerman-Blazic
jerman-blazic@ijs.si

Marko Bonac
marko.bonac@ijs.si
ARNES Executive Director

Denis Trcek
denis.trcek@ijs.si
ARNES

Serbia and Montenegro
Jagos Puric
xpmfd01@yubgss21.bitnet
EARN director for YU

Macedonia

Marjan Gusev
pmfmarj%nubsk@uni-lj.ac.mail.yu
or gusev@lut.ac.uk
Faculty for Natural Sciences,
Gazibaba, Skopje

Aspazija Hadzisce
rkntriasp%nubsk@uni-lj.ac.mail.yu
Ministry for Science and Technology,
Skopje

6.2. Canada

UUNET Canada

UUNET Canada serves all of Canada and offers international connectivity to the Internet via UUCP, Telnet, IP connections, and a corporate WAN service. This provider offers all the AlterNet services as well. It is a member of the CIX, and serves both the research and commercial communities.

For more information about UUNET Canada, contact:

UUNET Canada Inc.
1 Yonge Street
Suite 1801
Toronto, Ontario
M5E 1W7
CANADA
+1 416 368 6621
FAX: +1 416 369 0515
info@uunet.ca

CA*net

SRI thanks Eugene Siciunas of the University of Toronto for much of the information we present about CA*net.

Canada began implementation of its national research and academic network, called CA*net, in the summer of 1990. It is intended to interconnect the existing and emerging Canadian regional networks, and thereby to support data communications related to the research, academic, and technology transfer needs of Canada.

Following is information about CA*net and its ten-member regional networks.

CA*net
CA*net Information Centre
    Computing Services
    University of Toronto
    4 Bancroft Ave., Rm. 116
    Toronto, Ontario
    CANADA, M5S 1A1
    Attn: Eugene Siciunas
    416 978 5058
    FAX: 416 978 6620
    info@CAnet.ca
    eugene@vm.utcs.utoronto.ca

Quebec
RISQ Reseau Interordinateurs Scientifique
    Quebecois
    Centre de Recherche Informatique de
    Montreal (CRIM)
    3744, Jean-Brillant, Suite 500
    Montreal, Quebec
    CANADA, H3T 1P1
    Attn: Bernard Turcotte
    514 340 5700
    FAX: 514 340 5777
    turcotte@crim.ca

Ontario
ONet ONet Computing Services
    University of Toronto
    4 Bancroft Avenue, Rm. 116
    Toronto, Ontario,
    CANADA, M5S 1A1
    Attn: Eugene Siciunas
    416 978 5058
    FAX: 416 978 6620
    eugene@vm.utcs.utoronto.ca

Manitoba
MBnet
    Director, Computing Services
    University of Manitoba
    603 Engineering Building
    Winnipeg, Manitoba
    CANADA, R3T 2N2
    Attn: Gerry Miller
    204 474 8230
    FAX: 204 275 5420
    miller@ccm.UManitoba.ca

Saskatchewan
SASK#net
    Computing Services
    56 Physics
    University of Saskatchewan
    Saskatoon, Saskatchewan
    CANADA, S7N 0W0
    Dean Jones
    306 966 4860
    FAX: 306 966 4938
    jonesdc@admin.usask.ca

Alberta
ARnet
    Alberta Research Network
    Director of Information Systems
    Alberta Research Council
    Box 8330, Station F
    Edmonton, Alberta
    CANADA, T6H 5X2
    Attn: Walter Neilson
    403 450 5188
    FAX: 403 461 2651
    neilson@TITAN.arc.ab.ca

British Columbia
BCnet
    BCnet Headquarters
    Room 419 - 6356 Agricultural Road
    University of British Columbia
    Vancouver, B.C.
    CANADA, V6T 1W5
    Attn: Mike Patterson
    604 822 3932
    FAX: 604 822 5116
    Mike_Patterson@mtsg.ubc.ca

Newfoundland
NLnet
    Newfoundland and Labrador Network
    Director, Computing and Communica-
    tions
    Memorial University of Newfoundland
    St. John's, Newfoundland
    CANADA, A1C 5S7
    Attn: Wilf Bussey
    709 737 8329
    FAX: 709 737 4569
    wilf@kean.ucs.mun.ca

Nova Scotia
NSTN
    Nova Scotia Technology Network
    General Manager, NSTN Inc.
    900 Windmill Road, Suite 107
    Dartmouth, Nova Scotia
    CANADA, B3B 1P7
    Attn: Mike Martineau
    902 468 6786
    FAX: 902 468 3679
    martinea@hawk.nstn.ns.ca

Prince Edward Island
    Prince Edward Island Network
    University of Prince Edward Island
    Computer Services
    550 University Avenue
    Charlottetown, P.E.I.

CANADA, C1A 4P3
Attn: Jim Hancock
902 566 0450
FAX: 902 566 0958
hancock@upei.ca

New Brunswick
NBnet
    Director, Computing Services
    University of New Brunswick
    Fredericton, New Brunswick
    CANADA, E3B 5A3
    Attn: David Macneil
    506 453 4573
    FAX: 506 453 3590
    DGM@unb.ca

In addition, Mr. John Demco of the Computer Science Department of the University of British Columbia acts as the registrar for the CA domain (CA is the ISO 3166 two-letter country code designation for Canada). Mr. Demco can provide information to those sites interested in becoming a subdomain of CA.

For those already connected to the Internet, online information is available by anonymous FTP from host ftp.cdnnet.ca in the ca-domain directory. Included is an introduction to the domain, an application form, several indices, and a registration file for each organizational subdomain. The information is also available via e-mail from the archive server at archive-server@cdnnet.ca.

If you're not connected, but would like additional information about the CA domain or sites currently registered under CA, contact:

John Demco
Computer Science Dept.
University of British Columbia
Vancouver, B.C.
CANADA V6T 1Z2
demco@cs.ubc.ca
604 822 6724
FAX: 604 822 5485

6.3. Australia

connect.com.au Pty Ltd.

 connect.com.au Pty Ltd. provides local access to users in Melbourne and Sidney. Some of the services provided include SLIP, PPP, ISDN, UUCP, ftp, Telnet, NTP, and FTPmail. For further information contact:

> connect.com.au Pty Ltd.
> 29 Fitzgibbon Crescent
> Caufield, Victoria 3161
> AUSTRALIA
> +61 3 5282239
> FAX: +1 61 3 5285887
> connect@connect.com.au

AARNet

The Australian Academic and Research Network (AARNet) is a multi-protocol national network serving the Australian academic and research community. Our thanks to Geoff Huston for providing this information.

The network provides Internet services to the national academic and research sector as its primary objective, and also provides Internet services to any other organization with compatible interests to this sector on a fee-for-service basis.

AARNet was commissioned in May 1990, and currently uses 2-megabit capacity links across the major trunk routes interconnecting Adelaide, Melbourne, Canberra, Sydney, and Brisbane.

AARNet is connected to the U.S. Internet via a dedicated 512 kbps circuit to the United States, and also provides an Internet mail delivery service to Papua New Guinea and Thailand.

TCP/IP is the major supported protocol within AARNet. A national DECnet Phase IV network is supported, but it should be noted that there is no DECnet interconnection between this DECnet network and the HEP/SPAN DECnet.

X.25 is also supported on a regional basis, and an interconnection to the public X.400 mail service is also supported.

Further information regarding AARNet (including maps, a
more detailed description of the network, a list of connected institutions and organizations, and an Australian
network resource guide) is available via anonymous
ftp from the host aarnet.edu.au. The Australian resource
guide is also published in the Internet as a WAIS service.
The guide itself is maintained by Geoff Huston,
G.Huston@aarnet.edu.au.

For additional information regarding AARNet contact:

> Geoff Huston
> The Australian Academic and Research Network
> GPO Box 1142
> Canberra ACT 2601
> AUSTRALIA
> +61 6 249 3385
> G.Huston@aarnet.edu.au

PRO-NET

PRO-NET is a user-friendly communications system, fully
menu-driven at all levels, providing a comprehensive Australia-wide and international communications and resource
network.Computers, terminals, and workstations connect
easily to PRO-NET by modem. PRO-NET is wholly Austra-
lian-owned, and provides Australia-wide and international
e-mail (electronic mail) by modem dialup from anywhere
in Australia, together with software archives, Australia-
wide and international forums, real-time discussion
lounges, database storage, and retrieval.

For more information contact:

> Phone: +61 3 349 2266
> Fax: +61 3 349 1257.
> Mail: sysop@tanus.oz.au
> Pro-Net Australia
> P.O Box 186
> North Carlton, Vic., 3054
> Melbourne, Australia

6.4. Czechoslovakia

 SRI thanks Pavel Rosendorf for providing this information.

In Czechoslovakia, public X.25 networking services have been provided by the PTT only very recently, so the majority of connections are dialup lines. There is a great effort now being undertaken to build a national backbone based on 64 kbps lines, running the set of TCP/IP protocols via Cisoc routers. There is a project underway, launched by INRIA (Institut National de Recherche en Informatique et Automatique), and supported by the French government, which will assist with the tasks of building this national backbone and improving overall IP connectivity of some Eastern Europen countries.

Czechoslovakia is connected to two international networks—EUnet and EARN. Connection to the EUnet is realized by a 9600 kbps leased line between Bratislava and Vienna, Austria. The protocol currently in use is UUCP, but tests are being performed to switch to the TCP/IP protocols as soon as possible.

The connection to EARN is via a 19,200 kbps leased line between the cities of Prague, Czechoslovakia, and Linz, Austria. The current protocol for this connection is TCP/IP via Cisco routers. There is also a test TCP/IP connection between Praha and Linz using SLIP implemented on PC. E-mail and news services are currently available to all users and remote login and file transfer services are available on the test line.

There are two networking organizations in Czechoslovakia—the Czechoslovakian part of EUnet (CSUUG) and the Czechoslovakian part of EARN (CSERN).

There are also plans underway by the government of Czechoslovakia to establish a federal organization for networking in the country.

For additional information about networking in Czecho-slovakia or administration of the top-level domain CS, contact:

Pavel Rosendorf
University of Wisconsin
Dept. of Chemical Engineering
1415 Johnson Drive
Madison, Wisconsin 53706
U.S.A.
+1 608 263 6592
FAX: +1 608 262 0832
rosendorf@chera1.che.wisc.edu

6.5. Hungary

SRI thanks Balazs Martos for this information about networking in Hungary.

The IIF network center, operated by the Academic Computer Infrastructure Division of the Computer and Automation Institute (MTA-SZTAKI/ASZI), provides many types of services to a large Hungarian user community. This community includes people from education, research and development, government, healthcare, libraries and museums, etc. Services for these nonprofit organizations are free of charge, financed by the "Information Infrastructure Program" of the government. Commercial users pay a modest contribution to cover a part of the service costs.

Network services are provided mainly over the large X.25 network in Hungary, but leased lines running IP are also connected to the center. UUCP and PAD based services (mail, file transfer, news) are accessable for dialup users as well. The IIF network center runs the EUnet and EARN national node, so it also provides services to the Hungarian EUnet and EARN nodes.

Tens of thousands of people are using the most popular mail service. Internet services like FTP and Telnet are becoming more and more a dominant part of the international bandwidth.

Services include:

➢ Line mode terminal access (XXX)
➢ 327x full screen service
➢ Central e-mail service (called ELLA) with gateways to
  the Internet and BITNET, and with a built-in direc-
  tory system
➢ Central file server
➢ Central bulletin board
➢ Databases
➢ BITNET Listserv
➢ NetNews

IP services include:

➢ Domain Name Server

➢ Anonymous FTP

➢ Electronic mail

➢ Remote login

For more information, contact:

Balazs Martos
Head of the Academic Computer Infrastructure Division
Computer & Automation Institute
Hungarian Academy of Sciences (MTA-SZTAKI/ASZI)
Budapest, XIII
Victor Hugo u. 18-22
HUNGARY
martos@sztaki.hu
+361 1497532
FAX: +361 1297866

6.6. Bulgaria

BGnet

SRI thanks Daniel Kalchev for this information on networking in Bulgaria.

BGnet in Bulgaria is presently very small, but it is growing
more stable.

At present, sites in Bulgaria connect over UUCP dialup
links or use the national X.25 network to the national back-

bone in Varna. The backbone is connected to two other EUnet backbones—the Greek national backbone in Heraklion, Crete, and the European EUnet backbone in Amsterdam, The Netherlands. Both links are over the X.25 network, with dialup connections in reserve when the X.25 network is not operational.

The following additional background information is taken from a draft of the paper *Implementing Internationally Connected Computer Networks in Bulgaria* by Daniel Kalchev [31].

Danbo BBS, the first Bulletin Board System in Bulgaria, started in Varna in November 1989.

Shortly after that, Danbo BBS became a member of FidoNet. Having connected to FidoNet, the BBS could offer international e-mail, which was affordable and reachable for anyone with a computer and modem. This had a significant social effect and shortly thereafter many other BBSs opened all around the country.

Many Bulgarian users, mostly researchers, desired wider connectivity and services. Many alternatives for acquiring such services were considered, but the final choice was EUnet. In December 1990, a Bulgarian site (danbo.uucp) connected to EUnet.

As the demand for networking services was high, EUnet installed a national backbone in Bulgaria. Other sites connected in September 1991, and the EUnet network in Bulgaria started operation.

EUnet offered not only e-mail, but also news and InterEUnet (worldwide IP connectivity). To ease the future connection of the national network to the Internet, it was necessary to register the national top-level domain; Bulgaria's top-level domain BG was registered in November 1991.

Several other groups in Bulgaria began attempts to establish international connections with other networks, most notably with EARN. An EARN node was installed in Sofia.

There is a public X.25 network in Bulgaria called BULPAC. When the EUnet backbone connects to BULPAC, the other sites can dial a local access number, login to BULPAC and then connect to the backbone.

Here is some numerical data about the Bulgarian EUnet network. This data reflects the state of the network on May 1, 1992.

Number of operational sites:	12
Number of sites by type:	
Companies	6
Universities	2
Public Institutions	2
Research	1
Government	1

The majority of these sites are in Varna or Sofia, although Burgas, Plovdiv, Blagoevrgad, and Rousse each have at least one site.

For more information about BGnet, contact:

```
BGnet
Daniel Kalchev
c/o Digital Systems
Neofit Bozveli 6
Varna - 9000
Bulgaria
Voice and FAX: +359 52 234540
postmaster@Bulgaria.EU.net
```

6.7. Romania

 SRI thanks Florin Paunescu for this information about Romania.

Currently, Romania has no operational country-wide academic (or other) network. Romania is not connected to any international network either, except for an end-user connection from the Polytecnical Institute of Bucharest

(IPB) to the Technical University of Darmstadt in Germany. The only service provided is e-mail for a group of people from IPB.

A connection to EARN is planned by July 1992. It will be connected to the University of Linz, Austria. Although there are still problems with obtaining export licenses for both this node and TCP/IP routers, it is planned that the services available will be those currently offered by EARN.

The first users connected to this EARN node will be the Research Institute for Informatics in Bucharest (ICI), which is also hosting the node; the Research Institute for Atomic Physics (IFA); and IPB. There is a Romanian EARN Board.

To obtain a country-wide academic network in Romania, a TCP/IP backbone network is planned. The project is supported by the National Commission of Informatics (CNI), which is an interministerial governmental body whose main role is to propose to the Government strategies and policies for information in Romania.

For more information about networking in Romania, contact:

Florin Paunescu
Commission Nationale d'Iformatique
Piata VICTORIEI Nr.1
71 201 Bucarest, ROUMANIE
Tel.: +19 400 12 12 18
Fax.: +19 400 12 12 19
e-mail: florin@imag.fr

6.8. Ukraine

SRI thanks Igor Sviridov for this information about networking in Ukraine.

Most hosts in the Ukraine today started as part of the Relcom network, which was created in the U.S.S.R. in 1990. Services offered there today include mail feeds, access to news via a news-to-mail server, and news feeds.

These hosts are usually 386 PCs connected via dialup lines and UUCP. They provide users with access to e-mail (which is routed outside Relcom through Moscow, then to the host fuug.fi in Finland), as well as to Usenet news and Relcom news. There is also quite a young ukr.* news hierarchy. Users usually are equipped with DOS PCs, 2400 baud modems and UUCP flavors. There are more than 300 nodes in Ukraine and more than 10 hosts providing news feeds. There are also some direct UUCP connections to the West, though for now the Relcom link from Moscow to Finland is the most reliable.

A networking issue in Ukraine is the registration of the UA domain. Currently, UA is resolved only within Relcom, so traffic from outside Relcom must be routed through the host ussr.eu.net. For example, a user's address would be in the form:

user%domain.subdomain.ua@ussr.eu.net

Soon the administration of the UA domain will move from Moscow to a site in the Ukraine, although which organization will be assuming the responsibility is still unclear.

The Ukraine Unix Users Group (UUUG) was recently formed, and is now officially registered both in Ukraine and EUnet.

For more information about networking in the Ukraine, contact:

Igor Sviridov
App. 72, Prospekt 40 liet Oktyabrya, 108/2, 252127
Kiev, Ukraine
postmaster%cs.kiev.ua@ussr.eu.net
+7 044 2638770

6.9. Baltic Countries

BALTBONE

SRI thanks Ants Work for this information about networking in the Baltic countries.

The BALTBONE project is a joint project of Estonia, Latvia, and Lithuania to build a 64 kbps TCP/IP network backbone as soon as possible between Tartu, Tallinn, Riga, Vilnius, and Kaunas and to link the backbone to NORDUnet and the rest of the world via the current Tallinn to Helsinki connection. Cisco Systems AGS routers will be used as soon as export licenses have been acquired.

A digital microwave link of 34 Mbps between Tallinn and Helsinki is in operation, and one 64 kbps channel has been leased for the BALTBONE connection. As of May 1992, the Point-to-Point Protocol (PPP) runs on SUN 3/80. The 64K channel from Tallinn to Tartu is ready, and was built on 12-group analog voice channels. The digital 64K link from Vilnius to Kaunas is in operation (temporarily on X.25). The next difficult problem is to make the Vilnius-Riga-Tallinn connection.

Research and Education Networks in Estonia, Latvia, and Lithuania are called respectively ESTNET, LATNET, and LITNET, and they will use BALTBONE for international connectivity.

For more information about the BALTBONE project, contact:

Ants Work
Deputy Director
Institute of Cybernetics
Estonian Academy of Sciences
Akadeemie tee 21
EE 0108 Tallinn
ESTONIA
ants@ioc.ee
+007 0142 525622
FAX: +007 0142 527901

6.10. Russia

Relcom

 SRI thanks Dimitry (Dima) Volodin for this information about Relcom.

Demos provides UUCP access to the RELCOM network. The standard services are e-mail, Usenet and RELCOM news, and an archive service. Demos connects to the Internet via dialup IP link to Alternet (UUNET). The immediate plans are to start interactive (BBS and "public access Unix") dialup services, UUCP and interactive services via X.25, dialup IP and IP-over-X.25 services, fax-telex-e-mail gateways, and a fax box service. We plan to switch to a full-time leased line linked to Alternet to make the access to the Internet faster and easier for our customers.

Demos provides e-mail access not only to the RELCOM network, but to the Internet as a whole. TCP/IP access to Internet (Alternet-CIX-etc.) for users is planned for the near future.

For more information about Relcom or Demos, contact:

```
Demos
6 Ovchinnikovskaya nab.
113035 Moscow
Russia
postmaster@hq.demos.su
info@hq.demos.su
+7 095 231 2129
+7 095 231 6395
FAX: +7 095 233 5016
```

6.11. Former Yugoslavia

Yugoslav Academic and Research Network (YUNAC)

SRI thanks Borka Jerman-Blazic for this information regarding networking in what was formerly Yugoslavia.

The Yugoslav Academic and Research Network (YUNAC) was formed in 1990. After the political events in Yugoslavia in 1991, YUNAC reorganized itself as an international organization following the example of NORDUnet. YUNAC is an international member of RARE. New countries appeared on the territory of former Yugoslavia and new networking organizations formed within those countries.

In general all these networks provide a similar choice of services and are using the international IXI line that was granted to YUNAC. Services include:

➤ Electronic mail (DECnet and X.400)

➤ Computer conferencing

➤ Remote login

➤ Connection via gateways (IXI gate of DFN) to the international networks EARN/BITNET, EUnet/ USENET, and Internet.

Slovenia

The academic and research network of Slovenia is called ARNES. The infrastructure of ARNES is the following: PPSDN in the country, some leased lines, and one international 64 Kb line (the line granted to YUNAC) to IXI. ARNES is organized as a public institution and is governed by the body appointed by the Ministry of Science and Technology of Slovenia. ARNES is a member of RARE. The backbone of the Yugoslav part of EUnet is located in Slovenia. They use mainly UUCP protocol. Recently some new networks based on the TCP/IP suite became operational and provide international connectivity. They are members of RIPE.

Croatia

The academic and research network of Croatia is called CARNET. The infrastructure used by CARNET is similar to that used by ARNES (i.e., using a PPSDN with DECnet on top of it). CARNET is the YUNAC line to IXI for international traffic. CARNET is also a member of RARE.

Bosnia and Herzegovina

At the time of this writing, there is no networking activity in this part of former Yugoslavia.

Serbia and Montenegro

Serbia was connected with a leased line to Linz, and the University of Belgrad was a member of EARN. After the sanctions adopted by the U.N., this connection was cut off. Serbia can be reached by international public packet switched networks. The part of PPSDN—JUPAK—is still operational, as is the DECnet network within the country.

Macedonia

The part of the PPSDN in this former republic of Yugoslavia is also operational. The e-mail service is provided through the University of Ljubljana node and DECnet network. The academic and research networking organization is called MARNET. MARNET is currently seeking for direct connection to Internet and EARN.

For further general information about YUNAC and networking in these countries, contact:

```
Borka Jerman-Blazic
IJS E-5NET
Jamova 39
61000 Ljubljana
SLOVENIA
+38 61 159 199
FAX: +38 61 161 029
jerman-blazic@ijs.si
E-mail addresses for points of
 contact for other networks
mentioned in this section are:
ARNES: marco.bonac@ijs.si
EUnet: leon@ninurta.fer.yu
CARNET: p.pale@uni-zg.ac.mail.yu
MARNET: pmfmarj%nubsk@uni-lj.yu
EARN in Serbia: xpmfdo1@yubgss21.bitnet
```

6.12. France

EARN-France

EARN-France is the French portion of EARN/BITNET.

For more information about EARN-France, contact:

```
Dominique Dumas
EARN-France
950 rue de Saint Priest
34184 Montpellier Cedex 4
France
BRUCH@FRMOP11.BITNET
or
BRUCH%FRMOP11.BITNET@pucc.Princeton.EDU
+33 67 14 14 14
FAX: +33 67 52 57 63
```

Fnet

SRI thanks Annie Renard for this information about Fnet.

Fnet is the French part of EUnet, and INRIA (located near Versailles) is the organization that manages the Fnet backbone.

EUnet-FR is open to members of AFUU (French Unix users group), which is affiliated with EurOpen. One also needs to subscribe to the Fnet association to benefit from its services.

Fnet supports usage of TCP/IP over Transpac, leased lines, and telephone, with ISDN support coming soon. A service called InterEUnet (Internet for EUnet subscribers) is also provided, which allows these subscribers to get access to all authorized parts of the European and U.S. Internet. ("Authorized" meaning that the NSFNET might be inaccessible to a commercial company, but a U.S. commercial network could well be accessible to that site.) In addition, dialup IP access over a telephone ("DIP") is available on a pay-per-use basis.

Incoming calls to Fnet are supported at 1200 (V.22) (although this usage is discouraged now), 2400 (V.22-bis),

9600 (V.32), 14400 (V.32-bis), and other multiprotocol modems.

In addition, X.25 access is supported over PPSDN public network Transpac, and ISDN access is supported over ECMA 102 adaptors (which makes those adaptors look like 19200 full-duplex asynchronous modems).

For more information about Fnet, contact:

Sylvain Langlois
Fnet Association
11 rue Carnot
94270 Le Kemlin-Bicetre
FRANCE
contact@fnet.fr
+33 1 45 21 02 04
FAX: +33 1 46 58 94 20

6.13. Spain

RedIRIS

SRI thanks the Secretaria RedIRIS for this information about the RedIRIS network.

Since 1991, Higher Education and Research funding bodies in Spain have sponsored RedIRIS as the National Research and Academic Network organization. RedIRIS provides services for universities and research centers in Spain. The network is managed by Fundesco, a non-profit organization dealing with Information Technology and Telecommunication activities.

The number of RedIRIS user organizations has grown to 108, most of them belonging to the Higher Education and Public Research sectors. RedIRIS is the National Member representing Spain in the RARE Association, and participates in the COSINE Project.

RedIRIS services are supported on a private 64 kbps X.25 backbone called ARTIX, which links the main Research and Development sites, and connection to the PPSDN is also provided. An IP network service is tunneled over the common backbone as well. In a similar way a CLNS (ISO IP) service is provided, currently for experimental purposes. The ARTIX backbone expanded in the first half of 1992 to 9 regional nodes. Presently 50 RedIRIS member organizations (all mainly universities and research institutes in Spain) hold at least one access link to ARTIX. For 1993, plans are to upgrade the ARTIX infrastructure to 2 Mbps.

International communications are established through the COSINE IXI network for X.25 traffic, and through EBONE for IP and CLNS services. Present international bandwitdh is 2×64 kbps. A new 64 kbps digital link—Madrid to Amsterdam—was added in May as part of the EBONE infrastructure to supplement the former IXI (X.25) access point which was used for some time to carry all traffic types. Now the IXI line is used for X.25-based traffic (X.400, XXX, DECnet), whereas the EBONE tail link is kept for IP and CLNS traffic.

In June 1992, 40 RedIRIS member organizations reached full IP connectivity. Within the RedIRIS Autonomous System, there are now 57 IP connected networks (18 class B, 39 class C). More networks are in the process of getting IP connectivity.

Several user support and information services are now being implemented to provide users with available information and adequate tools. A principal aim is to help local managers at RedIRIS organizations run their own network services at each specific site. Anonymous ftp and an X.500 Directory are already available for that purpose. Other user-friendly interfaces such as WAIS and Gopher are under consideration.

For more information about RedIRIS, contact:

Secretaria RedIRIS
RedIRIS
Fundesco
Alcala 61
28014 Madrid
+34 1 435 1214
FAX: +34 1 578 1773
secretaria@rediris.es
C=es;ADMD=mensatex;PRMD=iris;O=rediris;S=secretaria

6.14. Germany

DFN

SRI thanks Martin Wilhelm for this information about the services provided by DFN.

The DFN (Deutsches Forschungsnetz) association provides a broad variety of communication services to its members and other interested parties. Consultancy services, manuals, and special software are provided to support the use of communication services. The association further supports projects for the development of data communication and encourages experiments with new applications. Special emphasis is put on the development of services at higher speeds (> 2 Mbps).

Communication within DFN is realized through a packet switched X.25 network using powerful and advanced technologies to provide access speeds of currently up to 2 Mbps. As of September 1992, WIN comprises 184 access points with 9.6 kbps, 164 access points with 64 kbps, and 17 access points with 2 Mbps.

International connectivity is established by connections to European backbone infrastructures and a high bandwidth connection to the U.S. internets.

Provision of additional value added services is another major concern of DFN. Gateway and relay services for electronic mail exchange between X.400, SMTP, and

BSMTP are provided. Currently, approximately half a million messages are handled monthly. Via the services of DFN, all the German universities, research institutes, Max-Planck-Society, Fraunhofer Society, database providers, libraries, and several research oriented departments of industry can be reached.

For additional information about the DFN Association, contact:

> DFN-Verein e. V.
> Geschaeftsstelle
> Pariser Strasse 44
> D - 1000 Berlin 15
> Germany
> dfn-verein@dfn.dbp.de
> wilhelm@dfn.dbp.de
> rauschenbach@dfn.dbp.de
> +49 30 88 42 99 22
> FAX: +49 30 88 42 99 70

6.15. Japan

The Widely Integrated Distributed Environment (WIDE) project was initiated in July 1987 by a group of researchers led by Professor Jun Murai of Keio University. The project was designed to provide a testbed for the development of large-scale distributed systems technologies, and was initially constructed by interconnecting several campus networks. The WIDE Internet has since provided a basis for Japanese computer science researchers to gain practical experience in advanced networking. The WIDE project operates as a non-government network with funding support from about 25 private companies.

The WIDE project sponsors a consortium to study various computer issues, including protocols, operating systems, computer security, ISDN technologies, home computing, mobile computing, satellite data communications, distributed applications, and internationalization of computer software. Their research results are annually published by the project and the resulting software is also distributed.

The WIDE Internet is composed of a variety of links, including voice grade leased lines, 64K kbps and 192 kbps digital leased lines, and ISDN. Currently, 52 user organizations, including universities and private companies, are connected to six operation centers through 64 kbps to 192 kbps leased lines. The backbone also passes traffic of other research networks, such as JUNET (Japan University Network), which is now JAIN (Japan Academic Inter-university Network), and JAIN does not have long-haul nationwide connectivity. The WIDE project has been providing connectivity to other networks, such as the University of Tokyo International Science Network (TISN), NACSIS Science Information Network (SINET), and BITNET-JAPAN. The WIDE Internet supports TCP/IP as its basic protocol suite.

WIDE operates in conjunction with the Pacific Communications Network (PACCOM) project to provide international links for Japanese researchers using 192 kbps undersea cable via the University of Hawaii to NASA Ames in Mountain View, CA.

WIDE Project contact:

> c/o Prof. Jun Murai
> Keio University
> 5322 Endo, Fujisawa, 252
> JAPAN
> jun@wide.ad.jp
> +81 466 47 5111 ext. 3330

6.16. Taiwan

TANet

SRI thanks Lui Zi-Di for this information about TANet.

TANet, The Taiwan Academic Network, is a pilot project undertaken by the Ministry of Education and Universities Computer Center to establish a common national academic network infrastructure.

To support research and academic institutions in Taiwan, TANet will provide access to unique resources and opportunities for collaborative work. TANet will be composed of most of the Taiwan Internet community, including industry networks such as SEEDNet (Software Engineering Environment Development Network).

The management structure of TANet is a two-layer hierarchy. The TANet network service center (TANSC) is to be responsible for the national backbone network and management of international links. Within each regional area, a regional network service center (RNSC) will provide necessary services and support connections to the TANet backbone from the local-area network/campus network of each university/institution. At present, TANSC is run by the Ministry of Education Computer Center, and each RNSC is run by a major local university.

The network protocols will initially focus on TCP/IP on the TANet backbone. Regional networks may support multiple protocols and additional facilities (including X.25 transport or dialup services) on a local basis in accordance with regional requirements. Support for OSI (CLNS) routing will be introduced in the near future. Existing Taiwan BITNET and ifNET (information NETwork) applications (including electronic mail delivery, NetNEWS, and file transfer) will be supported over TANet via IP connections.

A 256 kbps link will be installed from the Ministry of Education Computer Center to Princeton University at the end of 1992. This link will couple TANet to both JvNCnet and NSFNET.

For more information about TANet, contact:

Computer Center, Ministry of Education
12th Fl, No. 106
Sec. 2, Hoping E. Road
Taipei, Taiwan
Attention: Chen Wen-Sung
nisc@twnmoe10.edu.tw
nisc@twnmoe10.bitnet
+886 2 7377010
FAX: +886 2 7377043

6.17. Israel

ILAN, or Israeli Academic Network, is a network owned and operated by Machba - the Israeli Interuniversity Computer Center. ILAN was formed in November 1988 as an outgrowth of the BITNET network that existed in Israel. The initial network, established in 1984, grants Internet connectivity to institutes of higher education, cultural and academic organizations, as well as organizations involved in research and development.

There are two international links to sites outside of Israel. One starts at the Weizmann Institute of Science and ends in the United States within the NSF regional network called NYSERnet. The physical connection terminates in New York City. This link is a 64 kbps satellite link. The second connection is from Tel Aviv University to CERN in Geneva, Switzerland. This is also a 64 kbps link via an undersea fiber-optic cable called EMOS. The fiber-optic link is faster for Telnet connections since it does not suffer from satellite delays. Both these links are paid for and owned by Machba.

The ILAN network currently handles routing for IP, DECnet, and Appletalk between various universities.

For additional information about ILAN contact:

Hank Nussbacher
Israeli Academic Network Information Center
Computer Center
Tel Aviv University
Ramat Aviv
ISRAEL
hank@vm.tau.ac.il
+972 3 6408309

6.18. Italy

GARR

Our thanks to Antonio Blasco Bonito of CNUCE for the following information.

In Italy, The Ministry of University and Scientific Research supports and finances the GARR network. GARR is the acronym for "Group for the Harmonization of Research Networks" (Gruppo Armonizzazione delle Reti per la Ricerca). The aim of GARR is to interconnect the Italian research and academic networks and coordinate inter-country connections. GARR is currently composed of CNR (CNRnet), ENEA (ENET), INFN (INFNet), CILEA, CINECA, CSATA, and government research organizations. GARR is publicly financed and only allows research institutions to connect to it. IUnet in Italy (described below) is a non-profit institution and is open to the general public.

GARR provides the following facilities: electronic mail, file transfer, remote login, database access, remote job entry, remote terminal access, and USENET news.

All computers on GARR use Internet-style domain addresses for electronic mail.

Recognized vehicles of mail traffic are IP/SMTP and X.400. The electronic mail GARR task force (named GARR-PE) has adopted the policy of having every Italian domain registered through the DNS to be directly reachable through the Internet or indirectly through an SMTP/other protocol mail gateway. Another mail path is through the COSINE X.400 WEPS.

GARR has recently decided to organize a Network Information Service (NIS) which will act as the Italian Registration authority for IP addresses and Internet domains under IT. The GARR NIS will also provide support for managers of "GARR-regional" networks. The GARR-NIS will be in direct contact with the other major network information services, such as the InterNIC and RIPE-NCC. The GARR-NIS, located in Pisa, will run the IT top-level domain name server and the c=IT X.500 DSA.

The backbone of the GARR network provides four TDM channels over 2 Mbps lines, carrying IP, DECnet, SNA, and X.25 (IXI). There are seven primary sites on the network backbone. They are located in Milano, Pisa, Bologna, Roma, Frascati, and Bari. Sites on GARR employ a combination of protocols, including TCP/IP, X.25, SNA, DECnet, UUCP, and others.

The backbone, built up by the original seven primary sites, is gradually being extended as funds are made available. Many new sites are in the process of being added on the backbone. Other sites will be connected as secondaries attached to the primary sites at their own expenses.

GARR is composed by the interconnection of member networks, and is well connected to IUnet, the Italian part of EUnet/InterEUnet. GARR will also maintain connections to the major international research networks, including: RIPE/EASInet/Internet, EARN/BITNET, EUnet/UUNET, HEPnet, and others.

For additional information about GARR contact:

Gruppo Armonizzazione delle Reti per la Ricerca
Ufficio del Ministro per l'Universita' e la Ricerca
Scientifica e Tecnologica
Lungotevere Thaon di Revel, 76
I-00196 Roma
ITALY
+39 6 390095
FAX: +39 6 392209

IUnet

The Italian UNIX Systems User Group (I2U), a non-profit association of hardware manufacturers, software houses, universities, and research centers that share an interest for the diffusion of the UNIX operating system (as well as open systems), began in 1986 as a UUCP network. Totally reorganized in 1988, this network, subsequently named IUnet, has grown to become an important reality in the Italian networking landscape.

IUnet is the Italian segment of EUnet and today connects more than 80 sites in the Italian R&D community (both academic and industrial/commercial). While the IUnet NIC is hosted at the Computer Science Department of the University of Genoa (one of the founders of the I2U), IUnet receives no kind of government funding. All costs for the operation and improvement of the network infrastructure are covered by the user's fees.

IUnet is gradually evolving to become a TCP/IP network (about 30% of its sites have switched to the InterEUnet service, that is, have full access to the whole "European Internet"). EUnet is a participant to the CIX initiative. There are no limitations to the type of traffic that crosses IUnet, EUnet, or any other of the CIX networks. For this reason, unlike GARR, IUnet is ready to connect commercial/industrial enterprises, thus making possible a vital information exchange between academic research institutions and industry. IUnet members can also qualify for NSFNET access, provided they meet the requirements of the NSFNET Acceptable Use Policy.

TCP/IP access to IUnet is possible via leased lines, public X.25 and dialup, both SLIP and PPP (Points of Presence in Genoa, Milan, Turin, Rome—activation of the Bologna POP in 1993). International connectivity is via a leased line to INRIA in Sophia Antipolis, France. European and U.S. access is via the EUnet infrastructure.

IUnet offers UUCP mail, news, and archives via dialup and public X.25; access to the Internet via dialup, public X.25, and leased lines; a mailbox service; and database access to UNIX software and an electronic newsletter. IUnet plans to offer MHS X.400 services in 1993. The network operates the anonymous FTP archive host ftp.iunet.it.

For additional information about IUnet contact:

Alessandro Berni
IUnet
DIST, Universita' di Genova
Via Opera Pia, 11a
16145 Genova
ITALY
+39 10 3532747
FAX: +39 10 3532948
iunet@iunet.it

6.19. The Netherlands

SURFnet

 Our thanks to Peter Kokosky Deforchaux for the following information.

SURFnet bv is the Dutch national organization for the provision of information and communication services for research and higher education, including industrial research. It is a private not-for-profit company. The owners are the SURF Foundation (51%), representing the user community, and the Dutch PTT (49%).

The main services of SURFnet are:

➤ Megabit multi-protocol backbone services (IP and X.25) with IP rates up to 1.5 Mbps; CLNS will follow in 1992;

➤ E-mail, file transfer and remote access, both TCP/IP and OSI, including gateway services;

➤ Open Library Network in cooperation with the national organization for library automation Pica;

➤ File services and a variety of other information services e.g., NEWS (in cooperation with NLnet, the Dutch part of EUnet). In The Netherlands, SURFnet is responsible for EARN/NJE and HEPnet services.

The SURFnet services are managed in a one-stop shopping approach where total administrative and technical (e.g. help-desk), support is provided by SURFnet personnel. Operational management tasks are subcontracted, with SURFnet retaining the overall service provision responsibility vis-à-vis its customers.

The 1991 turnover was 7 M$. The 120 connected institutions and companies pay 5.5 M$ for operational services via volume independent tariffs. The remaining 1.5 M$ are related to forthcoming innovative services (i.e., pilots, development projects) and are financed by the government funded SURF Foundation.

SURFnet's activities are restricted to universities, colleges, research institutions including industrial research, scientific and public libraries, and academic hospitals.

SURFnet is strongly focused on international cooperation, both in operational and in innovative activities. International connectivity is presently achieved via the EBONE initiative and via IXI. SURFnet's employees are active in several international bodies and programs (i.e., RARE, Internet, COSINE).

Current development activities include:

➤ The development of an Open Library Network based on the VTP protocol;

➤ The connection of student work places at home via the TV cable infrastructure;

➤ Enhancement of the Megabit multi-protocol backbone in terms of topology (resiliency), introduction CLNS, introduction 34 Mbps trunks, upgrade of international connectivity, investigation of protocols like Frame Relay, DQDB and ATM, and integration of network management;

➤ Extension of the pilot X.500 directory service with full scale data management tests and interworking tests;

➤ Set up of an X.400 1988 extension of the present X.400 1984 infrastructure including interworking tests of new products;

➤ Set up of a file service based on FTAM and FTP with interworking tests of new products;

➤ Introduction of security procedures and facilities including the set up of a CERT NL (Computer Emergency Response Team);

➤ The set up of a pilot Full Image Document Delivery Server in cooperation with scientific libraries and publishers (under preparation).

For more information about SURFnet, contact:

P.O. Box 19035
3501 DA Utrecht,
THE NETHERLANDS
+31 30310290
admin@surfnet.nl
c=nl, ADMD=400net, PRMD=SURF, O=SURFnet, S=Admin

6.20. Switzerland

SWITCH

SWITCH is the Swiss Academic and Research Network. We thank Thomas Lenggenhager for the information contained in this section.

SWITCH is a foundation, sponsored by the Swiss government and Swiss universities, that provides teleinformatics services to all Swiss universities, technical high schools, and various research institutes by connecting to national and international resources. SWITCH started operation in October 1988.

SWITCHlan is a national backbone network which connects all universities using leased lines with speeds between 128 kbit/s and 2 Mbit/s. Most other organizations are connected via 64 kbit/s. For routing on these national leased lines SWITCH uses Cisco routers. The protocols supported are DECnet, TCP/IP, X.25, and ISO CLNS.

The resources connected to SWITCHlan are documented in the SWITCH Resource Guide, a collection similar to the Internet Resource Guide. It is accessible via anonymous FTP on nic.switch.ch [130.59.1.40] in /info_service/ SWITCH-resource-guide. The Swiss supercomputer sites and several library catalogs are connected to SWITCHlan.

International connections on the network level went into operation in January 1990. The current state today is:

➤ Two lines with TCP/IP to CERN each 2 Mbit/s. This gives access to EBONE, the European part of the Internet and via the EASIgate T1 link to the U.S. access to the NSFNET.

➤ TCP/IP and ISO CLNS connection to Nice, France, with 64 kbit/s, which also acts as the backup route to the Internet/NSFNET.

➤ A TCP/IP 64 kbit/s line to BelWue, a regional research network in southern Germany.

A 64 kbit/s connection to the COSINE/EMPB private X.25
network has been running since the first quarter of 1990.
This infrastructure is mainly used for TCP/IP over X.25 to
RedIRIS, DFN, and ACOnet. In addition, it is used for X.400
and X.500 traffic, as well as for pilot ISO CLNP over X.25
with the European Academic and Research Community.

SWITCHmail is the national X.400 MHS network which connects the universities and research institutes to the ADMD of
the Swiss PTT, and through COSINE-MHS to research MHS
networks in 31 countries. E-mail gateways to EARN/BITNET,
UUCP, and Internet are offered by SWITCH too.

SWITCHinfo is an information service accessible either via
anonymous FTP to nic.switch.ch [130.59.1.40] or interac-
tively with Telnet to the same host with the login name
info; no password required.

On behalf of RARE (Reseaux Associes pour la Recherche
Europeenne, European Research Network Organization),
SWITCH runs COSINE-MHS, an MHS coordination service
spanning 33 research networks in 31 countries. SWITCH
is an active partner in other COSINE pilot X.500 Directory
Service projects and the COSINE Information Service
project.

Any host on the network of a connected organization may
access the network, as long the usage complies with the
use policy of SWITCH. SWITCH networks can only be
used for academic and research traffic.

SWITCH services include:

➤ Mailbox accounts. Offering e-mail connectivity to the
X.400, Internet, BITNET, and UUCP world. Dialup to
the mailbox account is via modem or XXX (Pad).

➤ Direct X.400 MTA-MTA connection. This includes gateway services to the same community as for the mailboxes.

➤ Dialup UUCP.

➤ Usenet NEWS service.

➤ Leased line access to the Swiss IP network and the Internet for organizations cooperating with universities on research projects.

➤ Dialup SLIP access to the Internet has been available since summer 1992, ISDN access is planned for 1993.

➤ X.500 DSA/DUA access to the international X.500 pilot.

For additional information about the SWITCH network, contact:

> SWITCH Head Office
> Limmatquai 138
> CH-8001 Zurich
> SWITZERLAND
> +41 1 256 5454
> FAX: +41 1 261 8133
> postmaster@switch.ch
> C=CH;ADMD=arCom;PRMD=SWITCH;O=SWITCH;
> S=Postmaster

6.21. Greece

ARIADNE

SRI thanks Yannis Corovesis for the following information.

The ARIADNE Network (ARIADNet) is open to all members of the Research Academic Community in Greece. It is also open to industrial R&D companies. The ARIADNE Network Operations Center (NOC) is at the Demokritos Research Centre in Attiki.

Most research institutes and universities are connected via a private backbone of more than 20 leased analog circuits (9.6 kbps). Athens (Attiki) is in the center of the network, with the peripheries stretching to Thrace, Macedonia, Ipeiros, Peloponnese, and the Aegean.

Recently, there has been demand for ARIADNE services by a wider community, beyond that currently covered by state and CEC financing, and a study is underway to devise a financial cost/charging scheme to cover operational costs. A study group has been formed to look into the problem of networking coordination in the research and academic sector as the relevant ministry is restricting funds severely. This exercise brings together pioneering sites in networking as well as newcomers planning to support regional NOCs. A forum of all user sites is to complement the above activity.

The outcome is expected to merge the Greek part of EARN (Crete) and ARIADNE, producing a four NOC backbone (University of Crete, CTI at Patra, University of Thessaloniki, and Demokritos at Athens)

The International networks Internet (via ULCC/JANET), COSINE-MHS, IXI/EMPB, BITNET (University of Crete), EUnet (ITE), and the CERN DECnet (Demokritos) may be accessed from ARIADNE.

The ARIADNE Network currently offers the following services:

➤ Remote login via PAD or Telnet.

➤ E-mail (RFC 822, X.400, and gateway RFC 987).

➤ File transfer via FTP and Kermit, and anonymous FTP to fetch RFCs, FYIs, and UNIX configuration files.

➤ Dialup on 5 telephone lines for PC users (1200-9600 bps, MNP error correction), including provision of a mailbox. An order of another 10 lines has been placed with OTE (PTT).

➤ Pythia, an information server for browsing information on keywords about networks and related topics, currently at an embryonic stage. Also Dialdoc for PC users over dialup for information and software exchange.

➤ A supercomputer, CONVEX, currently installed in Demokritos and made available to ARIADNE users for projects in physics, meteorology, environmental pollution, space, and defense.

Plans for the ARIADNE Network include:

➤ Immediate plans are the upgrade of International connectivity to 64K. Also a leased line running TCP/IP to CERN is being installed. This is to be an EBONE line.

➤ ARIADNE backbone is to receive 10 Cisco routers (currently being installed, 5 in pilot operation).

➤ Build an X.400 backbone (10 sites) in 1992-1993 (currently the MTAs of NRCPS, CTI, AUEB, TPCI, and HEP are operational).

➤ Install 10 network servers over the backbone in 1993 (in order from HP).

➤ Mass publish a Network Users Guide fully in Greek, with examples and explanations (certain parts produced using other net's experience).

For additional information about ARIADNE network, contact:

ARIADNE Network Help Desk
+30 1 6513392
+30 1 6536351
FAX: +30 1 6532910
FAX: +30 1 6532175
postmaster@isosun.ariadne-t.gr
C=gr; ADMD= ; PRMD=ariadne-t; OU=isosun; S=postmaster;
Yannis Corovesis
ycor@isosun.ariadne-t.gr
C=gr; ADMD= ; PRMD=ariadne-t; OU=isosun; S=ycor
Takis Telonis
ttel@isosun.ariadne-t.gr

6.22. Turkey

TUVAKA

SRI thanks Esra Delen for this information about the TUVAKA Network.

TUVAKA stands for "Turkish University and Research Organizations' Network." It was established in 1987 just before Turkey joined EARN. The network initially consisted of 4 nodes running the BSC protocol on 9.6K lines. Now the network consists of 34 nodes affiliated with 29 organizations. The network initially had a star topology with the node TREARN being the center and the main international exit to EARN/BITNET. Now the network mainly runs the SNA protocol over 14.4K lines and is planning to migrate to IP on 64K lines very soon. Also, now the network has begun to lose its star shape as alternate routes and backup links have developed.

The major node and the starting point of the network is at Ege University in Izmir. This node has the id TREARN in the NJE world, and ege.edu.tr in the IP world. It holds the major international link, a 14.4K SNA link. In a very short time this line will be upgraded to a 64K VMNET line. Another international exit from TUVAKA is the Middle East Technical University in Ankara, and this is an IP/X.25 line to The Netherlands.

The host ege.edu.tr is the major governing node of the network. Almost all routing, addressing, and other modifications are done from there. This node gives the other nodes a lot of technical assistance, and help in all issues. The network mainly consists of IBM VM nodes, UNIX machines, and DEC VAXes. Ege.edu.tr holds two IBM mainframes and two UNIX workstations, all of them are defined in the network as separate nodes.

The technical personnel on the TUVAKA backbone nodes give courses and assistance to the newly connected nodes both nationally and internationally. The network holds several servers and all of them are accessible by mail and via interactive messages. Most nodes in the network have dialup and packet switched access.

For more information about TUVAKA, contact the Network Country Coordinators:

```
Sitki Aytac
aytac@ege.edu.tr
Esra Delen
esra@ege.edu.tr
TUVAKA
Ege University Computing Center
Bornova, Izmir 35100
TURKEY
+90 51 18 10 80
```

6.23. Mexico

SRI thanks Ing. Hugo E. Garcia Torres for providing the information about networking in Mexico.

MEXnet

The Mexican Academic network (MEXnet) is one of the participants of Mexico's national academic and research networks, SIRACyT (Sistema Nacional de Redes para la Ciencia y la Tecnologia). MEXnet is a not-for-profit organization whose mission is to provide a way to facilitate communication for the faculty and student community of its members in order to promote the exchange of non-commercial information. MEXnet is a fully terrestrial network with links going from 9.6 kbps to 64kbps.The following institutions are MEXnet's members and are already connected and fully operational:

➤ ITESM System (Instituto Tecnologico y de Estudios Superiores de Monterrey), UDLA (Universidad de las Americas)

➤ Universidad de Guadalajara

➤ ITESO (Instituto Tecnologico y de Estudios
Superiores de Occidente)

➤ Colegio de Postgraduados de Chapingo

➤ CIQA (Centro de Investigacion en Quimica Apliacada)

➤ CINVESTAV (Centro de Investigaciones Avanzadas)

➤ ITAM (Instituto Tecnologico Autonomo de Mexico)

➤ UAC (Universidad Autonoma de Coahuila)

➤ IPN (Instituto Politecnico Nacional)

➤ UAM (Universidad Autonoma Metropolitana)

➤ LANIA (Laboratorio Nacional de Informatica Avanzada)

➤ ITM (Instituto Tecnologico de Mexicali)

➤ Instituto de Ecologia de Xalapa

➤ UDEM (Universidad de Monterrey)

At this time the national system of state owned public
universities are in the process of being incorporated into
MEXnet or with any of the other networks that participate
in SIRACyT.

MEXnet has several international connections. ITESM connects with a terrestrial 56kbps link to ANSnet at MCI's POP
in Houston, Texas, and also to the University of Texas in
San Antonio with three leased lines (3 X 9600 bps). ITM
connects with a terrestrial 64kbps link to San Diego State
University in San Diego, California.

Other participants of SIRACyT are:

➤ Red UNAM (Universidad Nacional Autonoma de
Mexico) which has an international link to the Na-
tional Center for Atmospheric Research (NCAR) in
Boulder, Colorado, via a 64 kbps satellite connection.

> Red Cicese (Centro de Investigacion Cientifica y Educacion Superior) with an international link to the San Diego Supercomputer Center in San Diego, California, via a 64 kbps satellite connection.

> Red CETyS (Centro de Ensenanza Tecnica y Superior) has a terrestrial 56 kbps link to San Diego State University in California.

Following is an overview of the ITESM Network, one of MEXnet's participants.

ITESM

ITESM, Instituto Tecnologico y de Estudios Superiores de Monterrey (Monterrey Technological Institute of Higher Education), is a network of 27 multicampus higher education institutions located in 22 different cities in Mexico. Telecommunications for the whole system are via satellite using 64 kbps full duplex channels for voice and data. The network is arranged using a star topology with the central hub located at the Mexico City campus.

The ITESM network has three international links.

ITESM users have been BITNET members since 1986 and Internet members since 1987. The ITESM network consists of approximately 4000 nodes, with approximately 60% PCs and Macs, and 40% workstations, mainframes, and mini-computers.

In the near future, ITESM plans to increase the capacity of the link to ANSnet in Texas to a T1, pending all necessary approvals. Also, the ITESM is working to have higher bandwidth links to the most important campuses like the one that is already working between the Mexico City campus and the Monterrey campus (2 Mbps digital terrestrial link).

For further details about the ITESM network and MEXnet contact:

Ing. Hugo E. Garcia Torres
Director
Depto. de Telecomunicaciones y Redes
ITESM Campus Monterrey
E. Garza Sada #2501
Monterrey, N.L., C.P. 64849
MEXICO
+52 83 582 000, ext. 4130
FAX: +52 83 69-20-04
hgarcia@mexnet.mty.itesm.mx

6.24. Dominican Republic

REDID

SRI thanks Daniel Pimienta for this information about networking in the Dominican Republic.

The Dominican Republic has a UUCP node called REDID. The design is of a centralized UUCP based mailing system with access to Puerto Rico via a national X.25 network and a 9600 bps leased line. Puerto Rico conveys messages between REDID and the Internet.

REDID (Red Dominicana de Intercambio para el Desarrollo or the Dominican Network for Exchanges Toward Development) is the name of a user group formed as the result of an "open, transparent, and participative process directly conducted by future end-users."

For more information about REDID, contact:

Daniel Pimienta
Asesor Cientifico Union Latina
APTD0 2972
Santo Domingo
Republica Dominicana
pimienta!daniel@redid.org.do
+1 809 689 4973
+1 809 535 6614
FAX: +1 809 535 6646
TELEX: 1 346 0741

6.25. Caribbean Basin

This Caribbean Basin survey is provided to us courtesy of Daniel Pimienta, who wrote it.

The Caribbean Basin has not been left apart of the ongoing network growth within the region. If the user population, except for Puerto Rico and Costa Rica, is still low, infrastructures are in place which lead us to expect further developments in the coming months.

For several years, Costa Rica has been a key BITNET location and, furthermore, hosts the central UUCP node of a pilot project named HURACAN. HURACAN offers access to various researchers belonging to different Central American countries via their interconnected national X.25 networks. This project is a result of a cooperative effort started by Canadian Agencies and completed by the UNDP.

Bitnet
Guy de Teramond
gdeter@ucrvm2.bitnet
gdeter%ucrvm2.bitnet@cunyvm.cuny.edu
+506 34 10 13
+506 25 59 11
Huracan
Technical contact: Theodore Hope
hope@huracan.cr
+506 244734
+506 252467
Management contact: Edgardo Richards
richards@huracan.cr

Puerto Rico is presenting, as a result of years of investments and technical follow-up, a state-of-the-art network linking all the campuses with each other and with the Internet by high speed lines. It allows students to operate Telnet functions at fractions of seconds in several terminal areas spread over the country. CRACIN (Corporation for the National Academic Scientific and Research Network) can now concentrate on user support and make available some time to help its neighbors.

Puerto Rico is heading a sub-regional project, named CUNET for Caribbean Universities Network, which has put seeds virtually in all English speaking islands of the Caribbean. CUNET has a star design where UUCP nodes access, by switched connection, into the Puerto Rico network which gateways the traffic to the Internet. The number of users is reported to be steadily growing in various countries, such as Jamaica and Trinidad and Tobago. The project is sponsored by OAS, which pays for the experts to travel and for the dialup connections to Puerto Rico.

CRACIN and CUNET
Roberto Loran
R_Loran@racin.clu.net

Cuba is experiencing a spectacular growth of the network. The island has a traditionally strong science and technology sector, and is in a good position to present user applications and scientific databases. INFO93, a congress planned for May 1993 in La Habana, will focus on networking.

Cuba Jesus Martinez
jemar@ceniai.cu

Surprisingly, the **French West Indies** have remained outside of the area's growth in networking. There is a RIO (Orstom network) node, but a 1988 plan to have the University (UAG) join EARN-France has not yet been implemented. However, moves are underway to make it a playing actor in network related training.

University of **Nicaragua** is maintaining a UUCP node.

Nicaragua
Teresa Ortega
Project Manager
Red Academica y de Informacion Nicaraguense (RAIN)
tere@uni.ni
+505 2 672054
+505 2 670274
FAX: +505 2 673709

Dominican Republic's REDID was born last May. Also, one of the 25 Dominican universities (PUCMM) is maintaining a PC station connected to the CUNET project, and has been planning a BITNET node for some time.

Haiti was targeted to be part of the REDID creation process. The political turmoils jeopardized the process. Other alternatives, such as training a group of researchers outside the country, are currently under study to start an action. See also Section 6.24 for more information about networking in the Dominican Republic.

REDID
Daniel Pimienta
pimienta!daniel@redid.org.do
+11 809 689 4973

6.26. Argentina

ARNET

SRI thanks Jorge Marcelo Amodio for this information about ARNET.

ARNET, a TCP/IP network connected to the Internet, is the major science and research network of Argentina. It connects approximately 300 sites, mainly universities and research organizations. ARNET provides electronic mail, USENET News, file server, and electronic mailing list services.

Like other cooperative networks, ARNET has no central planning or central authority. The current international link and the top-level AR domain are managed by the UNDP (United Nations Development Programme) at the Ministry of Foreign Affairs (MREC), together with the Secretariat of Science and Technology (SECYT). For the time being, the top-level subdomains are administered by the UNDP/ MREC project.

ARNET is connected to the Internet through a satellite link to SURANet at the University of Maryland.

Most ARNET connections are over the public telephone network or the public packet-switching network, ARPAC, using the UUCP protocol in different environments. USENET news and most electronic mail traffic is brought to ARNET from uunet.uu.net via Internet.

There is a cooperation agreement between the UNDP/ MREC project and the SECYT to distribute Internet services in the future. The first stage will be the installation of a couple of Unix boxes at major regional sites, interconnected through the PSN ARPAC and national satellite links using UUCP. The second stage will be the migration from UUCP to TCP/IP. There are under study different ways to distribute Internet services throughout the country, and to upgrade the international link to the Internet.

For more information about ARNET, contact:

```
UNDP Project ARG-90-012
Ministerio de Relaciones Exteriores y Culto
Reconquista 1088 1er. Piso - Informatica
(1003) Capital Federal
Buenos Aires, Argentina
Attention: Jorge Marcelo Amodio
pete@atina.ar
+541 315 4804
FAX: +541 315 4824
```

6.27. Bolivia

UnBol/Bolnet

SRI thanks Sam Lanfranco for this information about networking in Bolivia.

Bolivia has electronic mail access to the Internet via a network called BolNet (in English) or UnBol (in Spanish). The network was originally established with the help of PeaceNet, a network administered by the Institute for Global Communications (IGC) (see Section 4.2). IGC provides MX forwarding for the unbo.bo domain.

UnBol is located at the Department of Electronic Engineering of the Universidad Mayor de San Andres in La Paz.

For more information about UnBol, contact:

Prof. Clifford Paravicini
Facultad de Ingenieria Electronica
Univ. Mayor de San Andres
La Paz, Bolivia
clifford@unbol.bo

6.28. Nordic Countries

NORDUnet

NORDUnet is an international network connecting the Nordic countries. It is administered by NORDUNET (note capitalization), a networking program in the Nordic countries funded by the Nordic Council of Ministers. The participating organizations are the Nordic national networks in Norway (UNINETT), Denmark (DENet), Finland (FUNET), Iceland (SURIS), and Sweden (SUNET). The goals of NORDUnet are to provide harmonized network services to Nordic research and development users in co-operation with these national networks and to establish good inter-Nordic relations in networking.

Much of this information regarding NORDUnet was taken from the article *Profile: NORDUnet,* which appeared in the November 1990 issue of *ConneXions: The Interoperability Report* [29]. (See Section 12.5 for more information about this journal.)

The NORDUnet idea was born in September 1987 and the network was officially opened in October 1989.

NORDUnet activities focus on provision of services, meaning its goal is to extend the services and interconnectivity to new networks to the benefit of its users. NORDUnet is also planning for an introduction of OSI-based services through pilots and experiments. These include X.500 Directory pilots, the harmonization of e-mail addresses, and development of national e-mail gateways.

NORDUnet also takes an active part in the RARE work and supports the goals of COSINE (see Section 10.1.5).

The NORDUnet transport network is a wide area network based on MAC-level bridges and "network-level" routers. They form a logical Ethernet connection through leased lines provided by the Swedish Telecomm International (STI) and the Scandinavian Telecommunications Services AB (STS). NORDUnet provides, through its interconnections to the U.S. and central Europe, access to the following networks: The Internet, BITNET/CREN, EUnet, EARN, HEPnet, SPAN, and the COSINE/RARE IXI pilot service. The U.S. connection is between The Royal Technical Institute (KTH) in Stockholm, Sweden, and the John von Neumann National Super-computer Center (JvNC) in Princeton, New Jersey. JvNCnet is an NSFNET mid-level network (see Chapter 4).

For those already connected to the Internet, NORDUnet provides a common resource through its "NIC" host nic.nordu.net. This host is the first European DNS root server machine and also contains a wealth of information available for anonymous FTP. Information concerning NSF, IETF, NETF (NORDUnet Engineering Task Force), statistics for NORDUnet, EEPG (European Engineering and Planning Group), and EBONE are some examples of information resident on this host.

For additional information about resources available on nic.nordu.net, send mail to hostmaster@nic.nordu.net.

Alternatively, you may use the following address for obtaining more information about the NORDUnet program:

NORDUnet
c/o SICS P.O. Box 1263
S-164 28 Kista
SWEDEN
+46 8 752 1563
FAX: +46 8 751 7230
NORDUnet@sics.se

6.29. Finland

DataNet

 SRI thanks Seppo Noppari for this description of the DataNet Service offered by Telecom Finland.

DataNet is a network service for interconnecting LANs. It is mainly targeted for closed corporate networks. Telecom Finland has been running the network since 1990. At present there are several TCP/IP networks, for example SWIPnet and TIPnet in Sweden, and PSInet, Alternet, and CERFnet in U.S.A. DataNet network covers the whole country in Finland with its 21 POPs. Currently there are more than 300 CPEs of about 80 customers. The network is still growing fast. DataNet also has international connections through CIX and InfoLAN. DataNet service, like InfoLAN, also has one key feature that separates it from other commercial TCP/IP offerings. DataNet is an end-to-end managed complete network service with a wide range of supported protocols.

Backbone Technology

In the first phase DataNet network was based on a backbone of leased lines and Cisco multiprotocol/multimedia routers. Now it also includes a Stratacom IPX based Frame Relay backbone. Customer LANs are connected with routers (= CPEs) to the nearest backbone routers or IPX Frame Relay switches with serial lines. Charging is based on access line speed which varies from 19.2 kbit/s to 2 Mbit/s. Also FDDI connections are available which means access speed up to 100 Mbit/s. Supported level 3 protocols are TCP/IP, DECnet, ISO CLNP, Novell IPX, AppleTalk, and X.25. IBM connectivity is provided by source route bridging of Token Ring LANs and SDLC tunneling. Network management is SNMP based.

Service Elements

DataNet is a complete service including customer network planning, implementation, and management. The CPEs are usually owned and managed by Telecom Finland and the customer pays a flat rate for the service. For example, a typical 64 kbit/s access to the network is $1800/month and this price includes the CPE, local loop, traffic, and hardware. DataNet is using a wide range of routers and other equipment from Cisco.

AGS or AGS+ routers are used mainly in the backbone, but of course our FDDI customers also have AGS+ routers at their sites. Usually customers are connected with an IGS but CGS and MGS boxes are also used for special needs. MSM terminal servers are used for customers who need asynchronous or SLIP services. Per customer X.25 gateways are based on CPTs.

Supported Protocols

Supported protocols are TCP/IP, DECnet Phase IV, SRB, X.25, Novell IPX AppleTalk, ISO CLNP, and bridging. AppleTalk, IPX, DECnet, and bridging are nowadays implemented over the Frame Relay backbone. Routing protocol is IGRP and the following network interfaces are supported: Ethernet, TokenRing, and FDDI. The BGP protocol is used between different AS networks.

International connections

DataNet is currently connected to CIX via a Frame Relay link from NordFrame network. This arrangement allows practically global commercial IP connectivity. Connections to European IP networks have been built via EBS—EBONE Boundary System, built with Frame Relay also. For customers who want international and closed networks, there is a gateway to the InfoLAN network.

For more information about DataNet contact:

> Seppo Noppari
> Telecom Finland
> P.O. Box 228
> Rautatienkatu 10
> 33101 Tampere
> Finland
> +358 31 243 2242
> FAX: +358 31 243 2211
> seppo.noppari@tele.fi

6.30. Sweden

TIPnet

SRI thanks Anders Halldin, TIPnet manager, for the following information.

TIPnet is Swedish Telecom's commercial public TCP/IP service. TIPnet is based on a Cisco router backbone. TIPnet is a member of EBONE, and has Frame Relay-based connections to Alternet in the U.S., DataNet in Finland, and INFOnet's router in Stockholm. Access to TIPnet is either via leased lines from 9.6 kbit to 2 Mbit, or via X.25 at 9.6 kbit or 64 kbit.

The TIPnet customer support and Network Control Center services are situated in Gothenburg:

> Hakan Hansson
> +46 31 7708072
> hakan@tipnet.se
>
> Support and NCC:
> NRE MUX, TIPnet
> 403 35 Gothenburg
> Sweden
> +46 31 7707470
> FAX: +46 31 112800
> nremux@tipnet.se

The TIPnet technical sales support organization is in Stockholm:

> Kjell Simenstad
> MegaCom AB
> Kjell Simenstad
> 121 80 Johanneshov
> Stockholm
> Sweden
> +46 8 780 5616
> FAX: +46 8 686 0213

SUNET (The Swedish University Network)

SRI thanks Hans Wallberg for this information about SUNET.

SUNET is a network for Swedish universities. SUNET interconnects local and regional networks at all the Swedish universities. Via NORDUnet, SUNET provides international connections to the Internet. SUNET is also connected to the two commercial IP networks—SWIPnet and TIPnet—that operate in Sweden.

SUNET is based on Cisco routers and 2 Mbps lines. It supports TCP/IP and DECnet (plus NJE over IP and DECnet) and is ready to support ISO/IP. There were more than 19,000 IP hosts and 650 DECnet hosts connected to SUNET as of August 1992.

For more information about SUNET,contact:

```
Hans Wallberg
Hans.Wallberg@umdac.umu.se
or
Bjorn Eriksen
ber@sunet.se
SUNET
UMDAC
S-901 87 Umea
Sweden
+46 90 16 56 45
FAX: +46 90 16 67 62
```

6.31. Norway

UNINETT

SRI thanks Knut L. Vik for this information about UNINETT, some of which also appears in the Internet Resource Guide.

UNINETT is the Norwegian academic and research data network. Its purpose is to support research and education, and collaborative work in and among academic and non-profit research organizations in Norway, by providing access to computer networks and network resources. As the Norwegian branch of the Internet, EARN/BITNET, the European academic DECnet, and OSInet/IXI, UNINETT offers a variety of services connecting the Norwegian academic society to the rest of the academic world.

Electronic mail, file transfer, terminal access, directory services, USENET Network News, and Gopher information service are among the services available on the UNINETT network.

By August 1992, about 103 academic and research organizations were connected to the UNINETT backbone, giving national and international connection to some 14,500 IP hosts, a few hundred DECnet hosts and X.400 MTAs, and 3 EARN/BITNET nodes.

UNINETT is a member of NORDUnet, which is a cooperative effort of the academic networks in all of the Nordic countries, and is connected internationally through the NORDUnet network.

The UNINETT activity is funded by The Norwegian Ministry of Education, Research, and Church Affairs; the day-to-day work is organized by a secretariat sited at SINTEF Delab, Trondheim.

UNINETT is a non-commercial network for academic and research traffic only. However, some (25) commercial (and governmental) organizations have gained access to the network, under restrictions that do not allow them to use the network for commercial purposes.

For more information about UNINETT, contact:

```
UNINETT secretariat
SINTEF Delab
N-7034 Trondheim
Norway
sekr@uninett.no
C=no;P=uninett;O=uninett;S=sekr
+47 7 592980
FAX: +47 7 532586
```

6.32. Denmark

DENet

 SRI thanks Jan P. Sorensen for this information about DENet.

DENet was initiated at the beginning of 1988 to connect the local networks at various education institutions in Denmark. DENet is almost a star-shaped network with the center at the Danish Computing Centre for Research and Education (UNI-C) in Lyngby, which is located about 15 kilometers north of the center of Copenhagen on the campus of the Technical University. As of Spring 1992, DENet contained about 50 connections.

DECnet and LAT protocols are only supported on DENet institutions belonging to the Department of Education. All other institutions are required to use TCP/IP on DENet. This restriction is imposed to reduce the necessary resources for maintenance and development of DENet. Administrative applications are also required to use TCP/IP. The protocol requirement is only enforced on DENet, on the local Ethernet segments all protocols may of course be used.

In addition to DENet, UNI-C has operated an EARN/RSCS network since the beginning of 1985. Today the network is limited to IBM-compatible computers and contains four connections, two of which are based on VMNET, which enables an RSCS connection to run on top of TCP/IP.

The network is financed by the Danish Computer Board with grants from the Department of Education.

The connected institutions pay a fixed yearly rate, which is graduated according to the size of the institution, and differentiated by whether or not the institution belongs to the Department of Education. Telnet, FTP, SMTP, and domain name service are supported for all DENet users. All

UNI-C mainframes support all the above services. In addition, the network supports DECnet and EARN services for some sites.

UNI-C operates mail gateways between SMTP, VMS MAIL, EARN, and X.400. Domain addresses are used throughout the network. For ease of use, the addresses are independent of the various network protocols. Hence, the users do not have to know which protocol is used on a particular computer.

Users without direct access to DENet may use dialup or X.25 connections to mainframes at UNI-C, which have full TCP/IP connections to DENet.

International network connections are based on a 256 kb/s NORDUnet line to Stockholm. This line supports TCP/IP, DECnet, and X.25, and has been in operation since the beginning of 1989. In addition, two international 9.6 kb/s lines are connected to Lyngby: an EARN/RSCS line to Russia, and a combined TCP/IP and EARN/RSCS line to Poland.

For more information about DENet, contact:

DENet, The Danish Network for Research and Education
Jan P. Sorensen
UNI-C, The Danish Computing Centre for Research and Education
Building 305, DTH
DK-2800 Lyngby
DENMARK
Jan.P.Sorensen@uni-c.dk
+45 45 93 83 55
FAX: +45 45 93 02 20

6.33. Finland

FUNET

SRI thanks Petri Ojala for this information about FUNET.

FUNET, the Finnish University and Research Network, is a project established in 1984 by the Ministry of Education. FUNET provides Internet connectivity to the academic and research community. The network is based on Cisco multiprotocol routers, and is mostly based on public Frame Relay service. The supported protocols are TCP/IP, NJE, DECNET, and OSI CLNS. In two major cities, FUNET connectivity is provided with single modem fiber FDDI rings. FUNET operates various application level gateways and services, including the largest public archive server in the Internet on the host nic.funet.fi. FUNET uses the Nordic University and Research Network, NORDUnet, for international connectivity.

For more information about FUNET, contact:

FUNET
Finnish University and Research Network
Markus Sadeniemi
PO Box 40
SF-02101 Espoo
Finland
sadeniemi@funet.fi
+358 0 457 2711
FAX: +358 0 457 2302

6.34. Iceland

ISnet

SRI thanks Marius Olafsson for this information about ISnet.

ISnet is a collective term for the Icelandic segments of the EUnet and NORDUnet. The network is run by the Icelandic Association of Research Networks (SURIS). The network operation is contracted to the University of Iceland, Computing Services, where the network equipment is located. ISnet is open to anyone that signs the ISnet Acceptable Use document.

ISnet currently has approximately 50 nodes with more than 800 hosts connected. These nodes are connected via dialup lines through UUCP; IP via leased lines; IP via dialup lines, and IP via X.25 and Ethernet. Connection to NORDUnet and EUnet is via IP over 56 kbit/s leased satellite link to the NORDUnet hub in Stockholm using Cisco routers.

ISnet provides its members access to standard Internet services, including mail (SMTP), USENET, file transfer (FTP), remote terminal (Telnet), access to publicly available software and information via FTP, mail-based archive servers, access to library catalogues, general information systems, and many others. ISnet also participates in the X.500 pilot project (PARADISE).

ISnet does not have a fixed rate schedule, but subscription fees are determined by the size of the organization wishing to join, the type of access, and the access speed.

For further information contact:

> SURIS
> co Marius Olafsson
> Taeknigardi
> Dunhaga 5
> 107 Reykjavik
> ICELAND
> +354 1 604747
> isnet-info@isgate.is

6.35. Pacific Rim

PACCOM

 In the Pacific, Australia, Japan, Korea, New Zealand, Hong Kong, and Hawaii have forged a Pacific Communications Network consortium called PACCOM. We thank Torben Nielsen for this information about PACCOM.

Begun in 1989, PACCOM was conceived as a means to develop a regional networking infrastructure in the Pacific Region. The Pacific Rim nations realized they needed Internet access. At the same time, awareness of the need for international network connectivity to serve science groups in the U.S. was also increasing. PACCOM is intended to meet the need for connectivity to scientific groups in the Pacific Region.

PACCOM consists of a variety of links, with bandwidths ranging from 64 kbps to T1. Links have been installed to Melbourne University in Australia, Keio University in Ja-

pan, the University of Tokyo in Japan, the University of
Waikato in New Zealand, the Korea Advanced Institute
for Science and Technology (KAIST) in Korea, and NASA
Ames Research Center in the U.S.

The link to Australia connects to the Australian Academic
and Research Network (AARNet) and the link to New
Zealand connects to the New Zealand University Network
(NZUNINET) at the University of Waikato. Two links to
Japan have been established. One connects to the Univer-
sity of Tokyo International Science Network (TISN) at the
University of Tokyo and the other to the Widely Integrated
Distributed Environment (WIDE) at Keio University. Both
links are in the Tokyo area, and they are all interconnected
within Japan.

The link to NASA Ames Research Center connects to an
interconnect network where the various agency networks
meet, and it provides connectivity to the agency networks.

For more information about PACCOM contact:

Torben Nielsen
University of Hawaii
Department of ICS
2565 The Mall
Honolulu, HI 96822
U.S.A.
+1 808 949 6395
torben@foralie.ics.hawaii.edu

6.36. South Africa

UNINET-ZA

UNINET-ZA is an academic and research network in southern Africa.

The mission of the UNINET project is the development,
implementation, and promotion of an academic and research network of computers in southern Africa, where it
is required as an essential element of the region's research
infrastructure. We thank Vic Shaw for this information regarding networking in South Africa.

The UNINET project started in late 1987 as a result of joint action by the Computer and Network Subcommittees of the Committee of University Principals and the Foundation for Research Development (FRD). The project staff at the FRD gets collaborative support, both academic and technical, from staff of the participating organizations.

UNINET supports electronic mail, computer conferencing, file transfer, newsfeeds, and remote login. Access to overseas networks is now implemented via a TCP/IP link to the Internet.

The UNINET project provides a focal point for the many individual efforts that are being put into network development among the participating organizations, as well as for developing and managing a central information base for the operation of the network. It also operates an information and support service for organizations participating in UNINET, as well as for individual users of the network.

Participation in UNINET is on a voluntary basis and is open to research organizations, tertiary institutions and museums. Participation is formally effected by the organization entering into an agreement with the FRD, which covers matters such as costs and obligations of each party.

The project is financed partly by fees from participating organizations, partly from payment for the use of specific data communication channels, and partly from FRD funds.

The first point of approach for information on UNINET should be the computing services section of the interested person's organization.

Contact with the UNINET office is possible by electronic mail for persons on the network; the UNINET office may also be reached by post, telephone, TELEX, or FAX.

The FRD contact persons and address are:

Manager: Mr. Vic Shaw
Technical Assistants:
Mrs. Gwen Heathfield
Miss Annemarie Marais
UNINET Project
Foundation for Research Development
P.O. Box 2600
Pretoria 0001
SOUTH AFRICA
uninet@frd.ac.za
+27 12 841 3542
+27 12 841 2597
FAX: +27 12 804 2679
TELEX: 321312 SA

6.37. Ireland

HEANET

SRI thanks Peter Flynn for this information about HEANET.

HEANET is the Higher Education Authority Network. It is the Irish academic network, and connects all seven universities via multiprotocol services (TCP/IP, OSI, DECnet). There is a gateway to EARN/BITNET at the University College Dublin, and a gateway to EUnet/UUCP at Trinity College Dublin, as well as connections to IXI and other international networks.

An experimental X.500 directory (Irish Elk) is accessible by Telnet to Paradise (128.86.8.56, login *dua*). There are moves towards a National Research Network (NRN) which will eventually incorporate other academic and research sites which are currently on EARN/BITNET or EUNET/UUCP nodes.

For more information about HEANET, contact:

John Hayden
Chairman, HEANET Management Committee
Higher Education Authority
Fitzwilliam Square, Dublin
Ireland
jhayden@vax1.tcd.ie
+353 1 761545
FAX: +353 1 610492

6.38. United Kingdom

UKnet

A parallel activity to the development of the JANET IP Service is the IP service offered by the UKnet backbone. UKnet has been the U.K. backbone of the worldwide UUCP and USENET news services for more than 10 years. About half its customers are commercial sites. The first site was linked in early March 1991 and more sites were added throughout the rest of the year.

UKnet offers two IP services: first over 9.6 or 64 kbp/s leased lines and secondly over British Telecom "PSS Plus" closed user group X.25 service. UKnet has worked closely with JANET for many years and this cooperation has continued with IP services. As a direct result of this cooperation, UKnet and JANET IP sites will be able to route datagrams to sites on each other's networks.

For more details regarding UKnet write to:

Uknet Support Group
Computing Laboratory
University of Kent
Canterbury
Kent CT2 7NF
UNITED KINGDOM

PIPEX

A new service called PIPEX has recently been established by Unipalm Ltd. in Cambridge, U.K. PIPEX stands for Public IP Exchange, and is a commercial IP access provider for the United Kingdom. PIPEX has no "acceptable use" policy for its network limiting the types of traffic that can be sent. PIPEX is the first non-U.S. member of the Commercial Internet Exchange (CIX) (see Section 10.1.2 for more information about CIX). PIPEX offers both network connections and dialup IP services.

We thank Richard Nuttal for the information about PIPEX. PIPEX offers a range of connection strategies and prices.

There is an online PIPEX discussion list called pipex-info@pipex.net; to join, send a message to pipex-info-request@pipex.net. The list carries announcements of new services and news of changes to the network.

For more information about PIPEX, contact:

> PIPEX
> Unipalm Ltd.
> Area served: U.K.
> Michael Howes (sales information)
> Richard Nuttall (technical information)
> +44 223 250120
> pipex@pipex.net
> FAX: +44 223 250121
> Services: Network connections, dialup IP.

PC User Group CONNECT

SRI thanks Alan Jay for this information about CONNECT.

CONNECT is a multi-line Bulletin Board System (BBS) provider offering dialup e-mail services. The main dial-in number is +44 0 81 863 6646. USENET news and electronic mail services, both for individuals and sites, are available, as is access to the Internet via Telnet, FTP, and other services such as Internet Relay Chat (IRC). The main node is based in the London area. There is an annual charge for the service, with discounts to members of the PC User Group. (Membership in the User Group is not required to use the service.) BBS services for third parties based on CONNECT's host cluster are also provided. This service is affiliated with the IBM PC User Group (IBMPCUG) in England.

For more information about CONNECT, contact:

> Alan Jay
> or
> Matther Farwell
> The IBM PC User Group
> PO Box 360,
> Harrow HA1 4LQ
> ENGLAND
> info@ibmpcug.co.uk
> +44 0 81 863 1191
> FAX: +44 0 81 863 6095

JANET

SRI thanks Bob Day for this information about JANET.

JANET (the Joint Academic NETwork)is a network in the United Kingdom serving its academic community. It runs several different protocols, including the TCP/IP protocols used on the Internet. This latter service (called the JANET IP Service, or JIPS) has only recently been introduced and, although the majority of universities connected to JANET have opted for TCP/IP access, not all of these have at the time of writing finished the work necessary to be able to offer the service. (See Section 6.38 for more information about JIPS.)

Historically, JANET services have been based on X.25 and a set of protocols specific to the U.K. academic community. Besides the introduction of services based on TCP/IP, there are now some ISO services becoming available. Because of the different protocols in use, JANET supports a number of gateway services so that users can interwork between the different protocols. The most widely used of these is the electronic mail gateway called nsfnet-relay.ac.uk. Many JANET sites use this to send mail to the Internet and to receive mail from the Internet. With the advent of the TCP/IP service, some sites now mail direct to Internet systems without the use of this gateway. However, Internet users do not need to worry about this because JANET operators make sure that the entries in the Domain Name System (DNS) for all systems on JANET with mail access are kept up to date, regardless of the protocols they use. Consequently, the correct action is taken automatically by Internet mailers to ensure delivery of a message.

File transfer and interactive login may be done directly to many sites on JANET, if the site has TCP/IP access. You can always check whether a site has such access by seeing if the name of the system concerned is known in the DNS. Note that users in the U.K. often quote the names of systems the opposite way round from those in the U.S. Thus, if you have been given a name starting with uk.ac—e.g., uk.ac.janet.news—you should type it as news.janet.ac.uk to FTP or to Telnet. If the site where the system is located has TCP/IP access, the name will be found in the DNS, and you will be able to make an FTP or Telnet connection.

Where direct interactive login with Telnet is not possible, a user on the Internet can make a Telnet connection to a gateway called sun.nsf.ac.uk. When connected, login with the standard username janet, no password. You are then prompted to type the name of a JANET host, in U.K. format (i.e., the opposite way from the U.S. format, as explained above). The program suggests the JANET NEWS host, uk.ac.janet.news, as a starting point.

Where direct file transfer with FTP is not possible, there is a file-transfer gateway available called ft-relay.ac.uk. Currently this only offers a service used from within JANET, but an extension to allow users on the Internet access is going to beta test at the time of this writing. This will allow a FTP call to be made to it, and files on JANET systems that do not have TCP/IP access will be able to be accessed in this way. In the meantime, there is also a guest FTP service available on sun.nsf.ac.uk, but this is very overloaded.

JANET hosts have information on network addresses, gateways to other networks, instructions for electronic mail, remote login, guides to mailing lists, document collections, and user groups, as well as bulletin boards for technical questions and employment opportunities, libraries, and education projects. There are also extensive files of news of computing-related activities, including minutes of meetings in all parts of the U.K., as well as in Europe and the U.S.

For more information about JANET, contact:

Joint Academic Network
JANET Liaison Desk
c/o Rutherford Appleton Laboratory
Chilton
Didcot
Oxon
OX11 OQX
United Kingdom
+44 235 44 5517
janet-liaison-desk@jnt.ac.uk
O=GB; ADMD= ; PRMD=uk.ac; O=jnt; G=JANET-LIAISON-DESK

The JANET IP Service (JIPS)

SRI thanks Dr. Bob Day for this information about the JANET IP Service (JIPS).

JIPS is an IP carrier service which runs over the X.25 service provided by JANET. The JIPS has run as an additional service over JANET since the beginning of November 1991.

The JIPS is available to all sites connected to JANET, although joining this additional service is optional. To date approximately 60 of the 150 or so sites connected to JANET have applied to join.

As a major IP network, the JIPS is connected to the rest of the global Internet. In the U.K. it is connected to UKNET, a public IP network run by GBnet Ltd. and subscribed to mainly by commercial organizations, and it will be connected to PIPEX, a similar network recently established by Unipalm Ltd. The JIPS is also connected to many other European IP research networks through the auspices of RIPE. Finally, it is connected to the NSFNET, and hence to the regional IP networks in the U.S.A. Connectivity to the Far East is also gained through this route.

The JANET IP Service was introduced as one avenue to provide JANET users with the services they need. An IP service will increase international connectivity because the predominant protocol set in the research community outside the U.K. is IP. Many computer manufacturers of interest to the research community are currently providing their highest level of support for IP protocols. Also, new application protocols often become available first over IP networks.

Within JANET, there is a large ongoing commitment to X.25. This de facto situation meant that there was a choice at the JIPS planning stage of whether to run IP over the X.25 infrastructure, or to use physical multiplexing of the raw bandwidth to provide separate channels for X.25 and IP, with each running alongside each other. It was decided to use the technique of encapsulating IP as data over a X.25 virtual circuit (often referred to as "IP tunneling"). The advantages of this were of cost savings, given the existing infrastructure, and of the ability to get effective dynamic bandwidth sharing, as all services running over the X.25 carrier service could then compete on the basis of demand.

The JIPS network is organized as a backbone of eight IP routers, with one connected to each major X.25 switch on the X.25 backbone. Thus the routers appear to be fully interconnected to each other, via the X.25 network.

Of the 60 or so sites that have currently applied to connect, approximately 40 are already connected. As a consequence, traffic through the backbone IP routers is now building up quickly. There is now of the order of 4 Gbytes traffic per day through the JIPS backbone routers. Although not all of this is switched onto the main JANET trunks, there is already a large component due to international connectivity. For example, the IP link to the NSFNET in the U.S.A. is now supporting over 1 Gbyte traffic per day.

The other notable trend is the growth of registrations in the Domain Name System (DNS), that is, the set of nameservers used in the IP community to perform name-to-address mapping and some mail routing. The number of registrations of end systems in the academic community part of the namespace (the ac.uk domain) is growing very quickly. It is also noticeable, however, that the commercial side of IP networking (the co.uk domain) is growing, albeit not at the same rate. This latter is no doubt a reflection of the growing interest in that community in connection to IP networks, both to interwork with the academic research community, and to gain connectivity with other companies for more directly commercial purposes.

For more information about JIPS, contact:

> Dr. Bob Day
> Joint Network Team
> c/o Rutherford Appleton Laboratory
> Chilton Didcot
> Oxon OX11 0QX
> United Kingdom
> r.a.day@jnt.ac.uk
> +44 235 44 5163
> or
> The JANET Liaison Desk
> +44 235 5517
> JANET-LIAISON-DESK@jnt.ac.uk
> O=GB; ADMD= ; PRMD=uk.ac; O=jnt;
> G=JANET-LIAISON-DESK

6.39. U.S. Providers with International Connections

This section lists those providers based in the U.S. who provide access to the Internet internationally. When known, countries to which they currently have connections are listed. Some NSFNET mid-level networks are listed here because there is a node on the NSFNET backbone at their sites to which an international site is connected. For complete information regarding NSFNET's international connections, contact the InterNIC or send a message to info@internic.net.

Advanced Network and Services, Inc. (ANS) and ANS CO+RE

info@ans.net
800 456 8267
+1 313 663 2482
Area Served: U.S. and International
Current international connections: Germany, Mexico

CERFnet

California Education and Research Federation Network
help@cerf.net
800 876 2373
+1 619 455 3900
FAX: +1 619 455 3990
Area Served: California and International
Current international connections: Korea, Mexico, Brazil

Compuserve Information System

sam@csi.compuserve.com
+1 614 457 8650
800 848 8990
Area Served: U.S. and International
Current international connections: Switzerland, United Kingdom,
Venezuela, Germany

Institute for Global Communications (IGC)

+1 415 442 0220
FAX: +1 415 546 1794
TELEX: 154205417
support@igc.apc.org
Area served: Worldwide
Services: Dialup e-mail; affiliated with PeaceNet, EcoNet, and ConflictNet;
member of the Association for Progressive Communications (APC).
Current international connections: shares resources with APC members
in Australia, Brazil, Canada, England, Germany, Nicaragua, Russia,
Sweden, and Uruguay.

JvNCnet

John von Neumann Center Network
Sergio F. Heker
Allison Pihl
800 358 4437
+1 609 258 2400
market@jvnc.net
Area Served: U.S. and International
Current international connections: Singapore, Taiwan, Tokyo,
Venezuela

NorthWestNet

Northwestern States Network
Eric Hood
+1 206 562 3000
ehood@nwnet.net
Area Served: U.S. and International
Current international connections: Canada

NYSERnet

New York State Education and Research Network
Jim Luckett
+1 315 443 4120
info@nysernet.org
Area Served: New York State and International
Current international connections: Germany, Israel

Performance Systems International, Inc. (PSI)
>   +1 703 620 6651
>   800 827 7482
>   FAX: +1 703 620 4586
>   info@psi.com
>   Area Served: U.S. and International
>   Current international connections: PSI provides connections to an
>   extensive list of countries depending upon the service requested.

Portal Communications, Inc.
>   +1 408 973 9111
>   cs@cup.portal.com
>   Services: Dialup e-mail. Area Served: San Francisco, CA, area, and
>   International
>   Current international connections: Portal is connected to the Public
>   Data Networks (PDNs) of over 70 foreign countries.

SESQUINET
>   Texas Sesquicentennial Network
>   Farrell Gerbode
>   +1 713 527 4988
>   farrell@rice.edu
>   Area Served: Texas and International
>   Current international connections: Mexico

SURAnet
>   Southeastern Universities Research Association Network
>   Deborah J. Nunn
>   +1 301 982 4600
>   marketing@sura.net
>   Area Served: Southeastern U.S. (Alabama, Florida, Georgia, Kentucky,
>   Louisiana, Mississippi, North Carolina, South Carolina, Tennessee,
>   Virginia, and West Virginia)
>   Current international connections: Puerto Rico

UUNET Technologies, Inc.
>   800 488 6384
>   +1 703 204 8000
>   info@uunet.uu.net
>   Area Served: U.S. and International
>   Services: Network connections, dialup e-mail.

In addition to the above providers, the following two providers concentrate on offering international connections to the Internet.

Infolan
>   George Abe
>   abe@infonet.com
>   +1 310 335 2600
>   FAX: +1 310 335 2876
>   Current international connections: Europe, Canada, Hong
>   Kong, Japan, Singapore, and Australia

Sprint NSFNET ICM
>   Sprint NSFNET International Connections Manager
>   Area Served: International
>   Robert Collet
>   +1 703 904 2230
>   rcollet@icm1.icp.net
>   Current international connections: EBONE (Europe), Japan,
>   France, U.K.

7

THE INTERNET—MORE INFORMATION

This chapter gives a more detailed idea of what the Internet is and where it came from. It provides a physical description of the Internet, traces its history, and gives some information illustrating its growth.

We drew on several resources for the information presented in this chapter. Deserving of special mention is Douglas Comer for his book *Internetworking with TCP/IP* [13].

7.1. Historical Background

The Internet started as a wide area, packet-switching network called the ARPANET. This network was created as an experimental testbed in 1969 by the Advanced Research Projects Agency (ARPA) of the U.S. Department of Defense (DoD). Its purpose was to provide efficient communication between different types of computers over a large geographic area. The goal was to allow a large community of users to share the resources that were available on these computers.

The ARPANET provided this service by connecting single hosts and terminal servers into a network. The network started with four hosts, which were located at the University of California at Los Angeles (UCLA), the University of California at Santa Barbara (UCSB), Stanford Research Institute (now SRI International), and the University of Utah. In the mid-1970s, by which time the ARPANET had proven to be an effective communications network between DoD and university research centers, ARPA became the Defense Advanced Research Projects Agency (DARPA), and continued to fund the expanding Internet.

By 1976, it became clear that other types of networks were proliferating, such as LANs based on shared broadcast cables, token ring networks, and wide area networks based on shared broadcast satellite channels. DARPA responded to this growth by exploring the use of packet-switching techniques to communicate with these other types of networks.

Packet Switch Nodes (PSNs) and internetwork gateways were employed to interconnect and forward packets between these dissimilar network technologies, not just from host-to-host as the original ARPANET had. PSNs work in such a way to transfer data to and from hosts, as well as to and from other PSNs. Each PSN connects to at least two other PSNs, as well as from 1 to 16 host computers.

TCP/IP Arrives

The ARPANET originally used the Network Control Program (NCP) as its host-to-host protocol. When it became clear that NCP would not be able to support the number of hosts and PSNs on the ARPANET, DARPA funded the development of a more general set of communications protocols, which would become the **Transmission Control Protocol** (TCP) and **Internet Protocol** (IP). These protocols and their related standards, commonly referred to as **TCP/IP** (after the names of its two main standards), were conceived around 1978-1979 and were first implemented by sites in 1980, thereby setting the stage for the very beginnings of the Internet.

In 1983, two significant events occurred. First, in January, DARPA required that all computers connected to ARPANET use TCP/IP. Second, toward the end of the year, it was decided to split the network administratively into two separate unclassified networks, ARPANET and MILNET. This last action was accomplished to meet the twin needs for an unclassified operational military network and an experimental research and development network. MILNET itself was built using DARPA Internet technology and in 1982 had adopted a single set of communication protocols based on the TCP/IP protocol suite. The ARPANET, along with MILNET, now became a subset of the Defense Data Network (DDN), an operational military network made up of several DoD computer networks connected to the Internet. The DDN is funded by the U.S. Department of Defense and managed by the Defense Information Systems Agency (DISA), formerly the Defense Communications Agency (DCA).

National Science Foundation

The success of internetworking and the TCP/IP technology led groups other than computer science researchers to adopt it. The National Science Foundation (NSF), a U.S. government agency, also realized that network communication would become a crucial part of scientific research and took an active role in expanding the Internet to reach as many scientists as possible. In 1985, it began a program to establish network access centered around its six supercomputer centers—the Jon von Neumann National Supercomputer Center in Princeton, NJ, the San Diego Supercomputer Center in San Diego, CA, the National Center for Supercomputing Applications in Champaign, IL, the Cornell National Supercomputer Facility in Ithaca, NY, the Pittsburgh Supercomputing Center in Pittsburgh, PA, and the Scientific Computing Division of the National Center for Atmospheric Research in Boulder, CO.

In 1986, NSF further expanded its networking efforts by funding the NSFNET, a new long-haul backbone network designed to connect supercomputer centers, as well as make them accessible from the ARPANET. This action was legitimized through a Memorandum of Agreement with DARPA and set the stage for mutual access by users of both networks.

The NSFNET has a three-level component structure consisting of a backbone, mid-level networks, and campus networks. The TCP/IP protocols, developed by DARPA, are used on the backbone and on most of the mid-level and campus networks. Some of the NSFNET networks, other than the backbone, run protocols in addition to TCP/IP, such as DECnet.

The NSFNET also shares networking facilities and bandwidth with other federal agencies that run networks to support scientific research such as the National Aeronautics and Space Administration (NASA), and the Department of Energy (DoE). Gateways are used to connect these networks with the research sites of DARPA.

NSFNET Upgrades

In November 1987, NSF awarded MERIT, Inc., a grant to manage and operate the backbone for five years. MERIT established joint study projects with IBM and MCI on network research and development. Their plans were to reengineer the backbone, install higher speed lines, and use new technology. As part of this effort, MCI provided leased lines for the backbone and expertise in circuit technology, while IBM provided hardware and software for NSFNET switching nodes and network management. By July 1988, an upgrade to T1 links was completed and all connections on the NSFNET backbone became point-to-point T1 links. With this move to T1 service on the backbone, bandwidth capacity increased 24-fold over the original speed. MERIT, MCI, and IBM continued their goals of improved connectivity and higher speeds. By the beginning of 1991, the overall speed and capacity of the NSFNET was increased once again through deployment of new T3 technology at several of its backbone end nodes. In December 1992 NSFNET completed the conversion of its backbone from T1 to T3 service.

Obviously, newer, faster network technology was replacing the original long-haul links used by ARPANET. Plans to phase out the ARPANET started in 1988, and in June 1990, the ARPANET was officially dissolved.

Because the NSFNET provided the academic community with the same kind of networking infrastructure and employed the ideas of resource sharing and collaboration among researchers, most sites formerly part of the ARPANET were absorbed by the NSFNET. Today, the NSFNET supplies a major backbone communication service and has become the national U.S. research network since the demise of the ARPANET.

The MILNET remains under the administration of DISA. Plans are now under way for the current networks to be upgraded and expanded. A Defense Research Internet (DRI) will meet defense needs, while the U.S.

Government's Office of Science and Technology Policy (OSTP) is working on the National Research and Education Network (NREN) project. It is hoped the NREN will unify government sponsorship and management of what are now separately-sponsored internets owned by NSF, NASA, DoE, and DoD into one project providing a national forum for research and education.

7.2. Physical Description

To understand what the Internet is, it is important first to understand the concept of networks in general. **Any set of computers** (which are often referred to as hosts) **that are connected in such a way that each of them can interoperate with the others is called a network**. The joining of these hosts involves two major components: **hardware and software**. The **hardware**, or physical connection, can be as simple as local telephone lines connecting two or three personal computers in a building, or as complex as long-haul telephone lines, satellite relays, fiber-optic cables, or radio signals linking computers spread over the world.

The **software component** is the set of computer programs that controls communication over the hardware links. This software may be run on the same or dissimilar host operating systems and is based on standards that define its operation. These standards are often referred to as **protocols**; they give the formulas for passing packets of data, specify the details of packet formats, and describe how to handle error conditions. The protocols hide the details of network hardware and permit computers of different hardware types, joined by different physical connections, to communicate despite their differences.

A Packet-Switched Network

Communication networks can be divided into two basic types: **circuit-switched** and **packet-switched**. **Circuit switched networks** operate by forming a dedicated connection, or circuit, between two points. When two entities want to communicate, a call is established between them, a message is sent from one to the other, and then the call is terminated. A good example of a circuit-switched communications network is the U.S. telephone system. A telephone call establishes a circuit from the originating phone through the local switching office, moves across trunk lines to a remote switching office, and then arrives at the destination telephone.

Packet-switched networks, the kind typically used to connect computers and the type on which the Internet was founded, take an entirely different approach. In a packet-switched network, the communications circuits are leased on a permanent basis, and several messages from different hosts are multiplexed, or transmitted simultaneously on the same circuit, onto high capacity inter-machine connections. Messages are divided into small segments of data, called packets. These packets carry identification that enable other computers on the network to know whether the data is destined for them or how to pass it on to its intended destination.

The chief advantage of packet-switching is that multiple communications among hosts can take place at the same time, with intermachine connections shared by all pairs of machines that are communicating. Another major motivation for packet-switched technology is cost and performance. Circuit costs are fixed, independent of traffic, thus avoiding much of the substantial overhead and delay associated with the establishment and termination of calls. For example, one pays a fixed rate when making a phone call, independent of how quickly the two parties talk.

Because several hosts can share a network when packet-switching technology is used, fewer interconnections are required and costs are kept low. In addition, engineers have been able to develop high speed network hardware, so that capacity is currently not a problem.

Network Connections

Based on the TCP/IP protocols, **the Internet itself is a packet-switched network**. However, not all networks connected to the Internet are connected in the same way. The typical connection traditionally has been for a site to lease a dedicated line to a point on the Internet and connect its local network to the greater Internet via a router. The site's local area network may or may not be based on the TCP/IP suite. The TCP/IP protocols were originally developed for wide-area application, so many local networks were and are based on other types of protocols. However, the router translates from one protocol suite to another and routes packets appropriately to the right destination, either to the local network, to the Internet, or to another network.

Although leased lines are the most common way of connecting networks, the interconnecting networks that comprise the Internet are connected via several different physical configurations or topologies. Important characteristics of network topology to mention are the size of the geographic area the network covers, and the technology used to support it.

With that in mind, here are some examples of the types of networks that make up the Internet:

Point-to-Point Networks

Use a single communication channel to connect two computers. The connection can be via a cable between two local hosts sitting side by side in a room or via a phone line and modem to connect two distant hosts separated by a continent.

Local Area Networks (LANs)

Includes Ethernet, token bus, token ring, and broadband network technology. LANs are used for connecting hosts inside single buildings or other small areas.

Wide Area Networks (WANs)

Employ telephone lines, radio transmission, satellites, or long-haul land lines to connect computers that are located over large geographic areas.

Gateways

We've seen that the **Internet** is a **collection of packet-switching networks that interconnect to function logically as a single, large, virtual network**. To have a viable internet, computers that are able to send packets from one network to another are required. The computers that fill this role were traditionally called Internet gateways, and are now usually referred to as **routers**. Routers play a key role in Internet communication because they provide interconnections between networks, not just between machines. They take a packet created on one network, translate that packet so that a different network can read it, and then send it on to that network. A workable internet's interconnected systems also agree to implement a set of standard protocols that allow the sharing of resources and services across the network. These are often called gateway protocols, or **inter-domain routing protocols**.

In addition to gateway and router, other terms that you will hear in this context are bridge and repeater. The differences between the items these terms refer to can be hard to distinguish, and sometimes different definitions of the same terms differ subtlety. One good source of general definitions is RFC 1208, *A Glossary of Networking Terms*, which was adapted from *The INTEROP Pocket Glossary of Networking Terms*, compiled by Interop Company [18]. Below are their definitions of several of these terms.

bridge A device that connects two or more physical networks and forwards packets between them. Bridges can usually be made to filter packets, that is, to forward only certain traffic. Related devices are: repeaters which simply forward electrical signals from one cable to another, and full-fledged routers which make routing decisions based on several criteria. In OSI terminology, a bridge is a Data Link Layer intermediate system. See repeater and router.

gateway The original Internet term for what is now called router or more precisely, IP router. In modern usage, the terms "gateway" and "application gateway" refer to systems which do translation from some native format to another. Examples include X.400 to/from RFC 822 electronic mail gateways. See router.

mail gateway A machine that connects two or more electronic mail systems (especially dissimilar mail systems on two different networks) and transfers messages between them. Sometimes the mapping and translation can be quite complex, and generally it requires a store-and-forward scheme whereby the message is received from one system completely before it is transmitted to the next system, after suitable translations.

repeater A device which propagates electrical signals from one cable to another without making routing decisions or providing packet filtering. In OSI terminology, a repeater is a Physical Layer intermediate system. See bridge and router.

router A system responsible for making decisions about which of several paths network (or Internet) traffic will follow. To do this it uses a routing protocol to gain information about the network, and algorithms to choose the best route based on several criteria known as "routing metrics." In OSI terminology, a router is a Network Layer intermediate system. See gateway, bridge, and repeater.

7.3. Growth of the Internet

The physical split and "demise" of the ARPANET in 1990 by no means meant the end of the Internet. On the contrary, the split contributed to its growth and led to its evolution as the largest operational superset of research-oriented internets. The current Internet has made the transition from a research environment, in which the users were the implementors, to a service environment, in which a variety of users throughout the world now depend on it for their day-to-day communications. Not only has the Internet grown in size and topology, but also in the number of different types and vendors of hosts and routers. Hosts range from PCs to supercomputers, with everything in between, and gateways vary from vendor to vendor. The Internet is now a true multi-vendor system.

If you are just now considering joining the Internet, it will probably be hard for you to imagine both how big it is now, and how small it used to be. RFC 1296, *Internet Growth (1981-1991)* [3], describes the size and growth of the Internet; from it we take the following data.

In August of 1981, approximately one year after the TCP/IP protocols had replaced the original Network Control Program, there were 213 hosts on the Internet (still called the ARPANET at that time). Today, 213 hosts would easily fit on one Class C network, and the Internet community is currently devising ways to deal with the decrease in the availability of the larger sized Class B networks.

In October of 1984, the year the Domain Name System (DNS) was introduced to the Internet, there were 1,024 hosts. Before the implementation of the DNS, the name and address of every host on the Internet had to be entered into a central host table. The example figures given here so far have all been taken from old host tables. Once the DNS was distributed in the Internet (see Section 8.5 for more discussion of domains), the whole DNS had to be searched to count the number of Internet hosts.

By using a program to search through the DNS, we know that as of April 1993, the Internet was approaching 1.5 million hosts!

The chart below shows the increase in the number of hosts on the Internet since 1981. These are hosts with at least one IP address assigned. Data was collected by the ZONE or census DNS searching programs, except where a host table reference is noted. Following is a graph of the data in this chart. It shows quite graphically the phenomenal rate of growth the Internet has experienced in the last few years.

Date	Hosts	Source
08/81	213	Host table #152
05/82	235	Host table #166
08/83	562	Host table #300
10/84	1,024	Host table #392
10/85	1,961	Host table #485
02/86	2,308	Host table #515
11/86	5,089	ZONE
12/87	28,174	ZONE
07/88	33,000	ZONE
10/88	56,000	ZONE
01/89	80,000	ZONE
07/89	130,000	ZONE
10/89	159,000	ZONE
10/90	313,000	ZONE
01/91	376,000	ZONE
07/91	535,000	ZONE
10/91	617,000	ZONE
01/92	727,000	ZONE
07/92	992,000	ZONE
10/92	1,136,000	ZONE

Table 7-1: Internet Growth Data

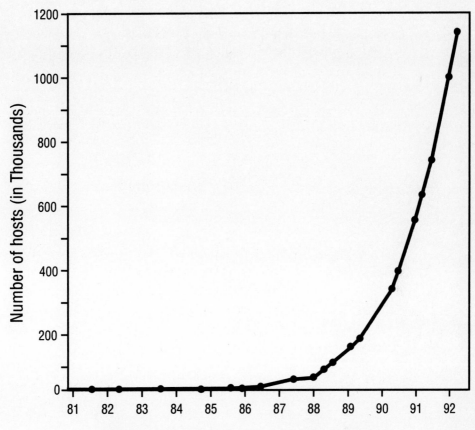

Figure 7-1: Internet Growth (1981–1992)

Basic Internet Concepts

Getting started on the Internet usually means facing a daunting number of new terms, references, and concepts, all of which seem to be required knowledge before you can proceed to get things done. Often it is unclear how much information about a new subject you need to know, and often the references you find provide a lot of details without any general overview.

In this chapter, we've chosen some Internet concepts we feel are basic to the level of understanding of the Internet you will need when you are just getting started. More technical documents abound, especially as RFCs, and these are cited in Chapter 12. We encourage you to look at these for more detailed information. This chapter offers instead an introduction to these topics for those for whom they are totally, or almost totally, new concepts. Some topics are discussed very briefly, while others, such as Internet security, the Domain Name System, and Internet addressing, are discussed in more depth. The concepts are not presented in any particular order.

8.1. RFCs, FYIs, and STDs

First we'll explain what RFCs, FYIs, and STDs are, why they're important, and how to get them.

8.1.1. RFCs

Some of the information in this section is taken from FYI 4, *FYI on Questions and Answers: Answers to Commonly asked "New Internet User" Questions* [7].

RFC stands for **R**equest **F**or **C**omments. RFCs are the technical and informational notes of the Internet research and development community. A document in this series may be about essentially any topic related to computer communication, and may be anything from a meeting report to the specification of a standard. They are traditionally online files, rather than paper documents, although they are often referred to as "RFC documents." They are freely available online from many Internet and non-Internet sites via anonymous file transfer (see Section 9.3.1 for an explanation of anonymous FTP). Many sites also make them available via electronic mail.

Dr. Jon Postel at the University of Southern California, Information Sciences Institute (USC ISI) is the RFC Editor. He reviews all RFCs before they are issued. Each time an RFC is issued, an announcement is made online of its availability. If you have electronic mail access to the Internet, you can join this announcement list by sending a message to *rfc-request@nic.ddn.mil*.

The RFC Editor assigns each RFC a unique, identifying number. Once a document is assigned an RFC number and published online, that RFC is never revised or re-issued with the same number. If the information in a particular RFC is updated, a new RFC is issued and assigned a new number. RFCs are often referred to by their numbers, sometimes even instead of by their names.

While RFCs are not refereed publications, they do receive technical review from either the Internet task forces, individual technical experts, or the RFC Editor, as appropriate. Currently, most Internet standards are published as RFCs, but not all RFCs specify standards.

When using an RFC as a reference for a protocol specification, it is important to verify that you have the most recent RFC on that protocol. The RFC titled *IAB Official Protocol Standards*, [8] currently RFC 1360 (but often updated with a new RFC number under the same title), is the reference for determining the correct RFC to refer to for the current specification of each protocol.

8.1.2. FYIs

FYI stands for For Your Information. FYIs are a subset of the RFC series of online documents.

FYI 1 states:

> The FYI series of notes is designed to provide Internet users with a central repository of information about any topics which relate to the Internet. FYI topics may range from historical memos on "Why it was done this way" to answers to commonly asked operational questions.
>
> The FYIs are intended for a wide audience. Some FYIs will cater to beginners, while others will discuss more advanced topics.

Very generally, FYI documents tend to be more information oriented, while RFCs are usually (but not always) more technically oriented.

FYI documents are assigned both an FYI number and an RFC number. As RFCs, if an FYI is ever updated, it is issued again with a new RFC number; however, its FYI number remains unchanged. This can be a little confusing at first, but the aim is to help users identify which FYIs are about which topics. For example, FYI 4, cited above, which discusses questions new Internet users commonly ask, will always be FYI 4, even though it may be updated several times and during that process receive different RFC numbers. Thus, a user has only to remember the FYI number to find the proper document. Of course, remembering titles often works as well.

8.1.3. STDs

The newest subseries of RFCs are the STDs (Standards). RFC 1311 [24], which introduces this subseries, states that the intent of STDs is to identify clearly those RFCs that document Internet standards. An STD number will be assigned only to those specifications that have completed the full process of standardization in the Internet. Existing Internet standards have been assigned STD numbers (see Section 8.3.4 for further discussion of Internet standards).

Like FYIs, once a standard has been assigned an STD number, that number will not change, even if the standard is reworked and re-specified and later issued with a new RFC number.

It is important to differentiate between a "standard" and a "document." Different RFC documents will always have different RFC numbers. However, sometimes, the complete specification for a standard will be contained in more than one RFC document. When this happens, each of the documents that is part of the specification for that standard will carry the same STD number. For example, the Domain Name System (DNS) is specified by the combination of RFC 1034 and RFC 1035; therefore, both of those RFCs are labeled STD 13.

The current STD Index is included in Appendix IV.

8.1.4. Identifying RFCs online

Sometimes you know you want information about a subject, but you don't know which RFCs discuss that subject. Until recently, there was no easy way to determine which particular RFC you might want. You could browse through the RFC Index or get one of the RFCs that provides summaries of the other RFCs (such as RFC 1000), but these are often time-consuming, hit-or-miss methods. Recently, however, a new RFC Information service has become available via electronic mail to host isi.edu. The following information about the RFC-INFO service was supplied by Jon Postel of USC Information Sciences Institute (ISI).

The RFC-INFO service

RFC-INFO is an e-mail based service to help in locating and retrieving RFCs, FYIs, and IMRs. Users can ask for "lists" of all RFCs, FYIs, and Internet Monthly Reports (IMRs) having certain attributes such as their ID, keywords, title, author, issuing organization, and date. (See Section 12.3 for more information about IMRs.)

To use the service send e-mail to rfc-info@isi.edu with your requests in the body of the message. Feel free to put anything in the Subject; the system ignores it. All is case independent.

To get started you may send a message to rfc-info@isi.edu with requests such as in the following examples (explanations in italics should not be included in the requests).

```
Help: Help              to get this information
List: FYI               list the FYI notes
List: RFC               list RFCs with "window" as keyword or
   in title Keywords: window
List: FYI               list FYIs about windows
   Keywords: window
List: *                 list both RFCs and FYIs about windows
   Keywords: window
List: *                 list all documents by Cooper
   Author: Cooper
List: RFC               list RFCs about ARPANET, ARPA NET-
   WORK, etc.
   Title: ARPA*NET
```

```
List: RFC              list RFCs issued by MITRE, dated 7+8/
   1991
   Organization: MITRE
   Dated-after: Jul-01-1991
   Dated-before: Aug-31-1991

List: RFC              list RFCs obsoleting a given RFC
   Obsoletes: RFC0010

List: RFC              list RFCs by authors starting with
   "Bracken"
   Author: Bracken*   * is a wild card that matches all
   endings

List: IMR              list the IMRs for the first 6 months
   of 92
   Dated-after: Jan-01-1992
   Dated-before: Jun-01-1992

Retrieve: RFC          retrieve RFC-822
   Doc-ID: RFC0822     note: always 4 digits in RFC#

Retrieve: IMR          retrieve May 1992 Internet Monthly
   Report
   Doc-ID: IMR9205     note, always 4 digits = YYMM

Help: Manual           to retrieve the long user manual, 30+
   pages

Help: List             how to use the LIST request

Help: Retrieve         how to use the RETRIEVE request

Help: Topics           list topics for which help is avail-
   able

Help: Dates            "Dates" is such a topic

List: Keywords         list the keywords in use

List: Organizations  list the organizations known to the
   system
```

Report problems to rfc-manager@isi.edu.

8.1.5. Getting RFCs, FYIs, and indexes

There are many Internet hosts around the world that act as online repositories for the RFCs and FYIs. These repositories make the RFCs available for anonymous file transfer. Many also have the RFCs available via electronic mail.

Following is a list of the hosts that make RFCs available online, directions for anonymous FTP (also illustrated in

Section 9.3), and directions for using the automatic mail server at SRI.

8.1.6. RFC repositories

This information is taken from the file in-notes/rfc-retrieval.txt available online from the host isi.edu. The full text of this file is included in Appendix VI. The Appendix contains details regarding the formats of the various files and about addressing the different mail servers.

If you can send electronic mail to the Internet, you can retrieve this information by sending a message to rfc-

"Primary" U.S. RFC Repositories that make RFCs available for FTP			
Site	**Host**	**Directory**	**E-Mail**
InterNIC Directory and Database Services	ds.internic.net	rfc	mailserv@ds.internic.net
SRI International Network Information Systems Center	ftp.nisc.sri.com	rfc	mail-server@nisc.sri.com.
NSFNET Information Center	nis.nsf.net	internet/documents/rfc	nis-info@nis.nsf.net.
JvNCNet Network Information Center	nisc.jvnc.net	rfc	sendrfc@jvnc.net
USC Information Sciences Institute	venera.isi.edu	in-notes	rfc-index@isi.edu.
Washington University, St. Louis	wuarchive.wustl.edu	info/rfc	N/A
Imperial College, London	src.doc.ic.ac.uk	rfc	info-server@doc.ic.ac.uk
CONCERT, North Carolina	ftp.concert.net	rfc	N/A

info@isi.edu with *help: ways_to_get_rfcs* in the body of the
message.

"Secondary" RFC repositories around the world:

Sweden

Site:	SUNET (Swedish University Network)
Host:	sunic.sunet.se
Directory:	rfc

Site:	Chalmers University of Technology
Host:	chalmers.se
Directory:	rfc

Germany

Site:	University of Dortmund
Host:	walhalla.informatik.uni-dortmund.de
Directory:	pub/documentation/rfc
Notes:	RFCs in compressed format

France

Site:	Institut National de la Recherche en Informatique et Automatique (INRIA)
Address:	info-server@inria.fr
Notes:	RFCs are available via e-mail to the above address.

Netherlands

Site:	EUnet (European Network)
Host:	mcsun.eu.net
Directory	rfc
Notes:	RFCs in compressed format

Finland

Site:	FUNET (Finnish University Network)
Host:	funet.fi
Directory	rfc
Notes:	RFCs in compressed format. Also provides e-mail access
	by sending mail to archive-server@funet.fi.

Norway

Site:	University of Trondheim
Host:	ugle.unit.no
Directory	pub/rfc

Denmark

Site:	University of Copenhagen
Host:	ftp.diku.dk (freja.diku.dk)
Directory	rfc

Australia and Pacific Rim

Site:	University of Melbourne
Host:	munnari.oz.au
Directory	rfc
Notes:	rfc's in compressed format rfcNNNN.Z PostScript rfc's rfcNNNN.ps.2

United States

Site:	CERFnet (California Research and Education Federation Network)
Host:	nic.cerf.net
Directory:	netinfo/rfc

Site:	uunet
Host:	ftp.uu.net
Directory	inet/rfc

United States / Mexico

Site:	SESQUINET
Host:	nic.sesqui.net
Directory:	pub/rfc

8.1.7. RFCs online from SRI

Here are specific instructions for getting RFCs online from SRI's repository. The general procedure outlined below is compatible with retrieving RFCs from any online repository, although file names, directory names, and FTP programs may vary slightly. In addition, some other repositories store RFCs in a compressed format, indicated by appending .Z to the file name.

RFCs can be obtained via anonymous FTP from the host ftp.nisc.sri.com. They are in the *rfc* directory. Each file is in the form *rfcNNNN.txt* or *rfcNNNN.ps*, where *NNNN* refers to the number of the RFC. It is not necessary to use leading zeroes if you need an RFC with a number less than 1000. The RFC Index is in the file *rfc-index.txt*.

FYI files are in the *fyi* directory in the form *fyiNN.txt* or *fyiNN.ps*, where *NN* refers to the number of the FYI without leading zeroes. The FYI Index is in the file *fyi-index.txt*. Case is significant here; use lowercase in the names of the files and directories.

Most RFCs are in ASCII text format, as indicated by the ".txt" extension in the file names. Some RFCs are also available in PostScript format. Those with extensions of ".ps" must be printed on a PostScript compatible printer. Most RFCs available in PostScript format are also available in text format; however, in some cases, graphic elements, charts, or graphs may not be included.

For anonymous FTP, you open a connection to the host that has the file you want, log in with the user name *anonymous* and use the password requested, such as your login name. Most repositories also accept the password *guest*. Change directories with the command *cd rfc* or *cd fyi*. Then "get" the file you want, e.g., *get rfc1000.txt*. For a demonstration of anonymous FTP, refer to Section 9.3.

SRI is one of the repositories that also provides an automatic mail service for those sites that cannot use FTP, but do have access to the Internet via electronic mail. Address the request to *mail-server@nisc.sri.com*. This is the Internet form of the address. If you are sending from a site that uses a different addressing scheme, you may need to change that address into a form your mailer will understand and route correctly. (See Section 9.1.6 for more information about sending mail to the Internet from several other networks.)

In the body of your message, indicate the RFC to be sent by typing *send rfcNNNN* or *send rfcNNNN.p* where *NNNN* is the RFC number. Multiple requests may be included in the same message by listing the *send* commands on separate lines. To request the RFC Index, the command should read *send rfc-index.txt*.

8.2 Security

The Internet has grown significantly and has become quite diverse. U.S. Government institutions and agencies, academic and research institutions, commercial network and electronic mail carriers, non-profit research centers, as well as many industrial organizations are users of and contributors to this technology. The network administrators, users, vendors, and service providers work together to keep the Internet functioning, and take responsibility for the operation of their individual networks.

For the most part, the Internet has been a voluntary system, in the sense that rules of operation and network etiquette have not been strictly enforced unless an action violated U.S. national laws. This voluntary aspect can be seen as both a strength and a weakness of the Internet. Over the past few years, however, procedures have become stricter and several guidelines have evolved that should be followed to contribute toward the security of the Internet. How did these guidelines evolve? What is considered ethical network use? How can a user do his part to maintain the security of the Internet and stay informed on security-related topics? This section will answer these questions.

8.2.1. The Internet worm

On the evening of November 2, 1988, the Internet, was severely compromised by the intrusion of a "worm." According to John Wack of the National Institute of Standards and Technology, a worm is a program or a command file that uses a computer network as a means for adversely affecting a system's integrity, reliability, or availability. A worm is generally a self-contained program that spreads to other computers over a network, as opposed to other files on one computer.

This "worm" was a self-replicating program that infected certain computers by capitalizing on known loopholes in two network programs. RFC 1135, *Helminthiasis of the Internet* [9], discusses the Internet worm in more detail. The worm was eradicated from most computers within 48 to 72 hours after it appeared, due to the efforts of computer science staffs at university research centers. However, the worm had lasting effects on the Internet community because it dramatically proved the vulnerability of the Internet.

It should be noted that the same voluntary aspect of the Internet that perhaps encouraged a looser atmosphere than is apparent today was also responsible for the swift analysis and eradication of the Internet worm in 1988. The Internet continues to be protected today by a close association of cooperating security response centers.

8.2.2. A new awareness

One apparent effect in the aftermath of the Internet worm is an increased awareness of the importance of security in the Internet. Toward that end, there was seen to be a need to develop ethical standards that would apply to the entire Internet community, and a need to implement strong laws that would be vigorously enforced when necessary.

Today, more people are aware of Internet security and are even knowledgeable about broad types of security problems. In general, there are two classes of security problems. The first type includes actual attacks, either via programs or by a person attempting to break into and compromise a system. The second type includes software, hardware, and procedural vulnerabilities. Often these vulnerabilities can be addressed before any hostile action is taken; for example, patches for software problems can be developed and implemented, users can change their passwords regularly, information regarding procedural weaknesses can be distributed, etc.

8.2.3. Ethics and the Internet

As a result of the Internet worm, many government agencies, organizations, and professional computer societies have issued policy statements.

In January 1989, the Internet Activities Board (IAB) issued RFC 1087, *Ethics and the Internet* [10], a policy statement concerning the proper uses of the resources of the Internet. The following is extracted from RFC 1087:

> The Internet is a national facility whose utility is largely a consequence of its wide availability and accessibility. Irresponsible

use of this critical resource poses an enormous threat to its continued availability to the technical community.

The U.S. Government sponsors of this system have a fiduciary responsibility to the public to allocate government resources wisely and effectively. Justification for the support of this system suffers when highly disruptive abuses occur. Access to and use of the Internet is a privilege and should be treated as such by all users of this system.

The IAB strongly endorses the view of the Division Advisory Panel of the National Science Foundation Division of Network Communications Research and Infrastructure which, in paraphrase, characterized as unethical and unacceptable any activity which purposely:

- seeks to gain unauthorized access to the resources of the Internet,

- disrupts the intended use of the Internet,

- wastes resources (people, capacity, computer) through such actions,

- destroys the integrity of the computer-based information, and/or

- compromises the privacy of users.

8.2.4. Response teams

Another direct response to the Internet worm was the formation of several security response teams; one of the earliest was the Computer Emergency Response Team (CERT). CERT is a group of computer experts that have been organized to facilitate response to security events that involve Internet hosts. The Defense Advanced Research Projects Agency (DARPA) created the CERT Coordination Center (CERT/CC) at the Software Engineering Institute at Carnegie Mellon University to coordinate and improve communications during these emergencies. This team is now called the Internet CERT. Other teams were created as well and are discussed in greater detail in Section 8.2.6.

8.2.5. User's role in Internet security

An individual Internet user can do many things to strengthen the security of the Internet. This section discusses some of those things. Site administrators should consult RFC 1244, FYI 8, *Site Security Handbook* [11], for more detailed discussion about how to increase the security of a particular site or network.

RFC 1281, *Guidelines for the Secure Operation of the Internet* [12], states that, "Security is understood to include protection of the privacy of information, protection of information against unauthorized modification, protection of systems against denial of service, and protection of systems against unauthorized access."

It is the individual Internet user's responsibility to understand the security policies and procedures of his computer and network site. Users observing the following guidelines can help ensure the security of their own data, as well as assist in the protection of their local network site.

➤ Users are responsible for all resources assigned to them, so sharing of any computer accounts and/or access to resources assigned to the user is strongly discouraged.

➤ Follow site security procedures for password protection. If your system relies on the password protection system, be sure to select a password carefully and change it often. Do not use an unmodified word from any language; this includes words spelled backwards. A simple modification involves prefixing a word with one or several numerals.

➤ Change your password as required by your site or, at the minimum, every six months.

➤ Do not write your password down on paper, or record it in a file stored on a computer disk, floppy disk, PC, or magnetic tape.

➤ Do not leave your terminal logged in or unattended.

➤ Know the protection mechanism used by your computer, and make sure that all your files are set up with appropriate protection modes. The recommended file protection default for directories is "no read and no write to outside users." In this case, a user can still make files accessible to outside users over the network, but must knowingly set the file and directory protections to make this happen.

8.2.6. Security response centers

Security response centers were established not only for reporting security incidents, but as a good source for obtaining information on computer security and guidelines for ensuring security at your network site. This section describes several major response centers, some of the services they offer, and how to contact each of them.

The Forum of Incident Response Teams

The Forum of Incident Response Teams (FIRST) (formerly the Computer Emergency Response Team (CERT) System) is a network of computer security incident response teams that work together voluntarily to coordinate security problems and their prevention. The following information is extracted from the *CERT System Operational Framework* of November 16, 1990. (The name of the CERT System was changed to the FIRST on August 9, 1991.)

The goals of the FIRST System are:

➤ fostering cooperation among information technology constituents in the effective prevention, detection, and recovery from computer security incidents;

> ➤ providing a means for the communication of alert and advisory information on potential threats and emerging incident situations;

> ➤ facilitating the actions and activities of the member CERTs including research, development, and operational activities; and

> ➤ facilitating the sharing of security-related information, tools, and techniques.

The following definitions clarify common security response center terms.

CERT Computer Emergency Response Team—an organization whose function is to assist an information technology community or other defined constituency in preventing and handling security- related incidents. An individual CERT also takes active steps to raise its constituents' level of awareness of computer security issues and to improve the security of its constituents' information technology resources.

CERT Constituency—a group of users or organizations that is served by a given CERT and that share specific characteristics, such as a specific organization, computer network, operating system, or other common interest.

CERT Representative (CR)—an individual who is the designated representative of a Member CERT. The CR may delegate this authority and must notify the Secretariat in writing of the delegation.

CERT System Member (also, Member CERT)—a CERT which is a member of the CERT System. In this framework, the terms Member and Member CERT are used interchangeably.

Incident—an event that has actual or potentially adverse effects on computer or network operations resulting in fraud, waste, or abuse; compromise of information; or loss or damage of property or information. Examples include penetration of a computer system, exploitation of technical vulnerabilities, or introduction of computer viruses or other forms of malicious software.

Liaison—an individual or a representative of an organization other than a CERT that has a legitimate interest in and value to the CERT System.

Secretariat—a CERT System Member or other group designated by a 2/3 vote of the Steering Committee to serve as an administrative distribution point for the CERT System, to coordinate CERT System meetings and workshops, maintain Member profile information, and provide general guidance to new Members and potential Members.

Steering Committee—a group of individuals responsible for general operating policy, procedures, and related matters affecting the CERT System as a whole.

For further information regarding the FIRST, contact:

National Computer Systems Laboratory
National Institute of Standards and Technology
A-216 Technology
Gaithersburg, MD 20899
+1 301 975 3359
csrc@nist.gov

The Internet CERT

The Internet CERT (formerly the Computer Emergency Response Team/Coordination Center (CERT/CC)) was established by the Defense Advanced Research Projects Agency (DARPA) in December 1988 to address Internet computer security issues and concerns. It is operated by the Software Engineering Institute (SEI) at Carnegie-Mellon University (CMU).

The CERT acts as a clearing house for reporting, identifying, and repairing security vulnerabilities. The team also works closely with vendors and users to increase security awareness and improve incident response procedures.

CERT operates a 24-hour hotline for reporting security problems as well as receiving up-to-date information about rumored security break-ins. Other valuable security information, along with security advisories, can be obtained by subscribing to the cert-advisory mailing list. To be added to this list, send a message to cert@cert.org. The material sent to the cert-advisory list is also available through the USENET newsgroup comp.security.announce. Past security advisories and other generally useful security information is available via anonymous FTP from the host cert.sei.cmu.edu. Get the README file for a list of what is available.

The CERT promotes the exchange of information on tools and techniques that benefit the secure operation of the Internet. Access to this information is available via the cert-tools list. To subscribe, send electronic mail to cert-tools-request@cert.sei.cmu.edu.

For further information about CERT services and other useful security information, contact:

> CERT
> Software Engineering Institute
> Carnegie Mellon University
> Pittsburgh, PA 15213-3890
> +1 412 268 7090
> cert@cert.org

DoE Computer Incident Advisory Capability

The Computer Incident Advisory Capability (CIAC) is operated by the Department of Energy (DoE) and located at the Lawrence Livermore National Laboratory in Livermore, California. CIAC's principal responsibility is to act as the primary coordination center for reporting computer-related security incidents at DoE sites.

CIAC is available on a 24-hour-a-day basis to provide technical assistance, keep sites informed of current events, act as a clearinghouse of information pertaining to known threats, deal proactively with computer security issues, and maintain liaisons with other response teams and agencies. CIAC can be reached at:

CIAC
+1 415 422 8193
(FTS) 532 8193
ciac@tiger.llnl.gov

DDN Security Coordination Center

The Defense Data Network (DDN) Security Coordination Center (SCC) serves as a central point of contact for reporting host/user security problems and fixes for the DDN and MILNET. The SCC works with the DDN Network Security Officer and the DDN Network Information Center to distribute security-related information to DDN sites and their users. The SCC also distributes the DDN Security Bulletins, which contain information on network and host security exposures, fixes, and concerns to security and management personnel at DDN sites. The bulletins are available via anonymous FTP from the host nic.ddn.mil, in scc/ddn-security-yy-nn.txt (where "yy" is the year and "nn" is the bulletin number). If assistance is required with a problem on the DDN, contact:

DDN Security Coordination Center
(800) 365-3642 (7:00 am to 7:00 pm, ET)
scc@nic.ddn.mil

NIST CSRC

The National Institute of Standards and Technology (NIST) is responsible for computer science and technology activities within the U.S. government. For this reason, NIST has played an active role in organizing the FIRST System and is now serving as the FIRST Secretariat. NIST also manages and maintains the Computer Security Resource and Response Center (CSRC) which is responsible for providing help and information with respect to computer security events and incidents, and raising awareness of computer security vulnerabilities.

The CSRC's hotline is available 24-hours-a-day at (301) 957-5200. Online publications and security information can be obtained via anonymous FTP Security from the host csrc.ncsl.nist.gov. A personal computer bulletin board that contains security information is also accessible by modem. To access this bulletin board, set your modem to 300/1200/2400 kbps, 1 stop bit, no parity, 8-bit characters, and call (301) 948-5717. Once you have registered, full access is given immediately.

NIST publishes and maintains several publications dealing with the subject of computer security in general, and computer viruses in particular. Some of these are available online. For further information, contact NIST at:

Computer Security Resource and Response Center
A-216 Technology
Gaithersburg, MD 20899
+1 301 975 3359
csrc@nist.gov

NASA Ames CNSRT

NASA Ames' Computer Network Security Response Team (CNSRT) operates much like the Internet CERT, only on a local level in that it primarily serves Ames users. The NASA Ames CNSRT works closely with other NASA Centers and federal agencies such as the DoE's CIAC team and the DARPA CERT. CNSRT can be reached on 24-hour basis:

+1 415 694 0571 (their pager number)
cnsrt@ames.arc.nasa.gov.

8.2.7. Sources for computer security information

In addition to response centers, several online mailing lists and discussion groups are available for users to find out anything from the most up-to-date information on current security problems, to new developments and products in computer security. Here are just a few sources of online information.

The Internet Engineering Task Force (IETF) Security Working Groups

The Internet Engineering Task Force (IETF) has several groups that have been organized to address security issues in the Internet. For information about current work being done in this area, contact one of the following:

Steve Crocker
IETF Security Area Director
crocker@tis.com
or
IETF Secretariat
Corporation for National Research Initiatives
(703) 620-8990
ietf-info@nri.reston.va.us

UNIX Security Mailing List

The UNIX Security mailing list is a restricted access mailing list. It is available only to principal site administrators. Requests to join the list can be sent only by the site personnel listed in the Defense Data Network's Network Information Center (DDN NIC) WHOIS database, or from the root account on one of the major site machines. Send a request to join the list to *security-request@cpd.com* and include information such as the destination address; the electronic mail address and voice telephone number of the site contact; and the name, address, and telephone number of the organization.

This list was established in order to notify system administrators of potential or proven security problems before they are publicly announced, and to provide security enhancement information.

RISKS Digest

The RISKS Digest is a constituent of the ACM Committee on Computers and Public Policy, moderated by Peter G. Neumann. To subscribe, send a request to *risks-request@csl.sri.com*. This list is also available through the USENET newsgroup as *comp.risks*.

RISKS provides a forum to discuss computer security and privacy issues as they apply to the general public. Such topics as air and railroad traffic control systems, or software engineering are quite often deliberated.

VIRUS-L

VIRUS-L is a discussion group for those interested in keeping abreast of such topics as computer virus experiences, protection software, and related topics. It is open to the public and is moderated. The majority of the information is related to personal computers; however, some information may be applicable to larger systems. To subscribe, send a request to *listserv%llebiibm1.bitnet @mitvma.mit.edu* and in the body of the message type "SUB VIRUS-L *your full name*". This list is also available through USENET as *comp.virus*.

Computer Underground Digest

The Computer Underground Digest "is an open forum dedicated to sharing information among computerists and to the presentation and debate of diverse views." Although it is not a security list, it does include discussion regarding privacy and other security-related topics. To subscribe to this list, send a request to *9tk0jut2%niu.bitnet @mitvma.mit.edu*. This list is also available through USENET as *alt.society.cu-digest*.

Miscellaneous USENET Newsgroups

The USENET newsgroups *misc.security* and *alt.security* contain discussion related to security issues. *misc.security* is moderated and includes discussion on physical security and locks. *alt.security* is unmoderated.

8.3.Protocols

 What is a protocol? Put very basically, **a network protocol is a rule defining how computers should interact**. The Internet is built on the TCP/IP protocol suite. This term refers not only to the Transmission Control Protocol (TCP) and Internet Protocol (IP) themselves, but to the other protocols within that "family" that govern the interactions of computers on the Internet. This section introduces these concepts and provides some basic background about the Internet protocols.

Born from a lot of hard work and extensive dialog among members of the DARPA research community, TCP/IP meets the needs of the diverse Internet community because it is a nonproprietary network protocol suite that can connect the hardware and operating systems of many different computer manufacturers.

The Internet Protocol and the Transmission Control Protocol form the nucleus of a TCP/IP network. The Internet Protocol defines the basic unit of data transfer, the datagram (also referred to as a "packet"), and the exact format of all data as it passes across the Internet. IP also provides software routines to route and store-and-forward data among hosts on the network. This task can be as simple as routing a single datagram between two hosts on a LAN, or as complicated as sending datagrams to a remote host in another country through several gateways. The Transmission Control Protocol defines data flow, acknowledges data, and retransmits lost or damaged data. It provides a reliable, byte-stream-oriented, virtual circuit on which many application protocols depend.

8.3.1. Protocol layers

Protocols are designed in layers or levels to keep the complexity of a network manageable. The layers build up from those near the hardware to those near the users.

When communication takes place, information is passed vertically across layer boundaries and laterally between peer layers, according to rules known to the two interacting layers. These rules, or protocols, constitute the interface between the two layers and permit hosts to communicate with each other. They are the standards that specify how data is being transferred from one machine to another. They define how the transfer occurs, how errors are detected, and how acknowledgements are passed.

TCP/IP is a layered set of protocols. Individually, protocols define a set of commands or rules, but they must be used in conjunction with other protocols in order for the entire communication service to work. The protocols are "stacked" vertically into layers or levels and each layer takes responsibility for handling one piece of the problem. Each layer uses the services of the layer below and provides services to the layer above, depending on the direction of the transmission. When passing a transmission from one host to another in a layered environment, the object of transmission is sent and received at the same layer. The benefit of this approach is that it allows a protocol designer to focus attention on one layer at a time, without worrying about how lower layers perform.

In general terms, the TCP/IP protocol suite is organized into four conceptual layers of protocol software. Starting with the highest layer level, or level 4, these are: the application layer, transport layer, Internet layer, and network interface layer (also referred to as the data link layer). All of these layers build on a fifth layer of hardware.

8.3.2. What's a "protocol suite"?

Because of the complexity of a data communication system such as the Internet, a whole set of cooperative protocols, often referred to as a "**protocol family**" or "**protocol suite**," is employed. The Transmission Control Protocol and the Internet Protocol are the best known of the suite of protocols that has been used longest on the Internet, it has become very common to use the term "TCP/IP protocols" to refer to the whole family.

Many different networking protocols have been defined over the years. Other examples of coordinated suites of protocols are IBM's SNA and Digital Equipment Corporation's DECnet. These particular protocol suites permit communication for a specific brand of compatible computing machinery. Protocol suites such as TCP/IP define a range of communications for "open" systems. An "open" systems architecture enables communication among *various* types of computers using *different* operating systems. These computers can be set up in different topologies at different locations. Another suite of protocols designed to accommodate "open" systems are the protocols built on the Reference Model for Open System Interconnection (OSI). These are often referred to as the OSI protocols and are discussed further in Section 8.3.5.

8.3.3. Other TCP/IP protocols

There are several protocols other than TCP and IP in the Internet protocol suite. Most often mentioned are the *File Transfer Protocol (FTP)*, the *Simple Mail Transfer Protocol (SMTP)* and the *Telnet Protocol*. As a very basic introduction, here is a short list of RFCs that specify important Internet standards and protocols.

The Internet Protocol has several important extensions. The basic protocol is specified in RFC 791 *Internet Protocol (IP)*. A required component is the *Internet Control Message Protocol (ICMP)*, as specified in RFC 792. Subnetting and broadcasting are defined in RFC 919, *Broadcasting Internet Datagrams*, RFC 922, *Broadcasting Internet Datagrams in the Presence of Subnets*, and RFC 950, *Internet Standard Subnetting Procedure*.

In addition to the *Transmission Control Protocol* (TCP) specified in RFC 793, the *User Datagram Protocol (UDP)* in RFC 768 is a transport layer standard.

Two important applications that differentiate the Internet from other networks are specified in RFC 959, the *File Transfer Protocol*, and RFC 854, *Telnet Protocol Specification*. There are several options to the Telnet protocol as well.

Electronic mail for the Internet is specified in RFC 821, *Simple Mail Transfer Protocol (SMTP)*, and RFC 822, *Standard for the Format of ARPA Internet Text Messages*. RFC 974 discusses *Mail Routing and the Domain System*.

The protocols that are Internet standards are now designated as STDs. STDs are discussed in Section 8.1.3. Appendix IV contains an index of all the standard Internet protocols as of this writing.

8.3.4. Standard Internet protocols

The Internet is a dynamic environment. As it grows, new problems in internetworking appear, and new solutions to these problems are proposed. Sometimes several solutions to the same problem are proposed, most of which appear as RFCs. How do you know the status of these protocols? How do you know if they are something you should implement or not?

To answer these questions, the Internet Architecture Board (IAB) publishes a special RFC called *IAB Official Protocol Standards*. This RFC is updated often; the current version is RFC 1360 [8]. This RFC identifies which RFCs specify Standards, Draft Standards, and Proposed Standards, as well as identifying the Standards as Required, Recommended, or Elective. These designations are arrived at after considering recommendations from the Internet Engineering Steering Group (IESG) and acknowledging the work of the Internet Engineering Task Force (IETF). This RFC is the guide you should consult whenever you have a question about the status of an RFC.

In addition, a new subseries of STD RFCs has recently been established. STDs (Standards) designate those specifications that have reached the final stage of the standardization process and are considered mature Internet Standards. Once reaching this stage, a specification is assigned an STD number. See Section 8.1.3 for further information on this RFC subseries.

The procedures for creating and documenting Internet Standards are described in RFC 1310 [25]. That RFC explains what the Internet Standards track is and the process of entering and advancing a specification through the track. Familiarity with this document may help clarify terms used in the descriptions of standards track specifications.

Appendix IV is a complete Index of all the Standards as of the writing of this book.

8.3.5. The OSI protocols

The International Organization for Standardization (ISO) is an international standards body that drafts, discusses, proposes, and specifies standards for network protocols. It is composed of representatives from national standards bodies of member countries. The American National Standards Institute (ANSI) is the usual U.S. delegate body to ISO.

In 1984 ISO published the Reference Model of Open System Interconnection. The OSI Reference Model is a seven-layered conceptual model whose goal is to provide the basis for specifying an internationally accepted suite of standards for networking. Such a suite will facilitate the building of new open networks and enable the orderly development of new networking products.

The seven layers of the ISO Reference Model are: the application layer (highest layer or layer 7), the presentation layer, the session layer, the transport layer, the network layer, the data link layer, and the physical layer. TCP/IP architecture generally conforms through layer 4 of the OSI Reference Model. IP operates at OSI level 3, the network layer, and TCP operates at OSI level 4, the transport layer.

Currently ISO is developing a set of protocols that follow this seven-layer reference model. At the transport level, there are five proposed transport standards known as TP-0, TP-1, TP-2, TP-3, and TP-4. TP-4 most closely resembles TCP and handles the same sorts of functions, such as data flow and problems of lost data and data that arrives out of sequence.

Because of the global scope of the Internet as it has evolved today, it is the general policy of most Internet developers and researchers to adopt international standards when feasible. This means that to attain compatibility with more systems, TCP/IP vendors must gradually migrate their products to the ISO standards, without sacrificing the functions, performance, and reliability that TCP/IP now offers. Currently, the standards based on the OSI Reference Model are considered Internet co-standards alongside the TCP/IP protocols.

The main difference that is usually seen between the OSI and TCP/IP suites are that the TCP/IP protocols are fielded and tested before they become standards, while the OSI protocols are developed based on a conceptual reference model.

Further information about both the TCP/IP and the OSI protocol layering models can be found in Comer, *Internetworking with TCP/IP* [13], which was also a resource for some of the information in this section.

8.3.6. GOSIP

The Government Open Systems Interconnection Profile (GOSIP), issued by the National Institute of Standards and Technology (NIST), is a document that describes the U.S. Government's requirements to incorporate protocols based on the OSI Reference Model into its networks. The goal is to add OSI-based functions to the Internet without sacrificing services now available to Internet users.

GOSIP became mandatory in applicable federal procurements in August 1990. GOSIP Version 2 became a Federal Information Processing Standard (FIPS 146-1) on April 3, 1991. The new functions contained in Version 2 will be mandatory in federal procurements initiated eighteen months after that date. Interested parties should obtain GOSIP Version 2.

RFC 1169, *Explaining the Role of GOSIP* [14], is a valuable resource for understanding the current commitment to integrating the OSI protocols into the Internet. Here is the abstract of that RFC.

Abstract

The Federal Networking Council (FNC), the Internet Architecture Board (IAB), and the Internet Engineering Task Force (IETF) have a firm commitment to responsible integration of OSI based upon sound network planning. This implies that OSI will be added to the Internet without sacrificing services now available to existing Internet users, and that a multi-protocol environment will exist in the Internet for a prolonged period. Planning is underway within the Internet community to enable integration of OSI, coexistence of OSI with TCP/IP, and interoperability between OSI and TCP/IP.

The U.S. Government OSI Profile (GOSIP) is a necessary tool for planning OSI integration. However, as the August 1990 requirement date for GOSIP compliance approaches, concern remains as to how GOSIP should be applied to near-term network planning.

The intent of this statement is to help explain the role and applicability of the GOSIP document, as well as to emphasize the government's commitment to an integrated interoperable OSI environment based on responsible planning.

The National Institute for Standards and Technology periodically issues an online message containing ordering and pricing information needed to obtain the U.S. GOSIP, NIST/OSI Implementors Workshop (OIW) documents, Government Network Management Profile (GNMP) documentation, GOSIP Users' Guide, and GOSIP testing documentation. For convenience, the latest version of this file is contained in Appendix IX.

8.4. Internet Addressing

In order to make the Internet an open communications system, a globally accepted method of identifying computers was needed. To solve this, each host on the Internet is assigned a unique 32-bit Internet address (commonly referred to as an IP address).

Host addresses contain four parts or fields, each separated by a period (called a dot). Each field is decimal and specifies 8 bits, or an octet of the 32-bit (binary digits) address space. Each address is divided into a network portion and a local portion. IP addresses are divided into different

Classes depending on how much of the address space is allocated to the network portion rather than the local portion. There are currently three commonly used classes of addresses: Class A, Class B, and Class C.

For Class A addresses, the first octet of the address represents the network portion, and the last three octets are the local portion. For example, the Merit network is network number 35.0.0.0. Sometimes in discussing the network portion of an address, the zeroes that represent the local portion are disregarded. So, the Merit network will also be referred to as network 35.

For Class B addresses, the first two octets of the address represent the network portion, and the last two octets represent the local portion of the address. For example, the address 128.5.0.0 is assigned to the Ford Motor Company.

For Class C addresses, the first three octets of the address represent the network portion, and the last octet represents the local portion of the address. For example, the Network Information Systems Center at SRI International was assigned the address 192.33.33.0.

The InterNIC Registration Service is responsible for assigning unique IP network addresses. They assign the network portion of the address; the local site assigns the local portion to specific machines on their network. When the site assigns a host its own address, it gets a number in the portion of the address represented by a zero in the examples above. So, the specific host called nis.nsf.net has the address 35.1.1.48 on the Class A network assigned to Merit. The host nic.ddn.mil has the address 192.112.36.5 within its Class C network.

See Section 2.3.1 for specific information on obtaining a unique IP address.

8.4.1. Identifying the class of an address

Here are the addresses for three different hosts:

```
26.31.0.73
128.18.1.1
192.33.33.22
```

They all have four numbers separated by dots. So, how can you tell what Class of network a host is on just by looking at its address? You can tell by the decimal number that represents the first octet of the address. (The first octet is the number before the first dot). The classes of a network number are arranged from 0-223 in the following manner.

Class A   The first octet ranges from 0 to 127.

In decimal format, the first octet of a Class A address must be less than 128. Because 0 and 127 are reserved numbers, only 126 Class A networks can exist, each of which can support 16,777,214 hosts.

Class B   The first octet ranges from 128 to 191.

This class is usually used for large networks, such as campus networks and some wide area networks.

In decimal format, the first octet of a Class B number must be greater than 128 but less than or equal to 191; the second octet must fall between 1 and 254. Therefore, Class B network numbers fall between the range of 128.1 and 191.254. (255 is also a reserved number used for "broadcasting" a message you want every system on the network to see.) A Class B network can support 65,532 hosts.

Class C   The first octet ranges from 192 to 223.

Class C addresses are those most commonly assigned to local area networks.

In decimal format, Class C addresses use the first three octets in the range 192.1.1. to 223.254.254. This allows only 254 hosts on each network, but there can be many Class C networks. One site may have more than one Class C address assigned to it.

There are two other special Classes of IP addresses:

Class D All four octets are reserved for Internet-wide multicast addresses.

Class E These addresses are reserved for experimental use.

8.4.2. Subnetting

When the Internet Protocol was first defined, the structure of having a network portion and a host portion of each IP address seemed adequate. No one at the time envisioned that individual sites would want to network extensive Local Area Networks (LANs), some consisting of hundreds or even thousands of hosts. However, before long, many sites on the Internet were connecting large LANs, and some were connecting small internets. For this type of site, each LAN is connected to other LANs via routers; therefore, each LAN is an independent network and needs a unique network address.

However, as there is usually only one or perhaps two routers between a site and the Internet, it is simpler, for Internet routing purposes, if each site is identified by only one network number no matter how many LANs they have internally.

This seeming conflict of needs was resolved by the implementation of subnetting. Subnetting allows a site to assign each LAN a unique number, while showing only one network address to the Internet. Subnetting adds an additional level between the network and local portions of an IP address. For a Class B address, for example, the first two octets would be the network portion, the third octet the subnet portion, and the last octet the host portion.

It may seem that by subnetting LANs, every host has to act as a router in order to route packets properly to destinations on their own subnets, on the site's greater network, or on the Internet. If this were true, subnetting would certainly not be an efficient answer to handling the growing number of IP networks. In fact, Internet subnetting is designed so that a host on a subnetted system need only determine if a particular packet is directed to a host on its own subnet or elsewhere. If elsewhere, it need only know the address of a router on its own network. It doesn't even matter if the router is the gateway between a host's subnet and the network for which the packet is destined. If a host targets an inappropriate router initially, that router will send the host back a message re-directing the packet to the appropriate router.

A host determines if a destination is on its own subnet by using a mechanism known as an Address Mask (or "net mask"). An Address Mask is a means of separating the host number field in an IP address from the network and subnet portions. In general, there is one Address Mask for every network. By comparing the Address Mask with its own address and with the destination address, a host can determine whether the destination is on its own network or on another network.

This discussion benefits greatly from an article by Jeffrey Mogul that appeared in the January 1989 issue of *ConneXions: The Interoperability Report*. (See Section 12.5 for further information about this journal.) The article, *Subnetting: A Brief Guide* [15], is an excellent introduction to the complex subject of subnetting, and goes into much more detail than we have here. Mogul makes these points regarding general implementation issues.

> Subnet implementation can be divided into two categories: host issues and gateway issues. Host IP software must have a means of obtaining the Address Mask, and must implement the ICMP Redirect messages; that is, a host must do the right thing when it receives a Redirect. Beyond that, the subnet-related per-datagram processing for outgoing datagrams is quite simple, consisting simply of the "local"/"remote" decision . . .

> Gateway IP software must be able to extract the subnet field from the destination IP address of a packet it is forwarding, and use this subnet field to choose a route for the packet. Therefore, a gateway must also implement a routing protocol that understands about subnets.

RFC 950, *Internet Standard Subnetting Procedure*, was authored by Mogul and Jon Postel. It presents the Internet standard method of subnetting and should be read by anyone planning to implement subnetting.

8.4.3. "Connected" vs. "unconnected" networks and RFC 1174

Formerly, networks were registered as either "connected" to the Internet or "unconnected" to the Internet. A network has been considered unconnected if it has no physical access to the Internet. Any site implementing an IP network should register for a unique IP number so that, in the event that they do connect to the Internet in the future, they will be spared the trouble and expense of reconfiguring the addresses of all the numbered devices on their network to a new number.

Based on the recommendations made in RFC 1174 [27], the distinction between connected and unconnected networks was discontinued.

8.4.4. A network "sponsor"

Until the distinction between connected and unconnected networks is formally abolished, the registration form that must be filled out when requesting a network number asks for all connected networks to indicate a "governmental sponsoring organization." This request is often confusing to users filling out the form, but it turns out to be easy to answer.

If your network will be independent of the Internet, this question does not apply to you and you do not need to worry about it.

If you will be connecting to the Internet, your network service provider will be able to tell you the correct information to include. Most often, during this period before RFC 1174 is fully implemented, the National Science Foundation acts as nominal sponsor of new sites. Again, as work is progressing rapidly toward full implementation of RFC 1174, by the time you read this book, this requirement may be obsolete as well.

8.4.5. The future of IP addressing

The division of the Internet address space into distinct Classes of networks was proposed at a time when the phenomenal growth of the Internet and of networks connecting many personal workstations and PCs was not foreseen. Today, the Internet is faced with router technology that strains to keep track of thousands of network addresses and the imminent exhaustion of Class B network address space.

Within the next several years, the IP addressing scheme described in this section will be changing. The ultimate goal is to have a classless Internet address space. As that goal will probably not be attainable before the Class B address space is exhausted, an interim solution that institutes some scheme to accommodate the need for a network address size larger than Class C, but smaller than a B will be implemented. At the time of this writing, several such interim solutions have been proposed by groups working within the Internet Engineering Task Force (IETF) structure. The IETF has yet to decide on one best solution for the interim.

Although registration procedures for IP addresses may change, and routing protocols may need to accommodate a slightly different addressing style, the IETF is committed to moving toward a technical solution that does not disrupt the operations of the Internet.

8.5. The Domain Name System (DNS)

Internet network software uses a 32-bit IP address to communicate with another host. However, users prefer to deal with computer names rather than numbers. In order to accommodate this preference, hosts are given names as well as addresses. Because people tend to use names to refer to hosts, while software tends to use addresses, there needs to be some mechanism to map a name to an address so that a program can carry out instructions from a user. The **Domain Name System** (DNS) was developed to meet this need in the growing Internet environment.

This section describes the hierarchical naming scheme, known as the Domain Name System (DNS), that the Internet uses to keep track of the names and addresses of the large set of machines that comprise the Internet. The section also discusses name servers, which are the mechanism that maps between these machine names and their IP addresses.

8.5.1. Background of the DNS

Historically, the Internet started out with a system inherited from the ARPANET, in which the Network Information Center maintained one centralized table called hosts.txt. This file was a list of the names and network (IP) addresses of all known "entities," such as hosts, gateways, and networks. As the Internet grew, the task of managing the name and address space in a centralized place became increasingly complex. Network traffic increased greatly as host administrators were forced to transfer the table from the central maintenance site regularly.

To solve these problems, a distributed service, the DNS, was defined in 1983, and has been modified and extended since then. Its main intent is to do away with the idea of a monolithic central "phone book," and replace it with a new system of hierarchically organized names. This system is called the Internet name space.

8.5.2. What is a domain?

 A domain is an administrative entity that allows distributed management of host naming and addressing. The DNS uses a hierarchical naming scheme (known as domain naming), or tree structure, to delegate host naming and addressing to the local level.

The DNS is a database. It is distributed throughout the Internet, with different domain administrators responsible locally for different parts (or "domains") of the database.

Distributing the responsibility of keeping track of the names and addresses of Internet hosts alleviates the need to have a centralized authority administer the naming and addressing information.

8.5.3. The difference between a domain and a network

People often confuse networks and domains. They often think that a domain is the name of a network. A network may well have a name, but that name is merely a mnemonic for its numerical address. A network name does not serve the same function as a domain name, and it is helpful to differentiate the two.

This confusion probably arises because most Internet hosts have both a unique address on a network and a name within the Domain Name System hierarchy. However, the higher up one travels on the domain tree, the clearer it is that one domain can include several networks. While all the hosts in the domain *nisc.sri.com* are on the same network, that is not true for the hosts in the domain *sri.com*. Hosts within the *sri.com* domain are on several different networks. It is also possible, although unusual in the case of a Class C network, for hosts connected to the same physical network to fall within different domains.

A network is a physical entity, identified by a unique number. A domain is a concept, an administrative means of delegating the authority for keeping track of the Internet name space.

8.5.4. Domain name representation

The DNS tree is "anchored" at the root and then divided into several top-level domains. The top-level domains consist of those which were organized some time ago in RFC 920, as well as the top-level domains allocated to each country. Every country has a 2-letter acronym reserved for it, whether it has been claimed (delegated) or not. These acronyms are based on the ISO 3166 standard of 2-letter country codes. (See Section 8.5.10 for a discussion of the top-level U.S. domain assigned to the United States.)

Appendix VIII describes international connectivity. The keys used in the file that is reproduced in Appendix VIII are the two-letter ISO country codes for each country. You can identify the top-level country code domains by browsing through that Appendix.

All top-level domains are then subdivided into second-level domains, which may be further subdivided into third-level domains, and so on, with each subdivision making the domain less general and more local.

Following is a list of the current top-level domains that are not based on a country code.

Domain	Purpose	Examples
COM	Commercial	SUN.COM
EDU	Educational	MIT.EDU, STANFORD.EDU
GOV	Other U.S. Government	NASA.GOV
MIL	U.S. Military	ARMY.MIL, NAVY.MIL, AF.MIL
NET	NICs and NOCs	NYSER.NET
ORG	Non-profit Organizations	MITRE.ORG
INT	International Organizations	NATO.INT

Table 8-1: List of Top-Level Domains

A particular domain is identified by its domain name. Again, the DNS hierarchical structure represents the name space as a tree with labels on the nodes of the tree. A particular node's domain name is the list of labels associated with all the nodes on the path from that node to the root of the tree. Labels are listed from left to right, with the leftmost label corresponding to the most specific node, and the last label to the least specific node. The following figure shows an example of what a piece of the domain tree might look like:

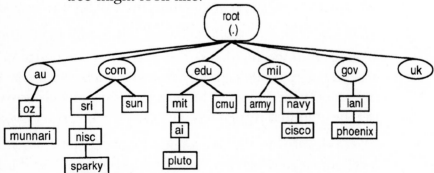

Figure 8-1: Sample Domain Tree

A user sees domain names expressed as text strings with dots used to separate the labels. For example, SPARKY.NISC.SRI.COM is a node with label SPARKY, under a node with label NISC, under a node with label SRI, under a node named COM. This example also illustrates that a domain is a subdomain of another domain if it is contained within that domain. NISC is a subdomain of SRI.COM, and SRI.COM is a subdomain of the top-level domain COM. The domain name SPARKY.NISC.SRI.COM contains four labels. The first three labels each represent a domain. The third-level domain is NISC.SRI.COM, the second-level domain is SRI.COM, and the top-level domain is COM. The fourth label represents the node name, SPARKY.

8.5.5. Choosing a top-level domain

At first, the abbreviations for the top-level domains can be confusing. However, with a little explanation of what each domain contains, most often it becomes clear under which top-level domain you should join. If your organization is not in the United States, you should join under the top-level domain designated to your country. If you do not know who administers this domain, contact InterNIC Registration Services (see Section 2.3.1 for contact information).

Most organizations in the United States join under one of the top-level domains described in Table 8.2.

8.5.6. The DNS approach

The most important function of the DNS is that host information is now distributed to local databases, and the authority to update information in the DNS database is distributed to many coordinators, rather than limited to one central site. This means that adding hosts, changing the names of hosts, reconfiguring IP addresses, or performing other database updates are now purely local matters. All

that is required is that the administrator of that local domain implement the changes in his part of the database.

The DNS depends not only on the maintenance and administration of these local databases, but also on the
implementation of two pieces of software: the domain
name server and the domain resolver.

8.5.7. Domain server and resolver

The DNS stores its information internally in the form of
Resource Records (RRs). Extracting data from the DNS is
done using a query/response model of resolver/server
program interaction. A program that needs DNS information and a program that provides DNS service interact by
exchanging one question and one answer (a query and a
response). These programs may be on the same host, but
usually are on different hosts. The program asking for information is called the resolver or client, and the program
providing information is called the server.

Once a resolver asks for information, the answer provided
may direct the resolver to ask another question, possibly
of another server that has knowledge of a different portion of the domain name database. In that case, another
query/response sequence occurs between the resolver and
the new server.

The process of mapping a host name to its Internet address involves querying name servers for appropriate information. Resource Records are returned to the resolver
in response to its DNS query. The resource records either
provide the IP address of the host in question, or provide
the IP address of a machine that does have address information or is at least closer to the address information. This
second machine is another name server. If the resolver is
referred to another server, it must make a separate query
to that server. These queries generally happen very, very
quickly, in a matter of seconds.

COM	This is the domain for commercial businesses and organizations that make a profit through a service or sale of a product. In September 1992, there were more than 304,000 hosts in the COM domain.
EDU	This is the domain for degree-granting educational institutions, such as colleges; universities; community colleges; libraries; research institutes; astronomical observatories; university-affiliated supercomputer centers; national academy-type organizations; national centers for research; local and state school districts; university chancellor's offices; university-affiliated health sciences centers, etc. In September 1992, there were more than 370,000 hosts in the EDU domain.
GOV	This domain is for non-military national government organizations, e.g., Veterans Administration, Department of Energy; national laboratories such as Lawrence Livermore National Laboratory. State government agencies also fit under this domain at the second level, e.g., CA.GOV or HAWAII.GOV.State agencies should be registered at the third level, e.g., WATER-DEPARTMENT.CA.GOV, rather than joining directly under the top-level GOV.
MIL	This is the domain for U.S. military organizations. Almost all of the major branches of the military have their own second-level domains under this domain: ARMY.MIL, AF.MIL, NAVY.MIL, etc.
NET	This is the domain for backbone systems—NICs, NOCs, gateways, etc. Only machines necessary for the actual operation of the network can be registered within this domain.
ORG	This is the domain for not-for-profit organizations. Any profit-making organization does not belong in this domain. It is also for technical-support groups; professional societies and associations; and computer users' groups. ORG also exists as a parent to subdomains that do not clearly fall under the other top-level domains.
U.S.	This domain is a top-level domain created for people in the United States who have computers at home, or small local corporations who wanted to register their hosts geographically. This domain is discussed further in Section 8.5.10.
INT	This domain is for special organizations of an international nature; few organizations are registered in this domain.

Table 8-2: Description of Top Level Domains

Sometimes a resolver has recently received the answer to some query and has saved, or "cached," it. Cached answers are provided immediately to the requester without the resolver having to query a DNS server.

Here is a list of a few frequently used RR types with a description of the type of information they provide. A complete list, and more in-depth explanation regarding

RRs, can be found in the domain specification RFCs, which are referenced in Chapter 12.

Designation	Full Name	Description
NS	Name Server	Name of host providing name service
A	Internet Address	IP address for a host
CNAME	Canonical Name	Formal name for a given nickname
MX	Mail Exchanger	Site to which mail for a domain should be sent
SOA	Start of Authority	Site of authoritative information for a zone
HINFO	Host Information	Information about a host, e.g., hardware type
WKS	Well Known Services	Services available at a certain address using a certain protocol

Table 8-3: Common RR Types

Here is a simple example of the type of information a server will return to a resolver. The format of the response is an abbreviated version of the "dig" program; other DNS search programs will output the same information in different formats.

```
;; QUESTIONS:
;;      paris.nisc.sri.com, type = ANY, class = ANY
;; ANSWERS:
paris.nisc.sri.com.       604800 A       192.33.33.109
```

You can see from this example that in response to a query for any information on the name *paris.nisc.sri.com*, the address 192.33.33.109 was provided.

8.5.8. MX resource records

The MX Resource Record is a good example of the difference between domains and networks because it is a means for a site without its own dedicated connection to the Internet (i.e., without its own Internet network) to have an Internet domain name. By using an MX record, a site can have electronic mail addressed to its own unique domain name. Such mail is actually received by an Internet host acting as a mail relay. This host holds the mail until the site obtains it, usually by accessing the relay host via a dialup connection. This mail gateway arrangement is transparent to Internet users, so no one has to remember that mail to Joe at SYZ Inc. has to be sent via ABC host. They just send to joe@syz.com, and the DNS takes care of letting the mail program know that mail for SYZ Inc. must be sent to host ABC.

What this means in terms of the DNS is that instead of linking SYZ Inc.'s host name to an address, an MX record is used to link to the domain syz.com with the host name of the intermediary host, abc.com. The intermediary host, e.g., abc.com, has an address record in the DNS, which mail programs use to determine where to direct electronic mail.

Here's an example of an MX record in the DNS. The format is an abbreviation of "dig" program output; other DNS search programs will output the same information in different formats.

```
;; QUESTIONS:
;;      macdavid.han.de, type = ANY, class = ANY
;; ANSWERS:
macdavid.han.de. 86400 MX 190 mail.Germany.EU.net.
;; ADDITIONAL RECORDS:
mail.Germany.EU.net. 86400 A 192.76.144.65
```

You can see that instead of returning the address for the host *macdavid.han.de*, the DNS shows an MX host of *mail.Germany.EU.net*. The DNS also provided the addresses of the relay host, so that the resolver would not have to make a second query. A mail program would send a message to the address of the relay host, and that host would then be responsible for ultimately delivering it to the target host.

8.5.9. The IN-ADDR domain

The structure of names in the domain system is set up in a hierarchical way such that the address of a name can be found by tracing down the domain tree and contacting a server for each label of the name. Because this indexing is based on names, there is no easy way to translate a host address back into its host name.

Therefore, a special domain was created to solve this problem. It is called the IN-ADDR (for "inverse addressing") domain. This domain allows the DNS to resolve IP addresses into host names. The important thing about this domain is that the hierarchy is by IP network number and host address, not by domain name. This hierarchy allows a resolver to get DNS data even if it knows only the network number or host address.

The IN-ADDR name is composed of the reversed octets of an IP or host address and a single, well-known place to start called IN-ADDR.ARPA.

Note: ARPA existed as a temporary top-level domain when the DNS was first conceived. It was created to facilitate the transition to the DNS from the host table. ARPA has since been phased out except for use by this special domain. Some network users feel it's rather "inelegant" to continue using it as a domain name, but whatever the opinion on the naming issue, the concept of inverse addressing is a very useful one.

If you wanted to find the host name that mapped to the address 192.33.33.109, you would search the DNS for the domain 109.33.33.192.IN-ADDR.ARPA. That is just the address in reverse, with IN-ADDR.ARPA added.

8.5.10. The U.S. domain

The U.S. domain was initially created to accommodate people in the United States who have computers at home, or small local corporations who wanted to register their hosts geographically. However, over the years since the first policies for the domain were written, other entities have been added, notably state and municipal government organizations. Today, any computer in the U.S. may be registered in the U.S. domain.

At present, Jon Postel (postel@isi.edu) sets the policy for the U.S. domain, and Ann Westine Cooper (cooper @isi.edu) administers the domain.

The U.S. domain name space is organized geographically; states occur directly under U.S., cities under states, and individual names under cities. For example, nri.reston.va.us represents the "nri" host in Reston, Virginia.

8.5.11. Commonly asked domain questions

Question: **Can you tell me what the minimum requirements are for establishing a domain?**

Answer: One of the first orders of business to be accomplished is to identify an individual who will act as the domain administrator. This person will have authority for the administration of the names within the domain, and will seriously take on the responsibility for the behavior of the hosts in the domain, plus their interactions with hosts outside the domain. It is assumed the domain administrator is already familiar with the overall concepts of the DNS and has the technical expertise to implement them. The domain administrator must also have the authority within the domain to see that problems are identified and fixed.

Secondly, it is required that there be a robust and reliable domain name lookup service. This requirement can be met by providing at least two independent domain servers for the domain. The domain database can be copied to each domain server, but the servers themselves should have no common point of failure; that is, they should not be on the same PSN, or connected to the same power source, or connected to the same local area network whose failure could simultaneously sever both servers from the Internet.

Question: **I've read all the pertinent domain RFCs and am ready to establish a domain for my site. Who do I contact for this?**

Answer: The InterNIC Registration Services provider is designated to provide registry services for the domain naming system on the Internet.

As registrar of U.S. top-level and some U.S. second-level domains, as well as administrator of the root domain name servers, InterNIC Registration Services is responsible for maintaining the root server zone files and their binary equivalents. In addition, the InterNIC is responsible for administering the top-level domains of COM, EDU, ORG, GOV, MIL, and NET, and for delegating the domains based on country codes.

If you're already connected to the Internet and you wish to register a new second-level domain, you must fill out the domain application and return the completed form to *hostmaster@rs.internic.net*. The application itself is available via FTP from the *rs.internic.net* host as *templates/domain-template.txt*.

There are alternate procedures for sites located on the public networks BITNET and UUCP, which are not connected to the Internet. The managements of these networks act as domain filters, processing domain applications for their own organizations. They pass pertinent information along periodically to the InterNIC for incorporation into the domain database and root server files. For further details regarding these alternate procedures, you can send a message to *hostmaster@rs.internic.net* or contact the InterNIC directly at (800) 444-4345 or +1 703 742-4777.

Question: **Is it possible to register a domain, even if my site is not directly connected to the Internet and is not a BITNET or UUCP member?**

Answer: It is possible to join the DNS without being directly connected to the Internet, if you can find a site that agrees to act as a mail forwarder for you. This involves having an MX (mail exchange) record established by the domain administrator of an officially registered domain to handle your mail routing. Also, you must comply with the requirements for establishing a domain; most notably, you must provide the addresses of two name server hosts on your domain application. Many access providers offer this type of mail forwarding service.

This MX record is one of the various resource record types (RRs), and provides a mechanism for non-Internet hosts to establish domains and to receive mail from Internet DNS users. The DNS users use DNS-style names to send mail to these non-Internet hosts. The details of how the path to a target host is determined are hidden from the DNS user, so he does not need to use complicated mail addresses involving relay hosts. The MX record allows a mail-sending host to deliver the message to a relay host. That relay host concerns itself with the details of the delivery to the final recipient-host. You must make sure there is a way for you to get your mail from the host acting as your gateway. Plus, you must make sure that those hosts acting as name servers for you insert your MX record into their portion of the DNS.

Question: **Can we establish a second-level domain with only one node?**

Answer: The general guideline for establishing a second-level domain is that it have more than 50 hosts. This is a very soft requirement. It makes sense that any major university, corporation, or organization be allowed to register a second-level domain even if it has just a few hosts. However, there is no edict to form a domain because one is over the minimum size.

Question: **What is meant by delegation of authority?**

Answer: The topmost level of the domain naming hierarchy partitions the namespace and delegates authority for the partitions or sub-domains. This means the topmost authority need not be bothered by changes within one sub-domain. This responsibility is delegated to the Domain Administrator of that particular sub-domain. This scheme is key to the overall goal of the DNS; i.e., the decentralization of the naming and addressing mechanism for the Internet.

Question: **Can subdomains of registered second-level domains be established? If so, how does one go about doing this?**

Answer: Each second-level domain may have many third-level domains, and each third-level domain may have many fourth-level domains, etc. For example: the second-level domain XCOLLEGE.EDU may also have MATH.XCOLLEGE.EDU, CHEM.XCOLLEGE.EDU, and PHYSICS.XCOLLEGE.EDU established. Every third-level domain (through the Nth level domain) must meet the requirements set by the domain administrator of the immediately higher-level domain. To join as a subdomain of a second-level domain, you must contact the administrator of that domain. The DDN NIC will have a list of administrators for every domain they've delegated. Contact them (see Section 2.3.1 for contact information) or use their WHOIS database to find out the name of the person you need to talk to. Using our example, any group wishing to establish a third-level domain under XCOLLEGE.EDU must contact the Domain Administrator for XCOLLEGE.EDU; any group requesting a sub-domain of MATH.XCOLLEGE.EDU would contact the domain administrator for MATH.XCOLLEGE.EDU, etc.

Question: **Does it cost anything to establish a domain?**

Answer: Currently, there is no cost associated with registering a domain because the work is supported by the National Science Foundation (NSF). The important thing to remember is that you contact the InterNIC to officially register a new top-level or second-level domain. If you wish to establish a sub-domain of an official second-level domain, you must contact the domain administrator for that particular second-level domain.

Question: **Is there a maximum length allowed when establishing a domain name?**

Answer: As described above, the domain name space is a tree structure. Each node of the tree is represented by a string of labels, read left to right and separated by dots. Although the domain system has no restrictions, other protocols such as SMTP do have name restrictions. Because of these restrictions, the labels must follow the rules for Internet host names. Domain names can start with a letter or digit, end with a letter or digit, and have as interior characters only letters, digits, and hyphens. Labels must be 63 characters or less and the sum of all label lengths is limited to 255. A good rule of thumb to follow, for the sake of simplicity and "easy-to-remember" names, is to keep each la-

bel to 8 characters or fewer; however, this is not a requirement.

Question: **How does one change the contact information, such as the administrative, technical, and zone contact, for a domain that has been officially registered with the InterNIC?**

Answer: Any updates or changes to domain information, including server data or modifications to contact information, should originate from the domain administrator and be sent online to *hostmaster@rs.internic.net*

Question: **Where do I go to find out more?**

Answer: In addition to the reading specified in Chapter 12, you can also get domain information online.

➤ The *namedroppers@nic.ddn.mil* mailing list discusses general DNS issues, specific software manage- ment, and application. To join, send a message to *namedroppers-request@nic.ddn.mil.*

➤ The *bind@ucbarpa.berkeley.edu* mailing list is a forum specific to topics relating to BIND domain software for UNIX sites. To join, send a message to *bind-request@ ucbarpa.berkeley.edu.*

8.6. Directory Services

Directory services refer to databases that list Internet enti- ties and allow you to look them up. Much like your tele- phone book, these services describe objects such as hu- mans, machines, organizations, distribution lists, network hardware, and application entities, such as electronic mail.

The Domain Name System is a directory service. It is also a distributed directory service because the responsibility for updating its data is distributed among many responsible parties.

There is also an OSI based directory services protocol called X.500, after the number of the CCITT Recommendation that specifies it. Another directory service often used are databases accessible via the WHOIS protocol. This protocol was first designed to be used with the WHOIS database maintained by the DDN Network Information Center. This is a centrally maintained directory, but there are client programs around the Internet that query it remotely. In addition, work is underway now to expand the basic WHOIS protocol to include distributed features.

This section will provide very brief overviews of X.500, WHOIS, and the RIPE Network Management Database.

8.6.1. X.500 directory services

The X.500 Directory Service is based on the joint ISO/CCITT International Standard ISO IS 9594, CCITT X.500. In very general terms, the OSI Directory specifies the standard for connecting directory services to form one distributed global directory. Distributed is the key word here because, unlike WHOIS, an X.500 directory does not have to be maintained at a central location. The X.500 protocol is similar to the DNS because it supports hierarchical name spaces, and decentralized maintenance of data. X.500 is also supported by searching and browsing facilities.

In the X.500 model, information is supplied by one or more servers called Directory System Agents (DSAs) to clients called Directory User Agents (DUAs), which act on behalf of users. Although information may be distributed among many DSAs, they work together to provide a single transparent view of the directory to DUAs and their users.

There are currently few implementations of the X.500 protocol, but research and development regarding using the protocol continues. FYI 11, *Catalog of Available X.500 Implementations* [20], is a useful reference that lists current known implementations of the X.500 protocol.

The Directory Information Services Infrastructure (DISI) Working Group in the User Services Area, and OSI Directory Services Working Group in the OSI Integration Area are working on integrating X.500 directory services into the Internet. These two Areas of the IETF collaborated on a document that provides an overview of the X.500 standard for people unfamiliar with the technology. It is FYI 13, *Executive Introduction to Directory Services Using the X.500 Protocol* [21], and it was a useful document in supporting this brief description. In addition, the groups have collaborated on a longer introductory document, FYI 14, *Technical Overview of Directory Services Using the X.500 Protocol* [26].

NIST OIW

In addition, the National Institute of Standards and Technology (NIST) has an OSI Implementors Working Group dedicated to X.500 development. For more information, contact:

Brenda Gray
OSI Implementors Workshop Registrar
Technology, B217
Gaithersburg, MD 20899
(301) 975-3664

There are currently several pilot implementations of X.500 databases.

PARADISE

One large X.500 pilot project is the PARADISE project originally supported by COSINE (see Section 10.1.7). This project provides an international directory service across

Europe with connectivity to North America and the rest of the world. It enables members of the academic, commercial and governmental research community to look up information about colleagues and find, for example, their electronic mail addresses.

The best first source of information about the PARADISE pilot is the PARADISE HelpDesk.

> PARADISE HelpDesk
> +44 71 405 8400 x432
> FAX: +44 71 242 1845
> helpdesk@paradise.ulcc.ac.uk

WPP Pilot

Another pilot implementation of the OSI X.500 standard is the White Pages Pilot Project sponsored by Performance Systems International, Inc. (PSI). This project collects personnel information from member organizations into a database, and provides online access to that data.

To access the data, telnet to wp.psi.com and login as *fred* (no password is necessary). You may now look up information on participating organizations. The program provides help on usage. For example, typing *help* will show you a list of commands, *manual* will give detailed documentation, and *whois* will provide information regarding how to find references to people. For a list of the organizations that are participating in the pilot project by providing information regarding their members, type *whois - org* *. For more information, send a message to *wp-info@psi.com*.

8.6.2. WHOIS

WHOIS is a program that looks up information in an electronic white pages of information about Internet users, hosts, domains, and networks. It can be used, for example, to find the administrative contact for a given domain or the electronic mail address of a colleague, if that colleague happens to be listed in the database. It provides a wide variety of information about those network entities registered by the InterNIC and is a useful first place to look for things such as domain names or network numbers. It is accessible either via Telnet, e-mail, or from a client program you would run on your own host. By Telnet, open a connection to *rs.internic.net* and choose one of the search options presented. Via e-mail, send a message to *mailserv@rs.internic.net*, with *whois help* as the subject of your message and you will be sent more information about using the program. Contact the InterNIC (see Section 2.3.1) for more in-depth assistance.

WHOIS is a standard client/server program which can be used to search other databases than those maintained by the InterNIC. Recently the InterNIC Directory and Database Services group have made it possible for their WHOIS server to search not only the *ds.internic.net* database, but also the *rs.internic.net* database and the *nic.ddn.mil* database. The latter two of these databases contain registration information; the first will contain the directory of directories information. To use this, it's best if you run a WHOIS client and point your queries to the *ds.internic.net* host. Contact the InterNIC for help in acquiring a WHOIS client if you need it (800 444-4345).

8.6.3. The RIPE network management database

One of the activities of RIPE is to maintain a database of European IP networks, DNS domains, and their contact persons. This database is called the RIPE Network Management Database or simply the "RIPE Database." Currently the RIPE database consists of IP networks, Domain Name System domains, and contact persons. The information in the database is currently maintained centrally by the RIPE NCC, but there are plans to distribute the maintenance and access of the database throughout Europe.

The RIPE database can be accessed via a WHOIS server on host *whois.ripe.net*. An example of accessing the database using WHOIS to get the DNS domain information for *ripe.net* would be with the command *whois -h whois.ripe.net ripe.net*.

The information in the RIPE database is also available from the Interactive Information Service provided by the RIPE NCC, by means of a browser and a full text search through the database. The Information Service is easily accessed from both the Internet and via IXI, and the Public Data Networks. From the Internet you type *telnet info.ripe.net*. You will see a menu, from which you can select the option of searching RIPE Database.

If you need more information about using the RIPE Database, contact the RIPE Network Coordination Center, *ncc@ripe.net*.

APPLICATIONS

From the Internet user's point of view, access to the network and its services is accomplished by invoking applications programs. It is not necessary for a user to fully understand the details of these applications programs (that's what programmers are for!). However, it might be helpful to be aware that when these programs are called upon, they use the underlying Internet protocols to provide the user with some particular network service. At the same time, it is also important to realize that having Internet standards for the applications encourages their widespread use in the Internet.

The most popular "traditional" services provided by TCP/IP are electronic mail, file transfer, and remote login via the Telnet Protocol. This chapter provides basic information on using these popular applications, and introduces several useful "information server" programs available to Internet users.

This chapter is intended only as an introduction to some popular applications; it is hardly a comprehensive resource guide of what is available, nor a user guide delineating specific procedures.

9.1. Electronic Mail

Electronic mail, or e-mail, allows a user to send messages electronically to individuals or groups of individuals. In addition, system programs accept and store mail messages that come in for users from other hosts. These programs automatically recognize the incoming traffic as electronic mail, translate it to a format compatible with the receiving mail program, and direct the message to the correct recipient. Most users have an online mail file where all messages addressed to them are stored. Internet mail makes mail delivery more reliable. Instead of relying on intermediate machines to relay mail messages, Internet mail delivery operates by having the sender's machine contact the receiver's machine directly.

Of course, the Internet is accessible to many other networks via e-mail. To send mail to some of these networks, you may have to explicitly address a gateway machine, or your message may go through a mail gateway by virtue of the fact that your target host is registered as an MX record in the Internet's Domain Name System (see Section 8.5 for more details).

Although there is a variety of electronic mail software supported by different computer systems, the format described in RFC 822, *Standard for the ARPA-Internet Text Messages,* is the standard used by the majority of research and development computer networks nationally and internationally. It is important that mail programs on the

Internet conform to the Internet standards in their mail headers, especially in their "reply-to" or "from" fields. A non-conformant "reply-to" field will mean that when people reply to a message, their reply won't be transmitted correctly.

This section explains some general concepts related to electronic mail and shows some address formats for sending mail to non-Internet networks. However, it is not a user's guide to a particular mail program and will not explain specific commands for starting a mail program or creating and sending a message. If you are just starting to use the Internet, your systems administrator should be able to steer you toward introductory material of this type. If you are a systems administrator installing a mail program, your vendor should have the supporting documentation you will need.

9.1.1. What mail looks like

In very basic terms, mail messages are broken down into two portions: the header and the body. There is an empty line that separates the two portions of the message, which is itself a requisite piece of the message format. The header lists information about the sender of the message, the recipient(s), the posting date of the message, and a subject field. The body holds the text of the message itself, usually in ASCII format (or EBCDIC for BITNET). Some sites set a limit on message size; some limits are as low as 10 kbs, although the general rule is 64 kbs. Another limitation to be aware of is line width; the general rule is 80 characters.

Figure 9-1 is an example of a message header and body. The body starts with "thanks."

```
From: june@nisc.sri.com (June Goldfarb)
To: ccalloc@nnsc.nsf.net (Chris Calloca)
Cc: june@nisc.sri.com (June Goldfarb)
Subject: online PACCOM info
Date: Fri, 28 Feb 92 13:49:01 PST

Thanks for your help in getting the information about PACCOM.
Have a great weekend!

—June
```

Figure 9-1: Example of an Electronic Mail Message

You can see that the header of the message identifies the message, tells who it is from, who it is to, who is getting a copy (cc), what the subject is, and the date and time it was sent. More complicated headers have additional information.

9.1.2. E-mail ethics

Electronic mail is a powerful communication tool that must be used with care. This section discusses some basic rules of thumb to remember when sending electronic mail.

Online mail tends to change a person's style of communication. Sending mail is so quick that it is tempting to send your immediate reaction to a message, rather than a more considered, appropriate response. It is a good idea to avoid using derogatory or inappropriate language in messages, especially those sent to discussion groups.

It is easy to forward mail you receive, but the writer may never have intended that anyone else read the message. For this reason, it is wise to check with the sender before forwarding a message.

In general, messages that are short and to the point are most appreciated. It is easy to send off a quick message, only to realize a moment later that you needed to say more. To avoid this, organize your thoughts and send a single message rather than several incomplete ones. This will make your mail far more useful to the recipients, and minimize the load on the network.

If you regularly send mail to a large group, learn how to create a mailing list. Otherwise, each recipient must scroll through a list of the mailboxes of all other recipients as a part of the message header.

Before sending a message, double check your headers to make sure you know who is receiving the message. Often personal replies are mistakenly sent to a group, which can be rather embarrassing.

When joining or leaving an established mailing list, send your message to the administrative contact rather than the whole list. Often, Internet lists will have a list-name-*request* mailbox for such messages. Sending administrative messages to the whole list will definitely annoy its readers!

You should always assume that other people may see what you write, even if you are simply sending a message to a friend.

9.1.3. Internet mail addressing

When addressing mail from the Internet to another user on the Internet, the form *user@host* is used. The **user** is the name of the user's mailbox or mail account, or the name of a distribution list that sends to many users. The **domain** is the fully qualified domain name of the host on which the user has a mail account, or of the host relaying mail to the user's host. Examples of Internet addresses are *brenly@nisc.sri.com, douglas@sfsu.edu,* and *lou_sinclair @xerox.com.*

Throughout this guide there are examples of Internet e-mail addresses. In some cases, these are role mailboxes, such as *nisc@nisc.sri.com*. "Nisc" is not a person; it is a generic mailbox that is a placeholder for a function that many people can fill. Using a role mailbox allows an organization to have a constant point of reference for users, rather than identifying a particular function with a particular person, who may leave the organization. Other examples of role mailboxes that follow the Internet addressing format are *nnsc@nnsc.nsf.net* and *hostmaster @nic.ddn.mil*.

9.1.4. Electronic mail addresses

A network provider usually allows a user to send mail not only to users on his own network and the Internet, but to users on other networks as well. Ideally there would be one format used for all electronic mail addressing; however, various mail systems have been developed, many of which have dissimilar forms of addressing. This section discusses the format of various types of electronic mail addresses. It focuses mainly on addresses used for sending mail outside of your local network. Sending mail within your local network, or even from one Internet site to another, is rarely that confusing.

As we have seen, Internet addresses have two parts separated by an @ (at-sign). The part to the left of the @ is the local part, and usually designates the person to whom a message is sent. It may also indicate a mailing list that includes several people. The part to the right of the @ indicates the destination host. The @ is a convention used in electronic mail based on the Simple Mail Transfer Protocol (SMTP). Addresses with @s are sometimes called *SMTP addresses* or, more often, *RFC 822 addresses*, after the RFC that specifies the standard format for Internet messages.

Other mail protocols use delimiters other than the @, but most retain a distinction between the user or mailing list portion and the destination host portion.

"Source routing" refers to the practice of indicating the route a message should take to travel from the sender to the destination. Explicit source routing is discouraged on the Internet (it is not necessary for sites implementing the Domain Name System), but some other networks do use it. When source routing is done, two or more hosts are indicated in the left-hand part of the address.

Here are examples of some address formats networks use.

user@host	The at-sign (@) is the most commonly used separator. The Internet, BITNET and JANET use this syntax in addresses.
host::user	The double colon (::) is prevalent in Digital's EASYnet and other DEC networks such as MFEnet and INFNET. Note that the order in which the host and user portion appear has been reversed.
host!user	The exclamation point, called "bang syntax," is used with UUCP mail. Many times it separates more than one element because the network implements source routing, which requires that each "hop" of a message be explicitly specified. Again, note the positions of the host and user portions of the address.
host1!host2!host3!user	
	Different UUCP hosts are separated by exclamation points due to source routing requirements.
user%host1@host2	
	The percent sign is often used when source routing is done from the Internet. This convention allows a user to specify a mail gateway (host2) for a message to travel through on its way to the target (host1). Prior to having MX records do this routing transparently, users were compelled to employ this format more often. The message is first routed to the host appearing after the @. Once there, the relay host interprets the first part of the message, and sends the message on to host1. Under these circumstances, host1 would not have its own direct Internet connection.

Figure 9-2: Common E-mail Address Formats

9.1.5. A brief word about X.400 addressing

Recommendation X.400 is the international standard for message handling developed by International Telegraph and Telephone Consultative Committee (CCITT—Comite Consultatif International Telegraphique et Telephonique) in cooperation with the International Organization for Standardization (ISO). Many networks support this electronic mail format or have plans to do so. It is currently being implemented by RARE (Reseaux Associes pour la Recherche Europeenne) networks in Europe, for example.

The X.400 standard supports not only normal text, but can contain other formats as well, such as FAX messages and voice recordings. Addressing is done by using a unique set of attributes for describing each recipient. These attributes are then used to search in an electronic directory, which is fashioned much like a telephone book for electronic mail domains and addresses. X.400 uses the following attributes in the address field of its messages:

Country	Country specification; uses the ISO country codes. Can be abbreviated as **C**.
ADMD	Administration Management Domain. This is the name of the public X.400 carrier. For example, in the UK, the national carrier is PTT British Telecom. Can be abbreviated **A** or **AD**.
PRMD	Private Management Domain. The private X.400 carrier that is being used, such as ATTMail, SprintMail, etc. Can be abbreviated **P** or **PD**.
Organization	The organization the recipient belongs to. This can be a company or university, etc. Can be abbreviated **O** or **OR**.
Org.Unit	This could be the department or "suborganization" within the organization the recipient belongs to, such as the chemistry department at a college or university. Can be abbreviated **OU**.
Surname	The family name, or last name, of the recipient. Can be abbreviated **S** or **SN**.
Givenname	The first name of the recipient, or the name used as a username. Can be abbreviated **G** or **GN**.

Figure 9-3: X.400 E-mail Address Attributes

In some systems, **PN** is used for Personal Name. In these systems, a person's whole name is designated under this attribute instead of using the Surname and Givenname attributes. The first names and last names of PNs are often separated by underscores or dots, such as Mary.Jones or John_A_Smith.

An address on an X.400 system would look something like:

```
C=CH; ADMD=arCom; PRMD=SWITCH; O=SWITCH; S=Lenggenhager;
```

From the Internet, users sending to an X.400 system would translate the X.400 attributes to an RFC 822 style of address, such as:

```
firstname.surname@orgunit.orgunit.org.prmd.admd.country
George.Wilson@acctng.admin.waxco.ibmmail.ibmx400.US
```

It is possible to send mail from the Internet to a user on a network that supports the X.400 message system if there is a gateway between the Internet and that user's network. In doing so, the X.400 syntax is used in the local part of the address, and the mail gateway is designated as the host part of the address. The X.400 syntax may change slightly to conform to the specific attributes used by the specific X.400 implementation. Here is one example of what such a message from the Internet to an X.400 mail user could look like:

```
/C=US/ADMD=IBMX400/PRMD=IBMMAIL/S=WARD/G=CAROL/@SRI.COM
```

9.1.6. Electronic mail to other networks

Figure 9.4 contains a few examples of how messages would be addressed in order to send mail to some non-TCP/IP networks with which Internet users commonly correspond. Two very good sources for addressing information are *The User's Directory of Computer Networks* by Tracy LaQuey [4], and *!%@:: A Directory of Electronic Mail Addressing and Networks* by Donnalyn Frey and Rick Adams [1]. In addition, a document available online, *The*

Internetworking Guide, by John Chew, provides helpful information on address formats [30].

9.2. Mailing Lists and Newsgroups

Electronic discussion forums are among the most useful features of the Internet. These forums are commonly known as newsgroups, bulletin boards, and mailing lists. Participation in these forums is easy.

9.2.1. Mailing lists

The simplest and most direct method is to subscribe to a special interest group mailing list. How do you find out what lists there are? A file containing a listing of Internet mailing lists can be found on ftp.nisc.sri.com in *netinfo/ interest-groups*. A hardcopy version of this file, *Internet: Mailing Lists*, is available as one of the volumes in the *SRI Internet Information Series* available from Prentice Hall. More than 800 lists are described in this book, and it is the best place to start. The listings cover almost every subject imaginable—from discussions of network protocols to the human genome project to birdwatching.

The general convention for being added to or deleted from a mailing list is to send a message to *list-request@host*. Lists that are maintained through an automated server mechanism like LISTSERV or majordomo usually have a central address such as *majordomo@greatcircle.com* to which administrative requests should be sent. Following these conventions will direct your request to the person or program who maintains the list, rather than to the membership of the entire mailing list.

Some lists may not provide this capability, but it is always best to check first. For example, *tcp-ip-request @nic.ddn.mil* is the address to which requests for changes to the TCP/IP mailing list should be addressed. After sub-

Internet user to Internet user:
username@host

Internet user to BITNET user:
user%site.bitnet@cunyvm.cuny.edu
(Note: there are gateways between BITNET and the Internet other than cunyvm.cuny.edu. If you often correspond with someone on BITNET, ask your colleague which BITNET gateway is best to use when routing to his host) or
user@host (for those BITNET sites that have DNS addresses.)

BITNET user to Internet user:
user@host (as in Internet addressing)

UUCP user to Internet user:
user@host (if gateway supports domain service) or
gateway!domain!user (using UUCP source routing)

Internet user to UUCP user:
user%host.UUCP@uunet.uu.net

SprintMail (X.400) user to Internet user:
(C:usa, A:telemail, P:internet, ID: <name(a)location>)
e.g., if the Internet form of the address is ajr@abc.cso.ggg.edu
then the SprintMail <name(a)location> would be
<AJR(a)abc.cso.ggg.edu>

Internet user to SprintMail user:
/G=Mary/S=Ng/O=co.abc/ADMD=SprintMail/C=US@SPRINT.COM
or /PN=Mary.Ng/O=co.abc/ADMD=SprintMail/C=US@SPRINT.COM
Case is significant.

Internet user to CompuServe user:
xxxx.xxxx@compuserve.com
Replace the comma in the CompuServe userid (represented with x's) with a period and add the compuserve.com domain name.

CompuServe user to Internet user:
>Internet:user@host
Insert >internet: before an Internet address
e.g., >internet:may@nisc.sri.com

Internet user to MCIMail user:
accountname@mcimail.com or
mci_id@mcimail.com or
full_user_name@mcimail.com.
e.g., 2671163@mcimail.com

MCIMail user to Internet user:
The following scenario applies:
create <CR>
TO: full user name EMS: INTERNET
MBX: user@host (as in Internet addressing)

Figure 9-4: E-Mail Addressing Between the Internet and other Networks

scribing to a list, messages that are sent to the mailing list will appear directly in your electronic mailbox.

There are several types of mailing lists. One type, commonly known as an unmoderated list, allows free-form discussion. There is no restriction on the messages sent to the list, and anyone can participate. This type of list is frequently the most active, since messages may turn around in a matter of minutes. However, the drawback is that these lists also often receive heavy traffic (some of the more prolific lists average more than 30 messages a day), and some of the messages may be junk (such as "Please remove me from this list").

Moderated lists are just that—messages which are sent to these lists are first read by a moderator. If the moderator feels that the message is appropriate, the moderator then forwards the message on to the list. The quality of messages on these lists is usually higher than those to an unmoderated list since junk messages are removed before they are circulated. However, there is usually a longer turnaround time for messages to this type of list. Also, since most moderators do not receive compensation for their efforts, this type of list is not as common as the unmoderated type.

Digests are another common type of list. Messages which are sent to such lists are gathered by the moderator into one big file, which he then mails as one message to the whole list. This type of list is usually used for topics that receive heavy traffic. It helps to minimize network traffic by reducing the number of messages that subscribers receive. Digests typically have a table of contents at the beginning of each message to show what has been included in that message.

9.2.2. Newsgroups

In addition to special interest group mailing lists, a useful information source can be found through USENET, also known as netnews. Netnews originated on UNIX-based systems as a way to exchange information in a common area. It is now available on many types of non-UNIX systems (Macintosh, PC, VAX, and local bulletin board systems).

Information in netnews is divided into newsgroups, which cover specific areas of interest. There are more than a thousand newsgroups, although not all newsgroups are available on every system. The newsgroups are arranged in a hierarchical (tree) fashion, with each root of the tree devoted to a major topic. Some of the major roots are:

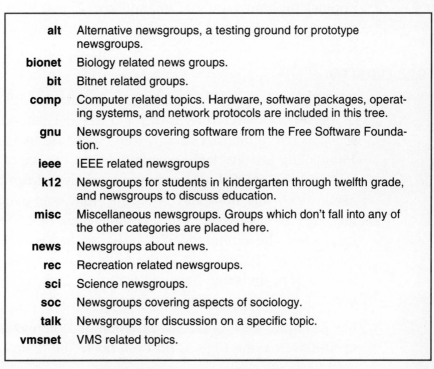

alt	Alternative newsgroups, a testing ground for prototype newsgroups.
bionet	Biology related news groups.
bit	Bitnet related groups.
comp	Computer related topics. Hardware, software packages, operating systems, and network protocols are included in this tree.
gnu	Newsgroups covering software from the Free Software Foundation.
ieee	IEEE related newsgroups
k12	Newsgroups for students in kindergarten through twelfth grade, and newsgroups to discuss education.
misc	Miscellaneous newsgroups. Groups which don't fall into any of the other categories are placed here.
news	Newsgroups about news.
rec	Recreation related newsgroups.
sci	Science newsgroups.
soc	Newsgroups covering aspects of sociology.
talk	Newsgroups for discussion on a specific topic.
vmsnet	VMS related topics.

Figure 9-5: Common Newsgroups

Like a tree, each of these roots has many branches, with each branch further defining the subject area. For example, the newsgroup discussing the TCP/IP protocols is called comp.protocols.tcp-ip; sci.space.shuttle is for space shuttle issues; and rec.juggling is devoted to people who juggle.

The list of the available newsgroups varies from site to site, as does the location of the file detailing which groups are available. Try looking in */usr/local/lib/news/news-groups* or */usr/local/news/lib/newsgroups*. If you can't find it, check with your systems administrator for the correct location.

Just as there are many programs that can be used to read electronic mail, there are also many programs that can be used to read news. On UNIX systems, some of the most popular programs are *rn*, *nn*, and *trn*. Check with your systems administrator to see what is available on your system.

9.2.3. LISTSERV

LISTSERV is an automatic mailing list maintainer. It is one of the services offered by EARN and BITNET, although it is accessible to Internet sites as well. There are more than 150 mailing lists available covering a broad range of subjects. Users can add and remove themselves from a list using electronic mail and issuing simple commands in the body of a message. For a complete list of LISTSERV lists, send the command *list global* to listserv@bitnic. educom.edu. Typing *help* in the body of a message and sending it to the same host will retrieve a help file listing some of the more general commands.

For example, here is the list of common commands the LISTSERVER at the BITNIC host returns to the "help" message:

Info	\<topicl?\>	Get detailed information files
List	\<DetaillShortlGlobal\>	Get a description of all lists
SUBscribe	listname \<full_name\>	Subscribe to a list
SIGNOFF	listname	Sign off from a list
SIGNOFF	* (NETWIDE)	Sign off from all lists on all servers
REView	listname \<options\>	Review a list
STats	listname \<options\>	Review list statistics
Query	listname	Query personal distribution options
SET	listname options	Set personal distribution options
INDex	\<filelist_name\>	Obtain a list of LISTSERV files
GET	filename filetype	Obtain a file from LISTSERV
REGister	full_namelOFF	Tell LISTSERV about your name

Figure 9-6: Common LISTSERV Commands

9.3. File Transfer Protocol (FTP)

The File Transfer Protocol (FTP) makes it possible to move a file from one computer to another, even if each computer has a different operating system and file storage format. Files may be data, programs, text—anything that can be stored online. Users are required to log in to each computer, thus ensuring they have the right to take or put files on those computers. File transfer across the Internet is reliable because the machines involved can communicate directly, without relying on intermediate machines to make copies of the file along the way.

Using FTP requires that you know the hostname or host address of the remote host, a username and password on that host, and the pathname of the file to be retrieved. A pathname is the location of a file on a particular host, and typically includes the name of the file and the names of the directory and any subdirectories in which the file is stored. FTP also requires that you have permission to access the files you wish to retrieve or transfer. Not every

file can be FTPed. Only files that have a protection per-
mitting transfer, i.e., allowing public read access, can be
FTPed.

These are the general steps for transferring a file:

➤ Log in to your local host and invoke the FTP program.

➤ Provide the hostname or host address for the remote
host.

➤ Once connected to the remote host, log in with
username and password.

➤ Issue commands to copy or send files.

➤ When finished, log out from the remote host and exit
from the FTP program.

Depending upon the implementation of FTP at the local
host and the remote host, it may also be possible to display a directory listing of public files on the remote host,
as well as system status information.

9.3.1. Anonymous FTP

Several hosts provide the username *anonymous* for FTP
retrieval of files from their system. This service is called
the FTP anonymous login convention. The hosts that allow anonymous login do so by establishing a special
anonymous login account, which works only with FTP,
and cannot be accessed for general use of that host. The
"anonymous" account is a special one with access limited
to the FTP archive offered by that host. Some hosts that
implement anonymous FTP act as repositories for Internet
information.

You cannot use the anonymous convention to *send* files
to a remote host as this requires a login account on that
host. You may only pull files from an Internet information
repository to your local workspace. Hosts that provide
information to the Internet via anonymous FTP are often

referred to as *FTP hosts*, *Internet repositories*, or *anonymous FTP archive sites*. The hosts listed as RFC Repositories in Section 8.1.6 all allow anonymous FTP, for example.

With anonymous FTP, the login name for a remote host will always be *anonymous*. The remote FTP program will often request a username as the password; most programs also accept *guest* as the password. If a host requests a user "ident," type your username rather than *guest*.

The other difference between anonymous FTP and the more general FTP is that with anonymous FTP, files can only be retrieved from an anonymous FTP repository, not deposited there.

9.3.2. How to FTP a file

 Following is an example of anonymous FTP from one UNIX host to another. Programs based on the FTP protocol can vary a great deal in implementation details. For instance, sometimes you may need to explicitly specify a local name for a file you are retrieving. Therefore, this example should be taken as a guideline; consult your local systems representatives for specific assistance with the particular FTP implementation on your host.

Make sure you are logged in locally to a directory to which you have permission to write files, otherwise you will get an error message (often "Permission denied") from the FTP program. In the following example, what the user types is **bold**, comments are in *italics*, and what you see on the computer is in this typeface.

```
paris%ftp ftp.nisc.sri.com
Connected to phoebus.nisc.sri.com.
220 phoebus FTP server (Version 2 Fri Apr 19 11:54 PDT
  1991) ready.
Name (ftp.nisc.sri.com:april): anonymous
331 Guest login ok, send ident as password.
Password:averill@myhost.com Password will not echo.
230 Guest login ok, access restrictions apply.
ftp>dir This command asks for a list of files in the current (anonymous)
  directory.
```

```
200 PORT command successful.
150 Opening ASCII mode data connection for file list.
rfc
netinfo
INDEX
iesg
internet-drafts
ietf
ien
fyi
226 Transfer complete.
134 bytes received in 0.056 seconds (2.3 Kbytes/s)
ftp> cd rfc This command connects you to the rfc directory.
250 CWD command successful.
ftp> get rfc-index.txt This command tells the program to start transfer-
    ring a specific file.
200 PORT command successful.
150 Opening ASCII mode data connection for rfc-index.txt
    (1641 bytes).
226 Transfer complete.
local: rfc-index.txt remote: rfc-index.txt
164250 bytes received in 2.6 seconds (61 Kbytes/s)
226 Transfer complete.
125 bytes received in 0.04 seconds (3.1 Kbytes/s)
ftp> quit This command quits the program.
paris%
```

9.4. Telnet

The **Telnet Protocol** allows an Internet user to log in to a remote host from his local host. Once connected and logged in to the remote host, a user can enter data, run programs, or do any other operation just as if he were logged in directly to the remote host. While running Telnet, the program effectively makes the local computer invisible during the session on the remote computer. Every keystroke the user types locally is sent directly to the remote system. When the remote login session terminates, the application returns the user to the local system. Telnet is a powerful tool in resource sharing.

The steps for running Telnet may be summarized as follows:

➤ Log in to your local host.

➤ Invoke the Telnet program on that host.

➤ Identify by hostname or host address the remote host you wish to access.

➤ Once connected to the remote host, log in with username and password for that host.

➤ When finished working on the remote host, type the command to log out. Then break the connection (if it is not broken automatically upon logout). You are now back where you began on the initial host.

Telnet has many other advanced features, too numerous to discuss here. Check your local Telnet user program for online documentation, or talk to your local systems support personnel for more information.

9.4.1. Publicly available programs

Some hosts make certain programs on their hosts available to the public by not requiring an individual account on the system to use the program. An example is the WHOIS program available on the nic.ddn.mil host. To use WHOIS, you need only telnet to the host and type *whois*. No other login procedures are required to use the program. (See Section 8.6.2 for more information about WHOIS.)

Another method of allowing public access is to publicize a certain account name (in much the same way that *whois* is the well-known name of the WHOIS account on nic.ddn.mil). For example, to use the White Pages service on host psi.com, you telnet to the host and login as *fred*, with no password. These are ways some Internet hosts make services available to the Internet public.

Often other services, such as access to supercomputer time or the ability to search certain databases, are also available via Telnet if you arrange for access in advance. Such arrangements usually include the assignment of an account name and password on the remote host, or access to a special guest account.

9.4.2. How to start a Telnet session

 In the following example, a user telnets from a local UNIX host to a remote UNIX host. Once the connection is made, the prompts, commands, and responses are those of the remote host. It looks to the user as though he is logged in directly to the remote computer.

After completing work on the remote host, the user gives the logout command. This returns the user to the Telnet program on the local computer, at which time he ends Telnet, and sees his local prompt.

In these examples, what the user types is **bold**, comments are in *italics*, and what you see on the computer is in `this typeface`.

Example 1

In the first example, a user logs in to a remote host on which he has an account.

`paris%`**telnet phoebus.nisc.sri.com**
User issues the telnet command, giving the name of the host he wishes to access over the network.
```
Trying 192.33.33.22
Connected to phoebus.nisc.sri.com
Escape character is '^]

SunOS UNIX (phoebus)

login:
```
 user types login name
```
Password:
```
 user types password; it will not show on screen
```
phoebus%
```

...USER SESSION...

`phoebus%`**logout**
```
Connection closed by foreign host.
paris%
```

Example 2

In the second example, a user telnets to the nic.ddn.mil host to use WHOIS.

paris%**telnet nic.ddn.mil**

> *User issues the telnet command, giving the name of the host he wishes to access over the network.*

```
Trying 192.112.36.5 ...
Connected to nic.ddn.mil.
Escape character is '^]'.
SunOS UNIX (nic.ddn.mil) (ttyp8)
* — DDN Network Information Center —
*
* For TAC news, type:    TACNEWS <return>
* For user and host information, type: WHOIS <return>
* For NIC information, type:    NIC <return>
*
* For user assistance call (800) 365-3642 or (703) 802-4535
* Please report system problems to ACTION@NIC.DDN.MIL
NIC, SunOS Release 4.1.1 (NIC) #1:
Cmdinter Ver 1.2 Wed Mar 4 17:48:25 1992 EST
```

@**whois**

```
Connecting to id Database . . . . . .
Connected to id Database
NIC WHOIS Version: 2.5 Wed, 4 Mar 92 17:49:52
```

> Enter a handle, name, mailbox, or other field, option-
> ally preceded by a keyword, like "host diis". Type "?"
> for short, 2-page details, "HELP" for full documenta-
> tion, or hit RETURN to exit.

```
—> Do ^E to show search progress, ^G to abort a search or
   output <—
Whois:
```
...USER SESSION....

@**logout**

```
Connection closed by foreign host.
paris%
```

9.5. Information Servers

In some ways, the Internet has grown faster than its ability to keep track of itself. Partly because there is no one central administrative authority, there is no central place to go to get a complete list of what is "out there." And partly because of the cooperative nature of the Internet, there is *a lot* "out there"!

Many hosts on the Internet have available collections of software, graphics images, digitized sound recordings, technical papers, or other information. It is possible for host administrators to make an Internet archive available to the entire Internet community using the anonymous FTP convention (see Section 9.3.1 for further information).

Currently, several efforts are underway to develop easy methods of discovering, locating, and retrieving information available freely on the Internet. Most of these efforts are in the early stages. Most of these efforts developed independently of the others and have only recently become aware of similar efforts. This section describes five of these information tracking projects: archie, Prospero, Worldwide Web (WWW), WAIS, and the Internet Gopher.

Because resource discovery is a rapidly developing area, the following information is deliberately sketchy. Our aim is simply to alert you to the fact that these services exist, describe them very briefly, and give you a place to inquire for the most up-to-date information about them.

Many of these services began as volunteer projects or projects focused on a specific community of users. Do not be surprised to find upon future inquiry that the services evolved into fee-based products once they grew to such an extent that their initial community could no longer fully support them.

9.5.1. Archie

Researchers originally at McGill University in Montreal, Canada, recognized that there was a multitude of information available on hosts acting as anonymous FTP archives, but that there was a big problem in finding out what that information is, who has it, where it is, and how to get it. In response to those needs, they designed ***archie***. Archie is "a collection of resource discovery tools that together provide an electronic directory service for locating information in an Internet environment" [17]. We would like to thank Peter Deutsch for information about archie.

At its simplest, archie is a means of locating files in anonymous FTP archives. It polls such archives regularly and compiles a database of references to available files. It makes this database available for searching, allowing users an entry point to the world of Internet resources. Searches are possible via Telnet, e-mail, or by using an archie client program. Archie can also be accessed through the Prospero system. Archie servers are replicated throughout the Internet. It is best to use one near you to reduce network load.

When you search the archie database, you are returned information about files that match your search criteria, including where they are located. This information makes it easy to retrieve what you need via the network.

Some of the archie servers and their locations known at the time of this writing are:

> archie.ans.net (USA [NY])
> archie.rutgers.edu (USA [NJ])
> archie.sura.net (USA [MD])
> archie.mcgill.ca (Canada)
> archie.funet.fi (Finland/Mainland Europe)
> archie.au (Australia)
> archie.doc.ic.ac.uk (Great Britain/Ireland)

To get started with archie, Telnet to a server near you and login as archie. When you see the archie prompt, try typing *help*. In the following example, a user telnets from a local UNIX host to one of the archie servers.

```
paris% telnet archie.ans.net  User makes the connection to the remote archie server
Trying 147.225.1.2 ...
Connected to nis.ans.net.
Escape character is '^]'.

AIX telnet (nis.ans.net)
```

```
IBM AIX Version 3 for RISC System/6000
(C) Copyrights by IBM and by others 1982, 1990.
login: archie log in as user "archie"
```

```
 — The default search method is set to "exact".
 — Type "help set search" for more details.

Other Servers:
archie.rutgers.edu
   128.6.18.15 (Rutgers University)
archie.sura.net  128.167.254.179 (SURANet server)
archie.unl.edu   129.93.1.14    (Univ of Nebraska in
   Lincoln)
archie.ans.net   147.225.1.2    (ANS server)
archie.au        139.130.4.6    (Australian server)
archie.funet.fi  128.214.6.100  (European server in Fin-
   land)
archie.doc.ic.ac.uk
   146.169.11.3 (UK/England server)
archie.ncu.edu.tw
   140.115.19.24 (Taiwan server)


o Questions/comments to archie-admin@ans.net, site add/
   delete requests to archie-updates@bunyip.com
   Client software is available on ftp.ans.net:/pub/archie/
   clients;documentation in /pub/archie/doc.
```

```
# term set to xterm 24 80
```

archie> **help** *This command displays help information about archie.*

```
Help gives you information about various topics, including
all the commands that are available and how to use them.
Telling archie about your terminal type and size (via the
"term" variable) and to use the pager (via the "pager" vari-
able) is not necessary to use help, but provides a somewhat
nicer interface.
Currently, the available help topics are:
        about    - a blurb about archie
        bugs     - known bugs and undesirable features
        bye      - same as "quit"
        email    - how to contact the archie email interface
        exit     - same as "quit"
        help     - this message
```

```
        list      - list the sites in the archie database
        mail      - mail output to a user
        nopager - *** use 'unset pager' instead
        pager     - *** use 'set pager' instead
        prog      - search the database for a file
        quit      - exit archie
        set       - set a variable
  Press return for more: Type carriage return here

        show      - display the value of a variable
        site      - list the files at an archive site
        term      - *** use 'set term ...' instead
        unset     - unset a variable
        whatis    - search for keyword in the software descrip-
    tion database
For information on one of these topics type:
  help <topic>

A '?' at the help prompt will list the available sub-topics.

Help topics available:

    about     bugs      bye       email
    list      mail      nopager   pager
    prog      regex     set       show
    site      term      unset     whatis
Help topic?
archie> whatis xterm This command looks for the keyword "xterm" in the
database
  colxterm    Color xterm (terminal emulator) for X11
  cxterm      Chinese capable xterm with input methods
              (Chinese language support)
  xlogin      Login via an xterm on a remote machine
  xterm       Terminal emulator for X window system
  xterm-250   Configing a 2/50 as an X terminal

archie> quit This commands ends the session.
Connection closed by foreign host.
paris%
```

The book *The Whole Internet User's Guide and Catalog* by Ed Krol [34] has a helpful chapter describing the use of archie. For the most current information about archie, contact:

Bunyip Information Systems
266 Blvd. Neptune
Dorval, Quebec H9S 2L4
CANADA
archie-info@bunyip.com
+1 514 398 3709
FAX: +1 514 398 6876

9.5.2. Prospero

Prospero is a distributed file system based on the Virtual System Model. Prospero is a tool that assists Internet users in organizing the large amount of information available on the Internet.

The Prospero file system supports a user centered view of files scattered across the Internet. It can be used to organize references to files as if they were on your local system, without the need to physically transfer them locally. Prospero also provides access to directories and indices that can be used to find files of interest that are available from Internet archive sites.

Prospero is being used to organize information on papers that are available by anonymous FTP. To use Prospero, you must install Prospero on your system. You need only install the clients, though you are certainly encouraged to install the server too.

Users are encouraged, though not required, to create directories containing references to their own papers. They are also encouraged to pick a topic in which they have expertise and to maintain a directory with references to the FTPable papers that they have found related to that topic. A user that is maintaining such a directory should send a message to pfs-administrator@cs.washington.edu to have that directory included at the appropriate place in the /papers/subjects or /papers/authors hierarchy.

At this writing, Prospero supports SUN's Network File System, the Andrew File System, and the File Transfer Protocol (FTP). It is also capable of retrieving directory information from independent indexing services, such as archie. Future plans include adding WAIS, WWW, and other indexing services.

A release of the Prospero file system is available via anonymous FTP from cs.washington.edu in the file pub/prospero.tar.Z (392 blocks).

The distribution contains the sources necessary to run the Prospero server and client. No special privileges are required to install the client. Papers describing Prospero can be found in the directory pub/pfs/doc.

Announcements of new releases are made to the mailing list info-prospero@isi.edu. If you would like to be added to that list send a message to *info-prospero-request @isi.edu.*

A second mailing list, prospero@isi.edu, is for general discussion of Prospero, as well as for announcements of new sites that have come on board, and new directories that people have created to organize the information already accessible. Requests for that list should be sent to prospero-request@isi.edu.

9.5.3. The World Wide Web Project (WWW or W3)

The World Wide Web (WWW or W3) Project was founded on the idea that much academic information should be made freely available to anyone. Its purpose is to allow global information sharing with "internationally dispersed teams," as well as the "dissemination of information by support groups." It "merges the techniques of information retrieval and hypertext to make an easy but powerful global information system."

Basically, W3 seeks to provide access to the web of information available. This web contains many types of documents, in many different formats. W3 considers documents to be either real, virtual, or indexes. Users need only provide keywords or other search criteria; they do not need to understand the various types or formats of documents.

Currently WWW sources and information are available for anonymous FTP from the host info.cern.ch in the */pub/ WWW* directory.

For further information about the World Wide Web Project contact:

```
Tim Berners-Lee
World Wide Web Project
CERN
1211 Geneva 23
SWITZERLAND
+41 22 767 3755
FAX: +41 22 767 7155
timbl@www3.cern.ch
```

9.5.4. Wide Area Information Server (WAIS)

The Wide Area Information Server (WAIS, pronounced "ways") began as an experimental joint venture developed by the alliance of four companies, all of which share a mutual interest in information retrieval. The four companies developing the prototype were Dow Jones & Co., Thinking Machines Corporation, Apple Computer, and KPMG Peat Marwick.

Some of the information in this section was taken from the article *An Information System for Corporate Users: Wide Area Information Servers* by Brewster Kahle and Art Medlar [16], which appeared in the November 1991 issue of *ConneXions: The Interoperability Report* (see Section 12.5 for more information about this journal).

WAIS is designed to retrieve full text documentation from various sources, either locally or via servers on other networks. WAIS uses a single user interface, through which a user can access multiple archives, thus sparing the user the need to be familiar with different operating systems or with different database management systems. The user has "transparent access to a multitude of local and remote databases."

The WAIS system has three parts: *Clients, Servers,* and the *Protocol* that connects them. The *Client* is the user interface, the *Server* retrieves and indexes the requested information, and the *Protocol* transmits the questions and responses.

In very basic terms, the system works much like going to the Reference Desk at your public library, but WAIS was designed to automate this procedure. The user formulates a question in English, selects the sources he wishes queried, and then receives responses to his question. WAIS knows to ask all servers for the necessary information, making this interaction transparent to the user. The responses are sorted and deposited in one spot that is easily accessible to the user. Responses can be in the form of text, picture, sound, video, etc. The user can examine the responses, mark those that are sufficient, and/or amend the original query and try again.

For further information about WAIS, contact:

Brewster Kahle
Thinking Machines Corporation
1010 El Camino Real, Suite 310
Menlo Park, CA 94025
+1 415 329 9300 ext 228
brewster@think.com

Thinking Machines Corporation
245 First Street
Cambridge, MA 02142
+1 617 234 1000

9.5.5. The Internet Gopher

Our thanks to Farhad Xerxes Anklesaria of the University of Minnesota for information about the Internet Gopher.

The Internet Gopher combines features of electronic bulletin board services and databases into an information distribution system that allows you to either browse a hierarchy of information or search for the information you need using full-text indexes. Gopher can store references to public Telnet sessions, phone book servers, finger-protocol information, and sounds.

The Internet Gopher software was developed by the Computer and Information Services Department of the University of Minnesota.

Gopher servers store a wealth of diverse information, including computer documentation, phone books, news, weather, library databases, books, recipes, and more.

How Does It Work?

Information is stored on multiple Gopher servers, which are connected together in a network. This allows for capacity to be added to the system in small, inexpensive increments. It also allows the Gopher system to cross institutional boundaries, since other servers can be "linked" into the system easily. Large indexes can be spread over multiple servers, resulting in significant speed-ups.

At the initial connection, the root server sends back a listing of the objects in its top-level directory. These objects can be: Directories, Text Files, CSO Phone Books, Search Engines, Telnet References, or Sounds.

Each object has associated with it a user displayable title, a unique "selector string", a hostname, and a port number. The client then presents the user with the list of titles, and lets him make a selection. The user does not have to remember hostnames, ports, or selector strings related to where information is on the Internet.

After the user makes a selection, the client contacts the given host at the given port and sends the selector string associated with the object.

Gopher Software

Client software for Macintoshes, PCs, NeXTs, X Windows, and UNIX terminals is available for anonymous ftp from the host boombox.micro.umn.edu in the directory /pub/ gopher.

Or, if you just want a quick look at the UNIX terminal client, Telnet to the host consultant.micro.umn.edu and login as *gopher*.

Running the client on a local personal computer or work-station is recommended. These local clients have a better response time and an easier user interface.

There is a mailing list that contains announcements of new software and new information available in Gopher. To subscribe to the *gopher-news* list, send an e-mail message to *gopher-news-request@boombox.micro.umn.edu*.

For more information, contact:

Internet Gopher Team
132 Shepherd Labs
100 Union St. SE
Minneapolis, MN 55455
+1 612 625 1300
gopher@boombox.micro.umn.edu.

10

INTERNET ORGANIZATIONS

New Internet users can be overwhelmed by references to the amazing number of organizations that are involved in some aspect of internetworking. To make matters worse, these organizations are normally referred to by their acronyms! This chapter helps prospective Internet users identify some major organizations and their roles in the Internet. We discuss standards organizations, network information centers, administrative organizations, government agencies, user groups, and network associations. Security response centers are described in Section 8.2.6.

10.1. Network Associations

10.1.1. FARNET

The Federation of American Research Networks (FARNET) was established in 1987. FARNET is a non-profit corporation whose mission is to advance the use of computer networks to improve research and education. Members of

FARNET are local, state, regional, national, and international providers of network services; for-profit and non-profit corporations; universities; supercomputer centers; and other organizations that support the mission of FARNET.

FARNET provides the following services to its members:

➤ Offers frequent educational programs.

➤ Works with other national and international organizations to improve the quality of information and services available to network users.

➤ Provides information about networking to interested consumers, the media, and decision makers.

➤ Negotiates discounts on products and services for its members.

➤ Provides a forum for the discussion of key technical and policy issues.

➤ Publishes a monthly online newsletter and regular proceedings of its meetings.

FARNET is governed by a Board of Directors elected by the membership. Membership in FARNET is open to any organization that supports its mission. Full members receive all of the services and benefits FARNET provides and are eligible to vote in elections for the Board of Directors. Associate members receive many of the same benefits but do not participate in Board elections.

For more information, contact:

Laura Breeden
Executive Director
FARNET
100 Fifth Avenue
Waltham, MA 02154
+1 617 890 5120
breeden@farnet.org

10.1.2. CIX

The Commercial Internet Exchange Association, Inc. (CIX), links Public Data Internets (PDIs). The CIX is an association open to all commercial Internet TCP/IP network providers and carriers. All CIX members agree to exchange traffic at a fixed and equal cost set by the association. The primary goal is to provide connectivity among cooperating TCP/IP carriers, each of which has no restrictions on the type of traffic allowed. In other words, network traffic is not restricted solely to research or academic pursuits.

Individuals do not join the CIX. However, if you are interested in sending traffic of the type CIX supports, you may want to investigate those service providers that are themselves members of CIX or ask your prospective providers if they are members.

CIX encourages the participation of all commercial and non-profit U.S. national, regional, and mid-level networks; federal and state government networks; and international network organizations.

Mitchell Kapor is the chairman of the CIX board of directors. For more information, contact:

> The CIX Association
> 3110 Fairview Park Drive
> Suite 590
> Falls Church, VA 22042
> +1 703 876 5050
> FAX:+1 703 876 5059
> info@cix.org

10.1.3. EDUCOM

EDUCOM is a non-profit consortium of colleges, universities, and other institutions founded to facilitate the introduction, use, and management of information technology in higher education. Through direct services and cooperative efforts, EDUCOM assists its members and provides leadership for addressing critical issues about the role of computing and related technology in higher education.

EDUCOM's membership includes virtually every major research university in the country, four-year private and public institutions, along with a number of two-year colleges, overseas campuses, foundations, consortia, and research laboratories.

For more information about EDUCOM, contact:

EDUCOM
1112 16th Street, N.W.
Suite 600
Washington, DC 20036
info@bitnic.educom.edu
+1 202 872 4200

10.1.4. CoSN

The Consortium for School Networking (CoSN) advocates access to, and facilitates the development of, national and international electronic networks as resources to K-12 (Kindergarten to 12th grade) educators and students.

Using these interconnected networks, CoSN will support educational goals by advocating equitable, low-cost, user-friendly access to communications services and information resources, and by stimulating collaborations among the K-12 educators and students, post-secondary researchers and scholars, and others groups and individuals concerned with K-12 education.

CoSN accepts both individual and institutional memberships.

For more information about CoSN, contact:

John R.B. Clement
1112 16th St. NW
Suite 600
Washington, DC 20036
clement@educom.edu
+1 202 872 4200
FAX: +1 202 872 4318

10.1.5. RARE

RARE, the Reseaux Associes pour la Recherche Europeenne, is the association of European networking organizations. Its purpose is to promote network services for the European research community, and especially to promote international interconnections of such services.

RARE sponsors working groups, which are responsible for developing coordination and cooperation in technical areas. RARE also sponsors an annual networkshop.

RARE also provides a user's voice on a number of European standardization and political bodies, for example European Workshop for Open Systems (EWOS), European Council of Telecommunication Users Association (ECTUA), and European Telecommunication Standards Institute (ETSI). On a broader scale, RARE represents the European participation on the Coordinating Committee for Intercontinental Research Networking (CCIRN).

In addition, RARE sponsors a group called RIPE, Reseaux IP Europeans (European IP Networks), and manages the Eureka COSINE project, both of which are described below.

For more information about RARE, contact:

RARE Secretariat
Singel 466-468
NL-1017 AW
AMSTERDAM
+31 20 639 1131
FAX: +31 20 639 3289
raresec@rare.nl

10.1.6. RIPE

RIPE is a RARE body that is responsible for European TCP/IP coordination activities. RIPE was formed in May 1988 in response to the pressing need for a total European connectivity plan with regards to the TCP/IP protocol.

RIPE's aim is to ensure the coordination necessary to allow the operation and expansion of a pan-European IP network. As such, RIPE acts as a forum for the exchange of technical information as well as for the promotion and coordination of interconnection of IP networks within Europe and to other continents.

The RIPE Network Coordination Centre (RIPE NCC) is an organization with the aim of putting some of the duties now being performed on a voluntary basis into a formal structure with employed personnel. See Section 6.1.1.6 for more information about the RIPE NIC.

The RIPE Network Management Database currently contains information on networks, domains, and contact persons. Section 8.6.3 discusses the RIPE Database and how to access it in more detail. RIPE also has an anonymous FTP archive and an interactive information service.

10.1.7. COSINE

COSINE (Cooperation for Open Systems Interconnection Networking in Europe) was established to provide an OSI-based standard computer communications infrastructure for the hundreds of scientific and industrial research institutes all over Europe. COSINE's goal is to make present-day research networks in Europe interoperate, so that a researcher in Finland can work easily with his colleague in France.

To this end, COSINE has initiated the IXI, CONCISE, and PARADISE projects.

IXI

The International X.25 Infrastructure (IXI) project is a X.25-based backbone connecting European countries. The IXI backbone is currently set up with 64 kbps connection points, with upgrades planned for the future. The IXI backbone is managed by the Netherlands PTT Telecom BV in cooperation with other national telcos and appointed access point managers.

IXI will become part of the European Multiprotocol Backbone (EMPB), which will include X.25, IP, and CLNP services.

CONCISE

CONCISE, COSINE Network's Central Information Service for Europe, aims to provide a pilot pan-European Information Service to the COSINE and the European Industrial Research Community based on an Open System Environment and accessible through OSI protocols.

Many countries already have national information services. The service provided by CONCISE will complement these national services by providing information Europe-wide and by providing information about these other existing services. Thus it will form the central focal point for users to obtain information about pan-European networking, research projects, products and services, as well as about COSINE itself.

A goal of this pilot project is to make the system architecture portable enough to allow other information services and special interest groups to adopt it and set up their own information servers elsewhere in Europe.

Knowledge gained from the running of the pilot system will be used to study the feasibility of providing a self-supporting information service in the future, as well as recommending ways in which the service might evolve.

It is anticipated that the recommendations made at the end of the project will make it possible to set up a self-supporting service for 1993 and beyond.

For more information, contact:

> COSINE Secretariat
> Commission of the European Communities
> Directorate-General XIII
> Office Breydel 11/213
> Rue de la Loi 200
> B-1049 Brussels
> BELGIUM
> +32 2 236 2075
> FAX: +32 2 235 0655
> COSINE_secretariat@eurokom.ie
>
> COSINE Project Management Unit (CPMU)
> c/o RARE Secretariat
> P.O. Box 41882
> 1009 DB Amsterdam
> +31 20 592 5078
> FAX: +31 20 592 5155
> raresec@rare.nl

PARADISE

PARADISE, the COSINE X.500 Directory Service pilot, was launched in November 1990 to coordinate the activities of the European national X.500 pilots and to provide a central operational service across Europe with access to North America and the rest of the world. PARADISE provides some services itself, such as a user interface to the Directory Service, and also liaises between national pilots across the countries participating in COSINE.

PARADISE is managed by University College London and involves the University of London Computer Centre (ULCC), X-Tel Services, and a group of service providers— PTT Telecom (Netherlands), PTT Switzerland, and Telecom Finland.

Online information regarding PARADISE is available from either the info-server, *info-server@paradise.ulcc.ac.uk*, or via anonymous ftp to the host *ftp.paradise.ulcc.ac.uk*.

For additional information, contact:

> PARADISE Helpdesk
> +44 71 405 8400 ext 432
> FAX: +44 71 242 1845
> helpdesk@paradise.ulcc.ac.uk
> S=helpdesk; OU=paradise; O=ulcc; P=uk.ac; A= ; C=gb;

10.1.8. CERN

CERN is the European Laboratory for Particle Physics, located on the Franco-Swiss border near Geneva. It provides facilities for particle physics experiments, mainly in the domain of high-energy particles. CERN is international in scope and supported by several member countries, including Austria, Belgium, Denmark, Germany, France, Greece, Italy, Netherlands, Norway, Portugal, Spain, Sweden, Switzerland, and the U.K. It also supports visiting scientists from throughout the world.

CERN is a key European site for external network connections. Institutes on three continents connect to CERN including a T1 link to Cornell University, which provides access to NSFNET.

Most of these links form an international network, the High Energy Physics Network (HEPnet), which is a leased line infrastructure covering Europe (CERN, France, Italy, Germany, Netherlands, Poland, Spain, Switzerland, U.K., and Scandinavian countries via NORDUnet); North America (U.S.A. and Canada); and Asia (Japan and India). HEPnet offers a wide range of services: a world-wide private X.25 network, the HEP DECnet in collaboration with SPAN from NASA and ESA, an IP network in collaboration with RIPE in Europe, and an SNA network.

CERN has also made connections to all the international multi-disciplinary academic and research networks, in addition to HEPnet, which provide connectivity to most of the physics sites collaborating on the CERN program. CERN's interconnectivity was established in 1984 with its connection to EARN. CERN is also the major hub of EASInet (European Academic Supercomputer Initiative of IBM).

In addition to its network connections, CERN also has considerable expertise in providing networking services and protocols, participating in various European working groups, and providing consultancy to the High Energy Physics Community as a whole. Traditional services such as remote login, file transfer, and electronic mail have been provided over conventional speed links at up to 64 kbps and more recently by 2 Mbps links. Electronic mail provides an essential means of communication between the geographically dispersed physics collaborations and CERN. CERN also operates mail gateways between EARN/BITNET, EUNET/USENET, DECnet, and the RARE Pilot X.400 network. CEARN, the Swiss International EARN node, and CERNVAX, a well-known EUNET backbone node, are located and managed at CERN.

The host info.cern.ch is a repository for a large amount of networking information, most of which is available via a wide variety of methods, such as World Wide Web, WAIS, and Gopher.

For additional information about CERN, contact:

>Brian Carpenter
>CERN-CN
>CH-1211 Geneva 23
>SWITZERLAND
>+41 22 767 4967
>brian@priam.cern.ch

10.1.9. EFF

The following description of the EFF (Electronic Frontier Foundation) was derived from its mission statement as it appears in the file eff.mission, on the host ftp.eff.org in the directory pub/EFF.

Computer-based communication media like electronic mail and computer conferencing are becoming the basis of new forms of community. These communities without a single, fixed geographical location comprise the first settlements on an electronic frontier.

While well-established legal principles and cultural norms give structure and coherence to uses of conventional media like newspapers, books, and telephones, the new digital media do not so easily fit into existing frameworks. Conflicts come about as the law struggles to define its application in a context where fundamental notions of speech, property, and place take profoundly new forms.

The Electronic Frontier Foundation has been established to help make the electronic frontier truly useful and beneficial not just to a technical elite, but to everyone. EFF is dedicated to the free and open flow of information and communication.

Electronic Frontier Foundation will:

① Engage in and support educational activities which increase popular understanding of the opportunities and challenges posed by developments in computing and telecommunications.

② Develop among policy makers a better understanding of the issues underlying free and open telecommunications, and support the creation of legal and structural approaches which will ease the assimilation of these new technologies by society.

③ Raise public awareness about civil liberties issues arising from the rapid advancement in the area of new computer-based communications media. Support litigation in the public interest to preserve, protect, and extend First Amendment rights within the realm of computing and telecommunications technology.

④ Encourage and support the development of new tools which will endow non-technical users with full and easy access to computer-based telecommunications.

There is an EFF mailing list. To subscribe, send e-mail to *eff-request@eff.org*. If your site subscribes to USENET, everything that goes over the EFF mailing list is also posted on the USENET list *comp.org.eff.news*.

For further information about EFF, contact:

The Electronic Frontier Foundation
155 Second Street
Cambridge, MA 02141
+1 617 864 0665
FAX: +1 617 864 0866
eff@eff.org

10.2. Network Administrative Organizations

10.2.1. FNC

The Federal Networking Council (FNC) was formed in 1990 out of a reorganization of the Federal Research Internet Coordinating Committee (FRICC). The FNC is the U.S. Federal Government's body for coordinating the agencies that support the Internet. It provides liaison to the Office of Science and Technology Policy (OSTP) (headed by the President's Science Advisor) which is responsible for setting science and technology policy affecting the Internet. It endorses and employs the existing planning and operational activities of the community-based bodies that have grown up to manage the Internet in the United States. The FNC plans to involve user and supplier communities through creation of an external advisory board and will coordinate Internet activities with other U.S. government initiatives ranging from the Human Genome and Global Change programs to educational applications. The FNC has also participated in planning for the creation of a National Research and Education Network in the U.S.

10.2.2. CCIRN

A Coordinating Committee for Intercontinental Research Networks (CCIRN) has been formed that includes the U.S. Federal Networking Council (FNC) and its counterparts in North America and Europe. Co-chaired by the executive directors of the FNC and the European Association of Research Networks (RARE), the CCIRN provides a forum for cooperative planning among the principal North American and European research networking bodies.

10.3. Administrative Bodies

10.3.1. IAB

The Internet Architecture Board, or IAB, provides the focus for much of the research and development that supports the Internet. The IAB was originally formed by DARPA in 1983 to determine the needs of the Internet, propose technical means to achieve them, and assist in the Internet's evolution by promoting exchange among researchers and professionals.

Today, the IAB exists as part of the Internet Society (ISOC). IAB members are committed to maintaining the effective functioning of the Internet, as well as developing it to meet a large-scale, high-speed future. The IAB focuses on the TCP/IP protocol suite, and extensions to the Internet system to support multiple sets of standards.

Before becoming part of the ISOC (see Section 10.3.2), the IAB was known as the Internet Activities Board.

Currently, the IAB has two principal subsidiary task forces: the Internet Engineering Task Force (IETF) and the Internet Research Task Force (IRTF). Each of these task forces is headed by an IAB chairman and guided by a Steering Group which reports to the IAB through its chairman. The work performed by each task force is carried out by a collection of working groups that usually have a narrow focus and are bounded by completion of specific tasks, although there are exceptions.

The IRTF is a group of network researchers formed by the IAB to promote research in networking and the development of new technology. Its members tend to be more concerned with understanding issues and areas of networking technology than with products or standard protocols.

Overall, the IAB performs the following functions:

① Sets Internet Standards.

② Manages the RFC publication process.

③ Reviews the operation of the IETF and IRTF.

④ Performs strategic planning for the Internet, identifying long-range problems and opportunities.

⑤ Acts as an international technical policy liaison and representative for the Internet community.

⑥ Resolves technical issues which cannot be treated within the IETF or IRTF frameworks.

The IAB meets quarterly to review the condition of the Internet as a whole, to review and approve any proposed changes or additions to the TCP/IP protocol suite, set technical development priorities, discuss policy matters, and agree on the addition or retirement of IAB members or task forces reporting to the IAB. All its decisions are made public, principally via the RFC process. Minutes of the IAB meetings are published in the online Internet Monthly Report and are stored online at host venera.isi.edu. (See Section 12.3 for further information regarding the Internet Monthly Report.)

10.3.2. The Internet Society

One of the important goals of the IAB is to prepare for and support the use of multiple protocols in a networked environment. Because the Internet is already a collection of cooperating, interconnected, multiprotocol networks spanning the globe, and because of its current scope and rapid rate of growth, it has been proposed that it will benefit from a more organized framework to support the objective of a multiprotocol environment. Therefore, the Internet Society has been formed to promote and support the evolution and growth of the Internet into a global research and development communications and information infrastructure.

The Internet Society will incorporate the IAB and its functions into its operation, as well as work with other organizations who are interested in supporting and assisting efforts to evolve the multiprotocol Internet. It will use the IETF and the IRTF to stimulate networking research and facilitate the evolution of the TCP/IP protocol suite and the integration of new protocols suites, such as Open Systems Interconnection (OSI) protocols, into the Internet architecture.

Other goals of the the Internet Society:

① To promote and support the technical evolution of the Internet as a research and education organization and to stimulate participation of the scientific community, industry, government and others in its evolution.

② To educate the scientific community, industry, and the public at large concerning the technology, use, and application of the Internet.

③ To promote scientific and educational applications of Internet technology for the benefit of government, colleges and universities, industry, and the public at large.

④ To provide a forum for exploring new Internet applications and fostering collaboration among organizations in their operation and use of the Internet.

The Internet Society has been organized to be a non-profit organization with its initial organizers to include the Corporation for National Research Initiatives (CNRI), EDUCOM, and RARE.

The Internet Society is a new, international, professional membership organization open to individuals, corporations, research and educational organizations, and government agencies.

To receive additional information about the Internet Society or to apply for membership, contact the following:

Internet Society
1895 Preston White Drive, Suite 100
Reston, VA 22091
+1 703 620 8990
FAX: +1 703 620 0913
isoc@nri.reston.va.us

10.3.3. Internet Engineering Task Force (IETF)

The Internet Engineering Task Force (IETF) is one of the task forces established by the Internet Architecture Board (IAB) to help coordinate the technical operation and evolution of the Internet.

The IETF is comprised of a large open community of network designers, operators, vendors, users, agency contractors, and researchers concerned with the Internet and the Internet protocol suite. It also serves as a forum for the exchange of information within the Internet community. There is no formal membership in the IETF, so anyone who shares these interests and is concerned with the smooth operation and evolution of the Internet can attend.

Technical activity on any specific topic in the IETF is addressed within Working Groups. All Working Groups are organized roughly by function into nine technical Areas. Each Area is led by an Area Director who has primary responsibility for that one area of IETF activity. Together with the Chair of the IETF, the Area Directors constitute the Internet Engineering Steering Group (IESG), which provides overall guidance and management of the IETF and reports to the IAB.

Many of the new standards developed for the Internet are produced as a result of activities in the working groups of the IETF. These working groups typically write Internet Draft documents that propose standards that will enhance technical aspects of the Internet or suggest procedures to strengthen the Internet infrastructure. Internet Draft documents are available for anonymous FTP at various repositories on the Internet. Anyone on the Internet can obtain one of these documents and provide comments and suggestions for improvements. Eventually, after a process of review by the Internet community, the IESG, the IAB, and the RFC Editor, many of these Drafts become RFCs.

There are currently three standard directories of online information made available by the IESG Secretariat: ietf, for general information about the IETF, including descriptions of its working groups and their charters, as well as information about the frequent IETF meetings; iesg, for the minutes of the IESG meetings; and internet-drafts, for the drafts themselves.

One of the online repositories for IETF information is ds.internic.net. For more information about these files or the IETF, contact:

IETF Secretariat
Corporation for National Research Initiatives
+1 703 620 8990
ietf-info@nri.reston.va.us

10.4. Standards Organizations

The following groups are those that have a role in creating standards, overseeing the process that coordinates standards efforts, or making standards documentation available. Addresses listed can be contacted for more information or to obtain that organization's standards.

10.4.1. American National Standards Institute (ANSI)

ANSI committees develop the U.S. position for participation in the International Organization for Standardization (ISO). Membership in ANSI is voluntary, and is typically drawn from the manufacturing and user communities.

ANSI documents are available from:

American National Standards Institute
11 W. 42nd Street
13th Floor
New York, NY 10036
USA
+1 212 354 3300
Sales: +1 212 642 4900
TELEX: 424396 ANSI UI
FAX: +1 212 302 1286

10.4.2. CCITT

CCITT, or International Telegraph and Telephone Consultative Committee, is an agency of the International Telecommunications Union (ITU) of the United Nations.

All CCITT Recommendations are published every four years in a series of books. Each book in the series is given the same color cover. The covers were orange in 1976, yellow in 1980, red in 1984, and blue in 1988. The recommendations for a given year are commonly referred to by color, so, for example, the 1988 CCITT Recommendations are called the Blue Books.

A new service called TELEDOC makes CCITT documents available online. It currently contains CCITT and CCIR administrative documents, lists of contributions to CCITT and CCIR study groups, lists of CCITT reports and Recommendations, summaries of CCITT new or revised Recommendations, and CCITT and CCIR meeting schedules, and other information concerning Study Groups structures and activities.

Starting early 1993, the full texts of all new and revised CCITT Recommendations (i.e., all standards approved after the publication of the Blue Books in 1988) will also be available from TELEDOC.

TELEDOC is based on a X.400 document server which processes requests sent in by electronic mail. TELEDOC can be used by sending a message to *teledoc@itu.arcom.ch* or *S=teledoc; P=itu; A=arcom; C=ch;* in X.400 format.

TELEDOC will be available on request, on a trial period of one year, at no access cost.

Hardcopies of CCITT Recommendations are available from:

Omnicom, Inc.
115 Park Street SE
Vienna, VA 22180-4607
USA
+1 703 281 1135
(800) 666-4266
FAX: +1 703 281 1505
TELEX: 279678 OMNI UR

Omnicom International, Ltd.
17 Park Place
Stevenage, Herts., SG1 1DU
UK
+44 438 742424
FAX: +44 438 740154
TELEX: 826903 OMINCM G

National Technical Information Service
5285 Port Royal Road
Springfield, VA 22161
USA
+1 703 487 4600

10.4.3. CEN/CENELEC

In English, this acronym stands for European Committee for Standardization/European Committee for Electrotechnical Standardization. This organization produces European standards, called ENs or ENVs.

CEN standards are available from:

Comite Europeean de Normalisation
Rue Brederode 2 Bte 5
1000 Brussels
BELGIUM
+32 2 513 59 30
TELEX: 26257 B

10.4.4. Corporation for Open Systems (COS)

The Corporation for Open Systems (COS) is a not-for-profit consortium established to "accelerate the introduction of interoperable, multivendor products and services based on OSI, ISDN, and related standards." COS does testing, evaluation, and certification of implementations for conformance.

For additional information about COS and the services it provides, contact:

> Corporation for Open Systems
> 1750 Old Meadowood Road
> Suite 400
> McLean, VA 22102-4306
> +1 703 883 2796

10.4.5. IEEE

The Institute of Electrical and Electronics Engineers, Inc. (IEEE) is another U.S. standards body. An example of one of its contributions to the networking arena is the IEEE 802 specifications for Local Area Networks (LANs).

IEEE standards are available from:

> Institute of Electrical and Electronics Engineers
> Service Center
> 445 Hoes Lane
> Piscataway, NJ 08854
> USA
> +1 210 562 3800
> (800) 678 4333

10.4.6. ISO

ISO is an international standardization body that handles networking issues.

As part of their efforts, in 1984 ISO published the ISO Reference Model for Open Systems Interconnection, a seven-layered conceptual model.

ISO Standards are available from:

> Omnicom, Inc.
> 115 Park Street SE
> Vienna, VA 22180-4607
> USA
> +1 703 2811135
> (800) 666-4266
> FAX: +1 703 281 1505
> TELEX: 279678 OMNI UR

> Omnicom International, Ltd.
> 17 Park Place
> Stevenage, Herts., SG1 1DU
> UK

+44 438 742424
FAX: +44 438 740154
TELEX: 826903 OMINCM G

American National Standards Institute
11 W. 42nd Street
13th Floor
New York, NY 10036
USA
+1 212 354 3300
Sales: +1 212 642 4900
TELEX: 424396 ANSI UI
FAX: +1 212 302 1286

10.4.7. Naval Publications and Forms Center

The Naval Publications and Forms Center (NavPubs) is the source for Military Standards (MIL-STDs). Five of the TCP/IP protocols were issued as MIL-STDs.

Internet Protocol (IP)	MIL-STD 1777
File Transfer Protocol (FTP)	MIL-STD 1780
Simple Mail Transfer Protocol (SMTP)	MIL-STD 1781
Telnet Protocol	MIL-STD 1782
Transmission Control Protocol (TCP)	MIL-STD 1778

For more information, contact:

Naval Publications & Forms Center
Code 3015
5801 Tabor Avenue
Philadelphia, PA 19120
+1 215 697 3321

10.4.8. National Institute for Standards and Technology (NIST)

Formerly called the National Bureau of Standards, this group publishes Federal Information Processing Standards (FIPS).

FIPS publications are available from:

FIPS Publication Sales
National Technical Information Service
5285 Port Royal Road
Springfield, VA 22161
USA
+1 703 487 4600

10.4.9. Open Software Foundation (OSF)

The Open Software Foundation (OSF) focuses mainly on the UNIX operating system. They are also interested in working toward the standardization of networking systems.

Additional information can be obtained from:

> Open Software Foundation
> 11 Cambridge Center
> Cambridge, MA 02139
> +1 617 621 8700

10.5. Network Information Centers (NICs)

10.5.1. The InterNIC

In cooperation with the Internet community, in the spring of 1992, the National Science Foundation developed and released a solicitation for one or more Network Information Services Managers (NIS Manager(s)) to provide and/ or coordinate services for the NSFNET community. As a result of this solicitation, three separate organizations were competitively selected to receive cooperative agreements in the three areas of Registration Services, Directory and Database Services, and Information Services.

Together these three awards constitute the InterNIC, which became operational in April 1993. Network Solutions, Inc. (NSI) provides Registration Services; AT&T provides Directory and Database Services; and General Atomics/ CERFnet provides Information Services. Each has a host dedicated to its tasks. The hosts are *rs.internic.net, ds.internic.net*, and *is.internic.net*. Each host supports remote logins (telnet) access to services and an anonymous FTP repository. In addition, InterNIC information is available via Gopher and WAIS interfaces.

InterNIC Registration Services is the Internet registration authority for the root domain and several top- and second-level domains, is the site of the Internet Registry (IR) for IP network numbers and Autonomous System Numbers (ASNs), and maintains a WHOIS database.

In addition to the services mentioned, the InterNIC has the role of being the first place to contact if you are unsure of a better source to answer your question.

All three portions of the InterNIC can be reached by calling (800) 444-4345 or by sending a message to *info@ internic.net*.

For more information, contact the InterNIC:

```
InterNIC
800 444 4345
info@internic.net
InterNIC Information Services
General Atomics
P.O. Box 85608
San Diego, CA

Information Services:
+1 619 455 4600
FAX: +1 619 455 3990
info@internic.net

Registration Services:
+1 703 742 4777
hostmaster@rs.internic.net

Directory and Database Services:
+1 908 668 6587
FAX: +1 908 668 3763
admin@ds.internic.net
```

10.5.2. DDN Network Information Center (DDN NIC)

The Defense Data Network (DDN) Network Information Center (NIC) is administered by Network Solutions, Inc., for the Defense Information Systems Agency (DISA) of the U.S. Department of Defense. The NIC's hostname is *nic.ddn.mil* and its host address is 192.112.36.5. The DDN NIC provides various user assistance services for DDN users, maintains the MIL domain and the official DoD Internet Host Table, and maintains a WHOIS database.

The NIC also has numerous publicly accessible information files available in directories such as *netinfo*.

Each directory has an index which lists the filenames available for anonymous FTP and a description of their contents. Most of these files are also available via the automatic mail server, *service@nic.ddn.mil*.

For more information, contact the DDN NIC:

> Network Solutions, Inc.
> Attn: Network Information Center
> 14200 Park Meadow Drive
> Suite 200
> Chantilly, VA 22021
> 800 365 3642
> +1 703 802 4535
> FAX: +1 703 802 8376
> nic@nic.ddn.mil

10.5.3. NASA NAIC

NASA's Network Applications and Information Center (NAIC) offers information services and application support for users of the NASA Science Internet (NSI), a worldwide, multiprotocol internet. It also offers information about NASA networking to other interested Internet users. The NAIC is tasked with facilitating a distributed NIC architecture for NASA, with NICs at NASA Centers providing primary user support.

NAIC information is accessible via Gopher, anonymous FTP, and telephone. Contact the NAIC for a more complete description of its services, or connect to the host *naic.nasa.gov* to access such information online.

For further information about NASA's NIC services, contact:

> Network Applications and Information Center (NAIC)
> NASA Ames Research Center
> M/S 233-18
> Moffett Field, CA 94035-1000
> 800 858 9947
> +1 415 604 0600
> FAX: +1 604 7300
> naic@nasa.gov

10.5.4. Merit Network Information Center

Merit Network, Inc., operates a Network Information Center that provides service to both MichNet members and NSFNET users. In addition to telephone and electronic mail consulting, Merit publishes two newsletters, the *Link Letter* and the *MichNet News.* Information is also made available for anonymous FTP from nic.merit.edu or via electronic mail at *nis-info@merit.edu.* Merit staff conduct informative seminars on the Internet several times a year at varying locations around the country (see Section 11.5).

For further information about Merit's NIC services, contact:

> Merit Network, Inc.
> 2901 Hubbard, Pod G
> Ann Arbor, MI 48105-2016
> 800 666 3748
> +1 313 936 3000
> FAX: +1 313 747 3185
> nsfnet-info@merit.edu
> info@merit.edu

10.5.5. BITNET Network Information Center (BITNIC)

The BITNET Network Information Center (BITNIC) is supported by EDUCOM and exists to promote the use of BITNET network in higher education. The BITNIC provides an online directory, conducts workshops, provides end-user documentation, and answers questions about using BITNET.

For more information, contact:

> BITNET Network Information Center
> EDUCOM
> Suite 600
> 112 16th Street, N.W.
> Washington, D.C. 20036-4823
> USA
> +1 202 872 4200
> info@bitnic.educom.edu

11

INTERNET RESOURCES

This chapter gives you a very, very brief glimpse of some resources available on the Internet. Our purpose in this chapter is not to list everything available on the Internet, nor even to give you exhaustive detail about those that we do list. As in previous chapters, we mainly wish to show you some of the tools available. This chapter includes references both to resources that may help you do your job better and to those that may help shed some light on the Internet itself.

This chapter is meant to be used in conjunction with Chapter 12, as that chapter identifies sources that specialize in listing Internet resources.

11.1. Merit's Cruise of the Internet

Merit's *Cruise of the Internet* is a computer-based tutorial for new as well as experienced Internet "navigators." The Cruise will introduce you to Internet resources as diverse as supercomputing, minorities, multimedia, and even cooking. It will also provide information about the tools needed to access those resources.

Versions of the tutorial are available free of charge for any Macintosh capable of displaying 256 colors, and for any IBM-DOS or DOS-compatible computer equipped to display 256 colors at an aspect ratio of 640 x 480.

More information about the Cruise, as well as the software itself, are available on the host nic.merit.edu. Get the READ.ME file first. For further help, contact cruise2feedback@merit.edu.

11.2. InternetCD

SRI International, Network Information Systems Center (SRI NISC) sells the Internet CD ROM, (formerly the TCP/IP CD), which features all the online RFCs, FYIs, STDs, and Internet Experimental Notes (IENs). Archives of the tcp-ip and namedroppers mailing lists are also included. A special program searches through indexes of these files to help users locate which files they need. Other public domain files, such as the GOSIP specification, and reports on the Internet worm are provided as well, although they are not indexed to be accessible to the IFIND search program. The CD also includes publicly available networking software such as NCSA Telnet and the X window system. The CD is updated regularly.

The Internet CD is an ISO-9660 (High Sierra) format compact disk. ASCII files are formatted for UNIX, MS-DOS, and

Mac systems, and may be readable on other systems supporting ISO-9660 filesystems.

Contact SRI NISC for complete details:

SRI International
Network Information Systems Center
333 Ravenswood Avenue, Room EJ290
Menlo Park, CA 94015
+1 415 859 6387
+1 415 859 3695
FAX: +1 415 859 6028
nisc@nisc.sri.com

11.3. Network Reading List

The *Network Reading List: TCP/IP, UNIX, and Ethernet* is available from the Network Information Center at the University of Texas. It is an annotated list of books and other resources concentrating in the areas of TCP/IP, UNIX, and Ethernet. There is a good blend of both introductory information for the novice and more technical articles for the veteran.

The list is available in PostScript or ASCII format from the host ftp.utexas.edu via anonymous ftp or e-mail from an archie server program. The files are in pub/netinfo/docs and pub/netinfo/ps directories as net-read.txt and net-read.ps, respectively. If your site does not have ftp capability you can request the same files using electronic mail from *archive-server@ftp.utexas.edu*. In the body of the message type the command line send ps net-read.ps for the PostScript version and send docs net-read.txt for ASCII text.

For further information, contact:

Charles Spurgeon
Computation Center
Networking Services
University of Texas at Austin
Austin, TX 78712
+1 512 471 3241 ext 265
E-Mail: c.spurgeon@utexas.edu

11.4. Online Libraries

Over the last several years, online library catalog systems have become available over the Internet. Presently, most major and many smaller universities have their libraries available on the Internet.

Some of the information for this section was taken from an article called *Another Use of the Internet: Libraries Online Catalogs* by Billy Barron, which appeared in the July 1991 issue of *ConneXions: The Interoperability Report* (see Section 12.5 for more information about this journal).

Many different groups of people use the Internet libraries, including librarians, faculty, students, and researchers. These Internet libraries are used for things such as:

1. Searching other libraries for books that you wish to acquire through Inter Library Loan (ILL). This online library access allows you to check the status of the book before submitting an ILL request.

2. Some ILL librarians use the online library systems because locally kept information is usually more accurate than the national databases.

3. The online library systems allow researchers access almost any time of the day instead of just during times a library is open.

4. Colleagues at different sites working on collaborative projects can check each others libraries' holdings.

5. The system can be used for verifying information for library acquisitions when some information is questionable.

Several useful documents, listed below, assist those who are interested in finding out more about Internet libraries.

UNT's Accessing On-line Bibliography Databases by Billy Barron, University of North Texas. This is a clear and concise guide to library systems available on the Internet, JANET, and THEnet (Texas Higher Education network).

Available via anonymous FTP on host vaxb.acs.unt.edu in the "library" directory. Submission for new or updated entries may be sent to billy@vaxb.acs.unt.edu.

Internet-Accessible Library Catalogs & Databases by Art St. George, University of New Mexico, and Ron Larsen, University of Maryland. A guide to Internet and JANET library systems and campus-wide information systems. Available via anonymous FTP from host ariel.unm.edu in the "library" directory. Submissions for new or updated entries can be sent to stgeorge@bootes.unm.edu.

AARNet Resources Guide. This is the equivalent to the ***Internet Resource Guide*** published by the NNSC for AARNET, the Australian part of the Internet. This information is also summarized in the Barron and St. George guides. Available for anonymous FTP from host aarnet.edu.au in the pub/resource-guide directory.

OPACS in the UK: A List of Interactive Library Catalogues on JANET Compiled for the JANET User Group for Libraries by the University of Sussex Library. This is the original source for accessing JANET libraries. It is included verbatim in the St. George guide and summarized in a format consistent with the rest of the information in the Barron guide.

There are also mailing lists that discuss library topics. The two listed below are particular to discussing library systems on the Internet:

PACS-L, moderated by Charles Bailey, University of Houston. The Public Access Computer Systems List (PACS-L) covers all aspects of patron computer use in libraries. Major updates to the documents listed above and library computer programs are normally announced on this mailing list. To subscribe, send mail to *listserv%uhupvm1. bitnet @cunyvm.cuny.edu,* with a body of "subscribe

PACS-L firstname lastname". Posts are mailed to *pacsl% uhupvm1.bitnet@cunyvm.cuny.edu.*

LIB_HYTELNET, moderated by Peter Scott, University of Saskatchewan. LIB_HYTELNET's primary purpose is to discuss the library program package called HYTELNET. However, the majority of the traffic is about new library and other information systems that are available on the Internet. To subscribe, send a message to *scott@sklib. usask.ca.* Messages for the list are sent to *lib_hytelnet @sask.usask.ca.*

11.5. Network Seminars

Several organizations provide seminars or tutorials regarding the Internet, its use, and technology. Some of these seminars are aimed at the specific constituency of the organization. However, many such seminars, even those offered by network service providers, are open to any interested user.

The following is a list of those organizations that we know offer or have offered informational seminars about using the Internet. Contact them directly for more information.

Other organizations, especially service providers, undoubtedly also offer seminars or tutorials. If you are joining the Internet and are interested in seminars, it is a good idea to ask your prospective network service provider if they offer this type of support.

InterNIC

InterNIC Information Services provides or coordinates seminars on different topics of interest to network users and administrations. In addition, they are working out agreements with other seminar providers for registration discounts.

For more information, contact:

> InterNIC Information Services
> 800 444 4345
> +1 619 455 4600
> FAX: +1 619 455 3990
> info@is.internic.net

CERFnet

CERFnet provides seminars for all its members and non-members. Seminars cover the following topics:

- Tools for Trouble Shooting Your Network
- Network Information Services
- Navigating the Internet
- Network Security
- Politics and Economics of Campus/Enterprise Nets

The contact information for CERFnet is:

> CERFnet
> 800 876 2373
> +1 619 455 3900
> help@cerf.net

CONCERT

From time to time CONCERT gives seminars at several levels: building basic LANs, fundamentals of TCP/IP networking, and advanced internet topics. These seminars are especially aimed at new sites being connected to CONCERT, but others may attend.

The contact information for CONCERT is:

> CONCERT
> Joe Ragland
> +1 919 248 1404
> jrr@concert.net

Interop Company

Interop Company was founded in 1985 as an educational organization to further the understanding of current and emerging standards and technologies within the fields of computer networking and communications.

Their approach is to identify the key issues and leading experts from industry, government, academic, and research communities to create new forums for facilitating education and progress. Their purpose is to be the conduit for dissemination of information and to promote cooperative efforts within the communications industry.

Their activities include the yearly Interop Conferences and Exhibitions, seminars and on-site training; protocol extension forums; marketing and consumer education; consulting; and publishing the technical journal, *ConneXions— The Interoperability Report.*

For additional information about the Interop Company, contact:

```
Interop Company
480 San Antonio Road #100
Mountain View, CA 94040
800 468 3767, ext 2502
+1 415 941 3399, ext 2502
FAX: +1 415 949 1779
info@interop.com (for general queries)
connexions@interop.com (for ConneXions subscription queries)
```

JvNCnet

JvNCnet runs a symposium series that is open to both JvNCnet members and the general public. The symposiums are held every other month, and usually take place at Princeton University. They are intended to cover both introductory and advanced networking topics. Topics in the past have included: Network Security, Introduction to TCP/IP, Applications of the Internet. Future topics will cover Domain Name Service, Network News, Mail, Network Operations, a repeat of Applications of the Internet, SNMP, etc.

Contact information for JvNCnet is:

```
JvNCnet
Sergio F. Heker
Allison Pihl
800 358 4437
+1 609 258 2400
market@jvnc.net
```

Merit Networking Seminars

Merit Network, Inc., manager of MichNet, Michigan's state-wide network, and the NSFNET backbone since 1987, sponsors seminars for beginning and intermediate Internet users.

In the area of education, presentations have focused on issues such as network applications in education from the elementary grades through the college level.

For beginning and intermediate network users, seminars on "navigating" the Internet and an introduction to internetworking and TCP/IP have been provided.

For further details, contact:

Merit Network, Inc.
1075 Beal Avenue
Ann Arbor, MI 48109-2112
800 666 3748
+1 313 936 3000
seminar@merit.edu

MIDnet

MIDnet will provide training to members for their technical staff and also to their information service or support staff. For the technical training MIDnet will cover topics such as how the network is configured, how the routers work and how to configure them, and guidelines on how to establish name service.

The informational training covers the basics of Telnet, FTP, and e-mail. In addition, pointers are given on where to look for information and resources that already exist.

For additional information about MIDnet contact:

MIDnet
Dale Finkelson
+1 402 472 5032
dmf@westie.unl.edu

NEARnet

NEARnet provides training for new members which covers topics such as IP, DNS, and mail configuration. They also provide user services training for member sites.

NEARnet holds periodic meetings which have included timely topics such as "Building the Open Road," NEARnet and NSFNET status reports, K-12 Educational planning, and technical topics such as Wide Area Information Services, Internet Security, and Privacy Enhanced Mail.

The contact information for NEARnet is:

> NEARnet
> +1 617 873 8730
> nearnet-staff@nic.near.net

NERComP Special Interest Group on Wide Area Networks (WAN)

NERComP, the New England Regional Computing Program, is a 52-college association promoting academic computing. In the past they have presented a hands-on workshop called "Navigating the Internet." Instructors from the Information Systems Department and Information Resource Center of Clark University in Worcester, Massachusetts, discuss, demonstrate, and propose various methods for supporting the Internet set of user tools as applied in a smaller university/college context.

Specific topics that are discussed include: an overview of the Internet, Internet mail, File Transfer Protocol (FTP), and Telnet.

Discussions are supported by hands-on access. Terminals are provided on each desk in order to allow attendees to enter network commands at the same time instruction is taking place.

For additional information about NERComP and this seminar, contact:

Robert Gibbs, President
NERComP, Inc.
350 Lincoln Street
Hingham, MA 02043
+1 617 740 0001
nercomp@dartmouth.edu

NorthwestNet

NorthwestNet provides annual seminars as events during their annual meeting. There are typically a half dozen topics covered in each of three categories: Technical Services, User Services, and Keynote Focus. The first category typically includes workshops addressing such topics as Domain Name Services, e-mail applications, X.500 directory services, telecommunications technology, etc. The second category includes topics such as user training, documentation resources, Internet tools tutorials, etc. And the final category addresses topics within the chosen keynote focus, for example, K-12, libraries, and health care.

The contact information for NorthWestNet is:

NorthWestNet
Eric Hood
+1 206 562 3000
ehood@nwnet.net

NYSERNet

NYSERNet provides several meetings, seminars, and tutorials for the broad range of their user community. NYSERNet User Meetings are held annually in conjunction with their board of directors meeting and give NYSERNet constituents a chance to address affiliate concerns and to showcase their institution's use of NYSERNet. The NYSERNet Library Networking Interest Group meets once or twice a year so representatives of more than 300 libraries can better bring the telecommunications technologies available through NYSERNet to their users. The NYSERNet Pre-College Networking Interest Group includes more than 400 educators in both college and pre-college communities and meets once or twice a year.

PSITech: The Tech User's Group, meets quarterly to allow NYSERNet affiliate technical contacts to meet face-to-face with PSInet network engineers and service providers so they can jointly shape the future of internetworking technology and service across PSINet.

PSI TCP/IP and OSI Internetworking Tutorials are offered three times per year, extend over a three-day period, and cover a broad range of topics, from basic network applications to network security and domain name service theory.

For more information about NYSERNet contact:

> NYSERNet
> +1 315 443 4120
> info@nysernet.org

OARnet

OARnet provides seminars covering what the Internet is, what kinds of resources are available through the Internet, and seminars that describe OARnet's services in particular.

Contact:

> OARnet
> +1 614 292 8100
> nic@.net

Performance Systems International, Inc. (PSI)

PSI offers tutorials for its customers three or four times a year. For more information, contact:

> Performance Systems International, Inc.
> 800 827 7482
> +1 703 620 6651
> FAX: +1 703 620 4586
> tutorial-register@psi.com

PREPnet

PREPnet has provided seminars on demand as training for its members, but does not have a pre-scheduled program. Presentations have included an overview of using the Internet, with specific information tailored to the member's requirements or desires.

For additional information, the contact for PREPnet is:

PREPnet
Thomas W. Bajzek
+1 412 268 7870
twb+@andrew.cmu.edu

WiscNet

WiscNet's User Services Committee provides training materials (model documents and special seminars) to user support staffs at member sites. A model User Guide document covers concepts of e-mail, remote login, and file transfer. Sections designed to be adapted locally by each site cover the site's particular policies and practices. In addition, general policies affecting network uses are explained.

Their training seminars are one-day sessions covering a similar range of topics, with additional materials of interest to local consulting staff, including e-mail gateways, nslookup, USENET, and setting up FTP servers.

For more information about WiscNet, contact:

WiscNet
Tad Pinkerton
+1 608 262 8874
tad@cs.wisc.edu

11.6. Supercomputer Centers

When the NSFNET was originally built in 1987, its purpose was to connect six NSF supercomputer centers via a cross-country backbone to facilitate the exchange of research and information between scientists nationally and internationally.

The line between supercomputers, mainframes, minicomputers, and workstations has been blurring more and more as improvements in technology speed up low-end systems. As recently as ten years ago, supercomputers were one to two hundred times faster than a typical mainframe computer. Today, the differential is as low as five or six. However, although the speed of a supercomputer's CPU may no longer be significantly greater than that of a workstation, they have special processors that allow them to do vector calculations many times more quickly than a mainframe or workstation. This advantage makes them an invaluable tool for large simulations.

At this writing there are seventeen supercomputer centers connected to the NSFNET; however, we've listed only a few of general interest. More detailed information about each and a complete list of all supercomputer centers can be obtained from the *Internet Resource Guide* [19].

Most of these supercomputer centers not only permit a variety of access methods to their computing facilities for qualified, approved researchers; they also often provide consulting services, newsletters, training services, documentation, and software. Costs for services vary; sometimes services are free to researchers and available to industry on a cost-recovery basis. Contact each center for specific information.

Cornell National Supercomputer Facility
Pat Colasurdo, User Accounts Coordinator
Center for Theory and Simulation in Science and Engineering
265 Olin Hall
Ithaca, NY 14853-5201
psfy@cornellf.tn.cornell.edu
+1 607 255 8686
Services: Supercomputing resources for researchers nationwide.
Proposals for time subject to peer review.

National Center for Atmospherical Research (NCAR)
Scientific Computing Division
John Adams
NCAR/SCD
P.O. Box 3000
Boulder, CO 90303
scdinfo@ncar.ucar.edu
+1 303 497 1225
Services: Supports research in atmospheric, oceanographic, and related sciences. Approved accounts are allocated time on a cost recovery basis to users with NSF grants.

National Center for Supercomputing Applications (NCSA)
National Center for Academic Computing
152 Computing Applications Building
605 E. Springfield Avenue
Champaign, IL 61820
consult@ncsaa.ncsa.uiuc.edu

+1 217 244 0072
Services: Open to any academic researcher; requests subject to peer
review.

National Energy Research Supercomputer Center
JoAnne Rivelli
revelli%nersc@nersc.gov
+1 415 422 4228
or
Anita Winfield
winfield%nersc@nersc.gov
+1 415 422 4022
Services: Open to researchers and collaborators with DoE sponsorship.

Ohio Supercomputer Center
Ohio Supercomputer Center
1224 Kinnear Road
Columbus, OH 43212
oschelp@osc.edu
+1 614 292 9248
Services: Supports research at Ohio State colleges and universities, but
also allows out-of-state researchers through its OSC Visitors Program,
and industry use of resources on a cost-recovery basis.

Pittsburgh Supercomputer Center
Pittsburgh Supercomputing Center
Mellon Institute Building
4400 Fifth Avenue
Pittsburgh, PA 15213
consult@a.psc.edu
+1 412 268 6350
Services: Open to all, supports a wide variety of
scientific and engineering disciplines.

San Diego Supercomputer Center
San Diego Supercomputer Center
P.O. Box 85608
San Diego, CA 92138-5608
consultant@sdsc.edu
+1 619 534 5000
Services: Open to all scientists and researchers.

Supercomputing Services, University of Calgary
SuperComputing Services
The University of Calgary
390-1620, 29th Street, N.W.
Calgary, Alberta, T2N 4L7
CANADA
(403) 221-8900
Services: Open to all scientists and researchers.

Arizona State University Supercomputing Services
ECA-311, ODP-0101
Arizona State University
Tempe, AZ 85287-0101
kgrmc@asucray.inre.asu.edu
+1 602 965 5677
Services: Supports Arizona State University users,
and commercial users on a cost-recovery basis.

FURTHER READING

This chapter provides references to further reading on many of the subjects discussed in this book. We mean it as a kind of informal, annotated bibliography that highlights some of the different types of references that we think would be most useful for new Internet users.

12.1. Introductory Books

The following books introduce the Internet. Many of them have brief sections on Internet access, but joining the Internet is not the primary focus of any of them. However, they are excellent resources once you are connected for discovering how to use the Internet, what resources the Internet holds, and with what networks you can communicate.

Kehoe, B. P. *Zen and the Art of the Internet: A Beginner's Guide.* Englewood Cliffs, NJ: Prentice-Hall, Inc.; 1993. 112 p.

Krol, E. *The Whole Internet User's Guide and Catalog.* Sebastopol, CA: O'Reilly and Associates; 1992 September. 376 p.

Frey, D.; Adams, R. *!%@:: A Directory of Electronic Mail Addressing and Networks.* Newton, MA: O'Reilly and Associates; 1989 August. 284 p.

Hardie, E.T.L.; Neou, V. *Internet: Mailing Lists.* Englewood Cliffs, NJ: Prentice-Hall, Inc.; 1993. 346 p.

LaQuey, T.; Ryer, J.C. *The Internet Companion: A Beginner's Guide to Global Networking.* Reading, MA: Addison-Wesley; 1992. 196 p.

LaQuey, T.L., ed. *Users' Directory of Computer Networks.* Bedford, MA: Digital Press; 1990 July. 630 p.

Quarterman, J.S. *The Matrix: Computer Networks and Conferencing Systems Worldwide.* Bedford, MA: Digital Press; 1990. 719 p.

The following books are excellent technical introductions to internetworking and networking protocols.

Comer, D.E. *Internetworking with TCP/IP, Volume I: Principles, Protocols, and Architecture, Second Edition.* Englewood Cliffs, NJ: Prentice-Hall, Inc.; 1990.

Comer, D.E.; Stevens, D.L. *Internetworking with TCP/IP, Volume II: Design, Implementation, and Internals.* Englewood Cliffs, NJ: Prentice-Hall, Inc.; 1991.

Comer, D.E.; Stevens, D.L. *Internetworking with TCP/IP, Volume III: Client-Server Programming and Applications–BSD Socket Version.* Englewood Cliffs, NJ: Prentice-Hall, Inc.; 1992.

12.2. Resource Guides

Many service providers and mid-level networks write the guides and make them available to users. Following is a list of several Internet resource guides that focus on alerting people to what the Internet offers. None of them is comprehensive (it is virtually impossible to have a comprehensive guide to the Internet), but users can learn something from each one. Although some of them are available in hardcopy, these were primarily designed to be available online.

Internet Resource Guide, 1992, [ca 250 p].

In 1989, the NSF Network Service Center (NNSC), which was the NSFNET Information Center before the InterNIC was established, created and published the first edition of the *Internet Resource Guide*. The goals of *Guide* were to increase the visibility of resources available via NSFNET and other parts of the Internet, and to expose users to those facilities that would help them do their work better. Sections of the document have been updated several times since its creation. Its editors hope that as copies of the guide are distributed throughout the community, additional organizations that maintain resources not yet mentioned will submit new descriptions for inclusion in the guide.

InterNIC Directory and Database Services now has responsibility for maintaining this guide. The guide is retrievable via anonymous FTP from host ds.internic.net in the directory resource-guide. The guide is also accessible via the InterNIC Gopher. For more information, send a message to *admin@ds.internic.net*.

This guide is a very helpful introduction to a great many Internet resources.

The Internet Passport: NorthWestNet's Guide to Our World Online. 4th ed. Kochmer, J. and NorthWestNet. Bellevue, WA: NorthWestNet Northwest Academic Computing Consortium, Inc. 1992 December.

and

NorthWestNet User Services Internet Resource Guide (NUSIRG). 1991 November, 300 p.

These guides were created by and are available from the people at NorthWestNet. *The Internet Passport* is NorthWestNet's more current information; NUSIRG was last updated November 1991, but will continue to be available for some time.

Contact NorthWestNet for the most up-to-date availability and pricing information for these useful guides.

NorthWestNet
NUSIRG Orders
15400 SE 30th Place
Suite 202
Bellevue, WA 98007
+1 206 562 3000
info@nwnet.net

Information Available on the Internet: A Guide to Selected Sources. SURAnet; 1992 April, 35 p.

This guide is available online via anonymous FTP from the host ftp.sura.net in the *nic* directory. It contains pointers to sources of information available on the Internet.

NYSERNet New User's Guide to Useful and Unique Resources on the Internet. NYSERNET; 1992, 137 p.

This guide includes information about fifty interesting internetworking resources and services, most of which are available via Telnet or FTP. The guide not only describes the services, but provides step-by-step instructions explaining how to access each service.

Version 2.2 is now available for anonymous FTP from the host nysernet.org in the directory */pub/guides*. The file is called *Guide.V.2.2.text*.

The guide is also available in hardcopy for $25 ($18 for NYSERNet members). Payment can be made by check, purchase order, or money order, payable to NYSERNet, Inc.

To order, or for more information, contact:

New User's Guide
NYSERNet, Inc.
111 College Place,
Syracuse, NY 13244-4100
editor@nysernet.org
315 443 4120

CICNet Resource Guide, Holbrook, J.P; Pruess, C.S., eds. 1992 June, 218 p.

This is a general guide to some useful Internet resources, with a focus on materials of interest to and available from the CICNet region. As the CICNet region includes most of the "Big 10" schools, these materials are also of interest to other users of the Internet. This guide began with a version of NYSERNet's guide, described above.

The CICNet Resource Guide will be available in electronic form and accessible using various online tools. For details about how to access this guide online, use anonymous FTP to access nic.cic.net, directory */pub/resourceguide*. This directory will contain the latest information on updates and online versions of this guide.

Paper copies of the guide are available for $27. To order via check or money order, or for additional information, contact:

CICNet, Inc.
Attn: Kim Shaffer
2901 Hubbard, Pod A
Ann Arbor, MI 48109
info@cic.net
+1 313 998 6103
FAX:+1 313 998 6105

12.3. Useful Online Files

This section serves as a catch-all to list several information files that are accessible via the Internet.

Internet Monthly Report (IMR)

The *Internet Monthly Report* is an online report that communicates to the Internet the accomplishments, milestones reached, or problems discovered by several organizations participating in the Internet. Many Internet organizations provide monthly updates of their activities for inclusion in this report.

You can receive the report online by joining the mailing list that distributes the report. Requests to be added or deleted from the *Internet Monthly Report* list should be sent to *cooper@isi.edu*.

Zen and the Art of the Internet: A Beginner's Guide to the Internet, Kehoe, B., ed. 1992 March, 100 p.

This first version of the later book is available online for anonymous FTP from the host ftp.cs.widener.edu in the *pub/zen* directory. Get the README file first, which provides an introduction and overview of the guide. This guide is not available in hardcopy, but was later updated and published as a book.

List of Lists

The *List of Lists* is the nickname for a file that lists electronic mail discussion groups. The list is maintained at SRI and contains descriptions of hundreds of special interest groups. For each, there is an explanation of how to join the discussion. The groups are extremely varied, ranging from technical computer topics to discussions about many scientific disciplines to educational subjects to many fun, hobby lists. The file is on the host ftp.nisc.sri.com as *netinfo/interest-groups*. It is the basis for the book *Internet: Mailing Lists* as well.

The Internetworking Guide, Chew, J.J. 1992, 10 p.

This useful file "documents methods of sending mail from one network to another. It represents the aggregate knowledge of the readers of *comp.mail.misc* and many contributors elsewhere." It is often posted to mailing lists, but is available for anonymous FTP from both *ftp.msstate.edu* as *pub/docs/internetwork-mail-guide* and on *ariel.unm.edu* as *library/network.guide*.

12.4. FYIs and RFCs

The following FYIs and RFCs are good places to start when learning about the Internet. See also Appendix III for a list of other FYI and RFCs that may be of interest. FYI documents are an excellent source of introductory information. Typically, several new FYIs are published each year, so be sure to check with a Network Information Center for the newest list. Remember that the index is probably out-of-date by the time you read this. In addition, several of these RFCs will probably have been updated, so be sure to get the most recent version.

FYI 19. Hoffman, E.; Jackson, L. *FYI on Introducing the Internet: A Short Bibliography of Introductory Internetworking Readings for the Network Novice.* 1993 May; Also RFC 1463. 4 p.

FYI 20. Krol, E.; Hoffman, E. *What is the Internet?* 1993 May; Also RFC 1462. 11 p.

FYI 3. Bowers, K.L.; LaQuey, T.L.; Reynolds, J.K.; Roubicek, K.; Stahl, M.K.; Yuan, A. *FYI on Where to Start: A Bibliography of Internetworking Information.* 1990 August; Also RFC 1175. 42 p. (This FYI will soon be updated.)

RFC 1118. Krol, E. *Hitchhikers Guide to the Internet.* 1989 September; 24 p. (This RFC is updated by his book.)

FYI 4. Malkin, G.S.; Marine, A.N. *FYI on Questions and Answers: Answers to Commonly Asked "New Internet User" Questions.* 1991 February; Also RFC 1325. 32 p.

FYI 7. Malkin, G.S.; Marine, A.N.; Reynolds, J.K. *FYI on Questions and Answers: Answers to Commonly Asked "Experienced Internet User" Questions.* 1991 February; Also RFC 1207. 15 p.

FYI 10. Martin, J. *There's Gold in Them Thar Networks! or Searching for Treasure in All the Wrong Places.* 1991 December; Also RFC 1290. 27 p.

RFC 1296. Lottor, M. *Internet Growth (1981-1991).* 1992 January; 9 p.

RFC 1087. Internet Activities Board. *Ethics and the Internet.* 1989 January, 2 p.

12.5. Newsletters and Journals

Many network providers offer newsletters as part of their services. These newsletters often highlight uses of the Internet or resources of particular interest. Often these newsletters are available online, or at no cost upon request, even if you are not a constituent of that particular network. Be sure to ask your service provider if they offer a newsletter. In addition, FYI 3 has a section that lists several newsletters that are available.

The following two newsletters offer substantial information about the Internet on a global scale. They may include some technical information as well.

Internet Society News, Internet Society. 1895 Preston White Drive, Suite 100, Reston, VA, 22091, USA.

Matrix News, Matrix Information and Directory Services, Inc. Building 2 Suite 300, 1120 South Capitol of Texas Highway, Austin, TX, 78746, USA.

ConneXions—The Interoperability Report. Several articles in this excellent journal proved helpful in writing this book. It often provides introductions to established and emerging Internet technologies. A free sample issue and list of back issues are available upon request.

ConneXions—The Interoperability Report is published monthly by:

Interop Company
480 San Antonio Road
Suite 100
Mountain View, CA 94040
USA
+1 415 941 3399
FAX: +1 415 949 1779
Toll-free (in USA):1-800-INTEROP
connexions@interop.com

12.6. Specific Topics

This section lists some RFCs that discuss specific topics that were addressed in this book. In addition, Appendix VII categorizes several RFCs by technical topic. Please refer there for references to RFCs on such topics as network management, exterior and interior gateway protocols, directory services (including the Domain Name System), and routing, as well as network, internet, and transport layer protocols. The Appendix also lists many utility and application protocols, including those related to file transfer, electronic mail, and Telnet.

Domain Name System

RFC 1034. Mockapetris, P.V. *Domain Names - Concepts and Facilities*. 1987 November; 55 p.

RFC 1101. Mockapetris, P.V. DNS *Encoding of Network Names and Other Types*. 1989 April; 14 p.

RFC 974. Partridge, C. *Mail Routing and the Domain System*. 1986 January; 7 p.

RFC 1032. Stahl, M.K. *Domain Administrators Guide*. 1987 November; 14 p.

RFC 1033. Lottor, M. *Domain Administrators Operations Guide*. 1987 November; 22 p.

Network Security

Note that RFC 1135 has an extensive bibliography of further reading, and that FYI 8 lists several sources for further security information.

FYI 8. Holbrook, J.P.; Reynolds, J.K., eds. *Site Security Handbook*. 1991 July; Also RFC 1244. 101 p.

RFC 1135. Reynolds, J.K. *Helminthiasis of the Internet*. 1989 December; 33 p.

RFC 1281. Pethia, R.D.; Crocker, S.D.; Fraser, B.Y. *Guidelines for the Secure Operation of the Internet*. 1991 November; 12 p.

RFC 1108. Kent, S.T. *U.S. Department of Defense Security Options for the Internet Protocol.* 1991 November; 17 p.

Some GOSIP Documentation

RFC 1169. Cerf, V.G.; Mills, K.L. *Explaining the role of GOSIP.* 1990 August; 15 p.

National Institute of Standards and Technology. *Government Open Systems Interconnection Profile (GOSIP).* 1991; FIPS-Pub 146-1. 83 p.

See also Appendix IX for more information on obtaining GOSIP documentation.

BIBLIOGRAPHY AND REFERENCES

References

[1] Frey, D.; Adams, R. *!%@:: A Directory of Electronic Mail Addressing and Networks*. Newton, MA: O'Reilly and Associates; 1989 August. 284 p.

[2] Quarterman, J.S. *The Matrix: Computer Networks and Conferencing Systems Worldwide*. Bedford, MA: Digital Press; 1990. 719 p.

[3] RFC 1296. Lottor, M. *Internet Growth (1981-1991)*. 1992 January; 9 p.

[4] LaQuey, T.L., ed. *Users' Directory of Computer Networks*. Bedford, MA: Digital Press; 1990 July. 630 p.

[5] *Internet Society News*, Internet Society. 1895 Preston White Drive, Suite 100, Reston, VA, 22091, USA.

[6] *Matrix News*, Matrix Information and Directory Services, Inc. Building 2 Suite 300, 1120 South Capitol of Texas Highway, Austin, TX, 78746, USA.

[7] FYI 4. Malkin, G.S.; Marine, A.N. *FYI on Questions and Answers: Answers to Commonly Asked "New Internet User" Questions*. 1991 February; Also RFC 1325. 42 p.

[8] RFC 1410. Chapin, A.L, ed. *IAB Official Protocol Standards*. 1993 March; 35 p.

[9]   RFC 1135. Reynolds, J.K. *Helminthiasis of the Internet.* 1989 December; 33 p.

[10] RFC 1087. Internet Activities Board. *Ethics and the Internet.* 1989 January; 2 p.

[11] FYI 8. Holbrook, J.P.; Reynolds, J.K., eds. *Site Security Handbook.* 1991 July; Also RFC 1244. 101 p.

[12] RFC 1281. Pethia, R.D.; Crocker, S.D.; Fraser, B.Y. *Guidelines for the Secure Operation of the Internet.* 1991 November; 12 p.

[13] Comer, D.E. *Internetworking with TCP/IP: Principles, Protocols, and Architecture.* Englewood Cliffs, NJ: Prentice-Hall, Inc.; 1988. 382 p.

[14] RFC 1169. Cerf, V.G.; Mills, K.L. *Explaining the Role of GOSIP.* 1990 August; 15 p.

[15] Mogul, J. *Subnetting: A Brief Guide.* Connexions: The Interoperability Report. 3(1): 2-9; 1989 January.

[16] Kahle, B.; Medlar, A. *An Information System for Corporate Users: Wide Area Information Servers.* Connexions: The Interoperability Report. 5(11): 2-9; 1991 November.

[17] Deutsch, P.; Emtage, A.; Heelan, B. *Archie: An Internet Electronic Directory Service.* Connexions: The Interoperability Report. 6(2): 2-9; 1992 February.

[18] RFC 1208. Jacobsen, O.J.; Lynch, D.C. *Glossary of Networking Terms.* 1991 March; 18 p.

[19] NSF Network Service Center. *Internet Resource Guide.* Cambridge, MA: BBN Systems and Technologies Corp; 1989.   [ca 250 p].

[20] FYI 11. Lang, R.; Wright, R. *Catalog of Available X.500 Implementations.* 1991 December; Also RFC 1292. 103 p.

[21] FYI 13. Weider, C.; Reynolds, J.K. *Executive Introduction of Directory Services Using the X.500 Protocol.* 1992 March; 4 p.

[22] Heijne, M.; Deforchaux, P.K.; Stals, B. *Guide to SURFnet.* 1989 December. 62 p.

[23] Barron, B. *Another Use of the Internet: Libraries Online Catalogs.* Connexions: The Interoperability Report. 5(7): 15-19; 1991 July.

[24] RFC 1311. Postel, J.B. ed. *Introduction to the STD Notes.* 1992 March; 5 p.

[25] RFC 1310. Chapin, A.L.; *Internet Standards Process.* 1992 March; 23 p.

[26] FYI 14. Weider, C.; Reynolds, J.K.; Heker, S. *Technical Overview of Directory Services Using the X.500 Protocol.* 1992 March; 16 p.

[27] RFC 1174. Cerf, V. *IAB Recommended Policy on Distributing Internet Identifier Assignment and IAB Recommended Policy Change to Internet "Connected" Status.* 1990 August; 9 p.

[28] Crowcroft, J. *UK Internet Protocol Connectivity Activities.* ConneXions: The Interoperability Report. 5(6): 20-23; 1991 June.

[29] Brunell, M. *Profile: NORDUnet.* ConneXions: The Interoperability Report. 4(11): 18-23; 1990 November.

[30] Chew, J.J. *The Internetworking Guide.* 1990. 10 p. On host ariel.unm.edu as *library/network.guide.*

[31] SRI International, Network Information Systems Center. *Internet Domain Survey.* 1990 October. 1 p. On host ftp.nisc.sri.com as *pub/ zone/report-9210.doc.*

[32] RARE Information Services and User Support Working Group. *User Support and Information Services In Europe: A Status Report.* 1992 October. 65 p. On host mailbase.ac.uk as */pub/rare-wg3-usis/rtr-usis- 92.*

[33] Sterba, M. *Overview of East and Central European Networking Activities.* 1992 November. 12 p. On host ftp.ripe.net as *ripe/docs/ ripe-drafts/ripe-draft-ece.v5.txt.*

[34] Krol, E. *The Whole Internet User's Guide and Catalog.* Newton, MA: O'Reilly and Associates; 1992 September. 376 p.

Bibliography

Bjork, S.; Fischer, N.; Marine, A.; Ward, C.; *DDN New User Guide.* Menlo Park, CA: SRI International, Network Information Systems Center; 1991 February. 79 p.

Carpenter, B.; Fluckiger, F. *Networking at CERN.* NSF Network News. No. 8: 1-4; 1990 September.

Chappell, D. *Components of OSI: A Taxonomy of the Players.* ConneXions: The Interoperability Report. 3(12): 2-10; 1989 December.

Comer, D.E. *Internetworking with TCP/IP, Volume I: Principles, Protocols, and Architecture, Second Edition.* Englewood Cliffs, NJ: Prentice-Hall, Inc.; 1990.

Comer, D.E.; Stevens, D.L. *Internetworking with TCP/IP, Volume II: Design, Implementation, and Internals.* Englewood Cliffs, NJ: Prentice-Hall, Inc.; 1991.

Comer, D.E.; Stevens, D.L. *Internetworking with TCP/IP, Volume III: Client-Server Programmering and Applications - BSD Socket Version.* Englewood Cliffs, NJ: Prentice-Hall, Inc.; 1992.

EUUG Becomes EurOpen. ConneXions: The Interoperability Report. 5(2): 11; 1991 February.

Goldstein, S.; Michau, C. *Convergence of European and North American Research and Academic Networking.* ConneXions: The Interoperability Report. 5(4): 20-27; 1991 April.

The Internet Gopher: A Distributed Information Service. ConneXions: The Interoperability Report. 5(11): 23; 1991 November.

Internetworking: An Introduction. The Wollongong Group, Inc.; 1988 April.

Introduction to the Internet Protocols. Computer Science Facilities Group. Rutgers University; 1988 October.

Kehoe, B. P. *Zen and the Art of the Internet: A Beginner's Guide.* Englewood Cliffs, NJ: Prentice-Hall, Inc.; 1993. 112 p.

LaQuey, T.; Ryer J.C. *The Internet Companion: A Beginner's Guide to Global Networking.* Reading, MA: Addison-Wesley; 1992. 196 p.

Malamud, C. *Exploring the Internet: A Technical Travelogue.* Englewood Cliffs, NJ: Prentice-Hall, Inc.; 1992 August. 376 p.

Mockapetris, P. *The Domain Name System. Proceedings of the IFIP 6.5 Working Conference on Computer Message Services, Nottingham, England, May 1984.* Also as ISI/RS-84-133, 1984 June.

Mockapetris, P. *Domains. In: Internet Protocol Handbook, Volume 4: The Domain Name System (DNS) Handbook.* Menlo Park, CA: SRI Network Information Systems Center; 1989.

Mockapetris, P. *Introducing Domains.* ConneXions: The Interoperability Report. 1(6): 2-4; 1987 October.

Mockapetris, P.; Postel, J.B.; Kirton, P. *Name Server Design for Distributed Systems.* Proceedings of the Seventh International Conference on Computer Communication, Sidney, Australia, 1984 October 30 to November 3. Also *ISI/RS-84-132*, 1984 June.

NNSC Provides a Tour of the Internet. NSF Network News. 10(11); 1991 August.

Perry, D.G.; Blumenthal, S.H.; Hinden, R.M. *The ARPANET and the DARPA Internet.* Library Hi Tech. 6(22): 51-62, 1988.

RFC 822. Crocker, D. *Standard for the Format of ARPA Internet Text Messages.* 1982 August; 47 p.

RFC 920. Postel, J.B.; Reynolds, J.K. *Domain Requirements.* 1984 October; 14 p.

RFC 1032. Stahl, M. *Domain Administrators Guide.* 1987 November; 14 p.

RFC 1033. Lottor, M. *Domain Administrators Operations Guide.* 1987 November; 22 p.

RFC 1034. Mockapetris, P. *Domain Names - Concepts and Facilities.* 1987 November; 55 p.

RFC 1108. Kent, S. *U. S. Department of Defense Security Options for the Internet Protocol.* 1991 November; 17 p.

RFC 1055. Romkey, J.L. *Nonstandard for Transmission of IP Datagrams over Serial Lines: SLIP.* 1988 June; 6 p.

RFC 1160. Cerf, V. *The Internet Activities Board.* 1990 May; 11 p.

RFC 1171. Perkins, D. *Point-to-Point Protocol for the Transmission of Multi-Protocol Datagrams over Point-to-Point Links.* 1990 July; 48 p.

RFC 1123. Braden, R.T.,ed. *Requirements for Internet Hosts - Application and Support.* 1989 October; 98 p.

RFC 1290. Martin, J. *There's Gold in Them Thar Networks! or Searching for Treasure in All the Wrong Places.* 1991 December; 26 p.

Special Issue: Network Management and Security. ConneXions: The
    Interoperability Report. (4)8; 1990 August.

Stockman, B. *Current Status on Networking in Europe.* ConneXions: The
    Interoperability Report. 5(7): 10-14; 1991 July.

Tennant, R.; Ober, J.; Lipow, A.G. *Crossing the Internet Threshold: An
    Instructional Handbook.* San Carlos, CA: Library Solutions Press; 1992
    October. 134 p.

ACRONYM LIST

This appendix presents a list of acronyms you will find in this document.

AARNet	Australian Academic and Research Network
ACONET	Austrian Network
ADMD	Administrative Management Domain
ANS	Advanced Network and Services, Inc.
ANSI	American National Standards Institute
ARPANET	Advanced Research Projects Agency Network
ASCII	American Standard Code for Information Interchange
ASN	Autonomous System Number
AUP	Acceptable Use Policy
BARRNET	Bay Area Regional Research Network
BBN	Bolt Beranek and Newman, Inc.
BIND	Berkeley Internet Name Domain
BGP	Border Gateway Protocol
CCIRN	Coordinating Committee for Intercontinental Research Networks
CCITT	International Telegraph and Telephone Consultative Committee

CEN	European Committee for Standardization
CENELEC	European Committee for Electrotechnical Standardization
CERFnet	California Education and Research Federation Network
CERN	Organisation Europeenne pour la Recherche Nuclearie
CERT	Computer Emergency Response Team
CIAC	Computer Incident Advisory Capability
CICnet	Committee on Institutional Cooperation Network
CIX	Commercial Internet Exchange
CNSRT	Computer Network Security Response Team
CONCERT	Communications for North Carolina Education, Research and Technology Network
CONCISE	COSINE Network's Central Information Service for Europe
COS	Cooperation for Open Systems
COSINE	Cooperation for Open Systems Interconnection Networking in Europe
CPMU	COSINE Project Management Unit
CREN	Corporation for Research and Education Networking
CRIM	Centre de Recherche Informatique de Montreal
CSERN	Czechoslovakian part of EARN
CSRC	Computer Security Resource and Response Center
CSUUG	Czechoslovakian part of EUnet
DARPA	Defense Advanced Research Projects Agency
DCA	Defense Communications Agency [now DISA]
DDN	Defense Data Network
DDN NIC	Defense Data Network Network Information Center
DDN SCC	Defense Data Network Security Coordination Center
DIGI	Deutsche Intressen Gemeinschaft Internet
DISA	Defense Information Systems Agency [formerly DCA]
DISI	Directory Information Services Infrastructure
DNS	Domain Name System
DoD	Department of Defense
DoE	Department of Energy
DRI	Defense Research Internet
DSA	Directory System Agent

DUA	Directory User Agent
EARN	European Academic Research Network
EBCDIC	Extended Binary Coded Decimal Interchange Code
EGP	Exterior Gateway Protocol
EUnet	Europe Network
EUUG	European Unix Users Group (now EurOpen)
FARNET	Federation of American Research Networks
FCCSET	Federal Coordinating Committee on Science, Engineering, and Technology
FDDI	Fiber Distributed Data Interface
FIPS	Federal Information Processing Standard
FNC	Federal Networking Council [formerly FRICC]
FRD	Foundation for Research Development
FRICC	Federal Research Internet Coordinating Committee [now FNC]
FTP	File Transfer Protocol
FYI	For Your Information
GARR	Gruppo Armonizzazione delle Reti per la Ricerca
GNMP	Government Network Management Profile
GOSIP	Government Open Systems Interconnection Profile
HEANET	Higher Education Authority Network
HEPnet	High Energy Physics Network
IAB	Internet Architecture Board [formerly Internet Activities Board]
ICM	International Connections Manager
ICMP	Intrnet Control Message Protocol
IEEE	Institute of Electrical and Electronics Engineers
IEN	Internet Experimental Note
IESG	Internet Engineering Steering Group
IETF	Internet Engineering Task Force
ILAN	Israel Network
IMR	Internet Monthly Report
IN-ADDR	Inverse Addressing
INet	Indiana Network
IP	Internet Protocol
IR	Internet Registry

IRSG	Internet Research Steering Group
IRTF	Internet Research Task Force
IS	International Standard
ISO	International Organization for Standardization
ISOC	Internet Society
ITESM	Instituto Tecnologico y de Estudios Superiores de Monterrey
ITS	Internet Technology Series
IUnet	Italian segment of EUnet
IXI	International X.25 Infrastructure
JAIN	Japan Academic Inter-university Network
JANET	Joint Academic Network
JUNET	Japan University Network (now JAIN)
JvNCnet	John von Neumann Center Network
K-12	Kindergarten through 12th grade
LAN	Local Area Network
MEXnet	Mexico Network
MFEnet	Magnetic Fusion Energy Network
MIB	Management Information Base
MIDnet	Midwest Network
MILNET	Military Network
MIL STD	Military Standard
NAIC	Network Applications and Information Center
NASA	National Aeronautics and Space Administration
NBnet	New Brunswick Network
NBS	National Bureau of Standards [now NIST]
NCC	Network Coordination Center
NCP	Network Control Program
NEARnet	New England Academic and Research Network
NERComP	New England Regional Computing Program
NIC	Network Information Center
NIST	National Institute of Standards and Technology [formerly NBS]
NNSC	NSF Network Service Center
NLnet	Newfoundland and Labrador Network

NNTP	Network News Transfer Protocol
NOC	Network Operations Center
NORDUnet	Nordic countries network
NREN	National Research and Education Network
NS	Name Server
NSF	National Science Foundation
NSFNET	National Science Foundation Network
NSI	NASA Science Internet
NSTN	Nova Scotia Technology Network
NVT	Network Virtual Terminal
NYSERNet	New York State Education and Research Network
NZUNINET	New Zealand University Network
OARnet	Ohio Academic Research Network
OIW	OSI Implementors Workshop
ONet	Ontario Network
OSI	Open Systems Interconnection
OSTP	Office of Science and Technology Policy
PACCOM	Pacific Computer Communications
PC	Personal Computer
PIPEX	Public IP Exchange
PPP	Point-to-Point Protocol
PREPnet	Pennsylvania Research and Economic Partnership Network
PSCNet	Pittsburgh Supercomputing Center Network
PSI	Performance Systems International, Inc.
PSN	Packet Switch Node
RARE	Reseaux Associes pour la Recherche Europeenne (Association of European Research Networks)
RFC	Request For Comments
RIPE	Reseaux IP Europeans
RIPE NCC	RIPE Network Coordination Center
RR	Resource Record
RISQ	Reseau Interordinatuears Scientifique Quebecois
SASK#net	Saskatchewan Network
SDSCnet	San Diego Supercomputer Center

SESQUINET	Texas Sesquicentennial Network
SFTP	Simple File Transfer Protocol
SINET	NACSIS Science Information Network
SLIP	Serial Line Internet Protocol
SMTP	Simple Mail Transfer Protocol
SNA	Systems Network Architecture
SPAN	Space Physics Analysis Network
SRI NISC	SRI International, Network Information Systems Center
STD RFC	Standard RFC
SUNET	Swedish Network
SURAnet	Southeastern Universities Research Association Network
SURFnet	Netherlands Network
SURIS	Iceland Network
SWITCH	Switzerland Network
TCP	Transmission Control Protocol
THEnet	Texas Higher Education Network
TISN	University of Tokyo International Science Network
TP	Transport Protocol
UDP	User Datagram Protocol
ULCC	University of London Computer Centre
UNINET-ZA	South African Academic and Research Network
UNINETT	Norway Network
UUCP	Unix to Unix Copy Program
VERnet	Virginia Education and Research Network
W3	World Wide Web
WAIS	Wide Area Information Server
WELL	Whole Earth 'lectronic Link
WIDE	Widely Integrated Distributed Environment
WVNET	West Virginia Network
WWW	World Wide Web
YUNAC	Yugoslav Academic and Research Network

ALL PROVIDERS ALPHABETICALLY

This appendix lists all the service providers that appear in Chapter 4 and Chapter 7 in alphabetical order by name of the network or provider. Complete contact information is presented here, including postal addresses. Information regarding the area a provider serves is also included. U.S. provider listings also note the access services they offer. Non-U.S. provider access services are not listed because they often do not fall into the neat categories we used for U.S. providers. Please consult the fuller descriptions of these providers that are presented in Chapter 7.

SRI is aware that this list is not comprehensive. We often seek new information for it, and are always happy to accept references for new listings. Please send such information to nisc@nisc.sri.com or to the address in the Overview.

AARNet
Geoff Huston
The Australian Academic and Research Network
GPO Box 1142
Canberra ACT 2601
AUSTRALIA
+61 6 249 3385
G.Huston@aarnet.edu.au
Area Served: Australia

a2i communications
1211 Park Avenue #202
San Jose, CA 95126-2924
info@rahul.net
Area Served: San Jose, CA, area (408 area code)
Services: Dialup e-mail, SunOS software development environment.

Advanced Network and Services, Inc.
(ANS) and ANS CO+RE
2901 Hubbard Rd.
Ann Arbor, MI 48105
800 456 8267
+1 313 663 2482
info@ans.net
Area Served: U.S. and International
Services: Network connections. ANS
CO+RE is a wholly owned, taxable
subsidiary of ANS. ANS is a not-for-profit
organization.

AlterNet
3110 Fairview Park Drive
Suite 570
Falls Church, VA 22042
800 488 6383
+1 703 204 8000
FAX: +1 703 204 8001
alternet-info@uunet.uu.net
Area Served: U.S.
Services: Network connections; a product
of UUNET Technologies.

America Online, Inc.
8619 Westwood Center Drive
Vienna, VA 22182-2285
800 827 6364
+1 703 8933 6288
info@aol.com
Area Served: U.S. and Canada
Services: Dialup e-mail.

Anterior Technology
P.O. Box 1206
Menlo Park, CA 94026-1206
+1 415 328 5615
FAX: +1 415 322 1753
info@radiomail.net
Area Served: San Francisco Bay area
Services: Dialup e-mail; RadioMail.

ARIADNE
ARIADNE Network Help Desk
NRCPS Demokritos, 153 10 Athens
GREECE
+30 1 6513392
+30 1 6536351
FAX: +30 1 6532910
FAX: +30 1 6532175
postmaster@isosun.ariadne-t.gr
postmast@grathdem
S=postmaster; OU=isosun; O=ariadne-t;
P=ariadne-t; C=gr;
Yannis Corovesis
ycor@isosun.ariadne-t.gr
C=gr; ADMD= ; PRMD=ariadne-t;
OU=iosun; S=corovesis; G=yannis;
Takis Telonis
ttel@isosun.ariadne-t.gr
Area Served: Greece

ARnet
Alberta Research Network
Director of Information Systems
Alberta Research Council
Box 8330, Station F
Edmonton, Alberta
CANADA, T6H 5X2
Attn: Walter Neilson
+1 403 450 5188
FAX: +1 403 461 2651
neilson@TITAN.arc.ab.ca
Area Served: Alberta, Canada

ARNET
UNDP Project ARG-86-026
Ministerio de Relaciones Exteriores y
Culto
Reconquista 1088 1er. Piso - Informatica
(1003) Capital Federal
Buenos Aires
ARGENTINA
Attention: Jorge Marcelo Amodio
pete@atina.ar
+541 313 8082
FAX: +541 814 4824
Area Served: Argentina

BALTBONE
Ants Work
Deputy Dirctor
Institute of Cybernetics
Estonian Academy of Sciences
Akadeemie tee 21
EE 0108 TALLINN
ESTONIA
ants@ioc.ee
+007 0142 525622
FAX: +007 0142 527901
Area Served: Baltic countries: Estonia,
Lithuania, Latvia.

BARRNet
Bay Area Regional Research Network
Pine Hall Rm. 115
Stanford, CA 94305-4122
Paul Baer
+1 415 723 7520
info@nic.barrnet.net
Area Served: San Francisco Bay area,
Northern California
Services: Network connections, dialup IP,
dialup e-mail.

BCnet
BCnet Headquarters
Room 419 - 6356 Agricultural Road
University of British Columbia
Vancouver, B.C.
CANADA, V6T 1W5
Attn: Mike Patterson
+1 604 822 3932
FAX: +1 604 822 5116

Mike_Patterson@mtsg.ubc.ca
Area Served: British Columbia, Canada

BGnet
Daniel Kalchev
c/o Digital Systems
Neofit Bozveli 6
Varna - 9000
BULGARIA
Voice and FAX: +359 52 234540
postmaster@Bulgaria.EU.net
Area Served: Bulgaria

Big Sky Telegraph
Jon Robinson
Western Montana College
Box 11
Dillon, MT 59725-3598
800 982 6668 (in Montana only)
+1 406 683 7338
jrobin@csn.org
Area Served: Montana
Services: Dialup e-mail.

BIX
Anthony Lockwood
General Videotex Corporation
1030 Massachusetts Avenue
Cambridge, MA 02139
800 695 4775
+1 617 354 4137
tjl@mhis.bix.com
Area Served: Area code 617; local dialup
connections outside 617 are
available through TYMNET.
Services: Dialup e-mail.

CA*net
CA*net Information Centre
Computing Services
University of Toronto
4 Bancroft Ave., Rm 116
Toronto, Ontario
CANADA, M5S 1A1
Attn: Eugene Siciunas
+1 416 978 5058
FAX: +1 416 978 6620
info@CAnet.ca
eugene@vm.utcs.utoronto.ca
Area Served: Canada

CAPCON Connect
1320 19th St. N.W.
Suite 400
Washington, D.C. 20036
+1 202 331 5771
FAX: +1 202 797 7719
jhagermn@capcon.net
Area Served: Washington, D.C. area
Services: Dialup e-mail

CERFnet
California Education and Research
Federation Network
P.O. Box 85608
San Diego, CA 92186-9784
800 876 2373
+1 619 455 3900
FAX: +1 619 455 3990
help@cerf.net
Area Served: California and International
Services: Network connections, national
dialup IP, dialup e-mail.

Channel 1
David Whitehorn
P.O. Box 338
Cambridge, MA 02238
+1 617 864 0100
whitehrn@channel1.com
Area Served: Area code 617
Services: Dialup e-mail.

CICNet
Committee on Institutional Cooperation
Network
ITI Building
2901 Hubbard Drive
Pod G
Ann Arbor, MI 48105
John Hankins
+1 313 998 6102
hankins@cic.net
Area Served: Minnesota, Wisconsin,
Iowa, Illinois, Indiana, Michigan,
and Ohio
Services: Network connections.

CONNECT
Alan Jay
Matther Farwell
The IBM PC User Group
PO Box 360
Harrow HA1 4LQ
ENGLAND
info@ibmpcug.co.uk
+44 0 81 863 1191
FAX: +44 0 81 863 6095
Area served: London area.

CLASS
Cooperative Agency for Library Systems
and Services
1415 Koll Circle
Suite 101
San Jose, CA 95112-4698
800 488 4559
+1 408 453 0444
FAX: +1 408 453 5379
class@class.org
Area Served: U.S.
Services: Dialup access for libraries in
the U.S.

Colorado SuperNet
Colorado SuperNet
CSM Computing Center
Colorado School Mines
1500 Illinois
Golden, Colorado 80401
Ken Harmon
+1 303 273 3471
FAX: +1 303 273 3475
kharmon@csn.org
info@csn.org
Area Served: Colorado
Services: Network connections, dialup IP.

Community News Service
1715 Monterey Road
Colorado Springs, CO 80910
+1 719 579 9120
klaus@cscns.com
Area Served: Colorado Springs (719 area code)
Services: Dialup e-mail.

CompuServe Information System
5000 Arlington Center Boulevard
P.O. Box 20212
Columbus, OH 43220
800 848 8990
+1 614 457 0802
postmaster@csi.compuserve.com
Area Served: U.S. and International
Services: Dialup e-mail, other services.

CONCERT
Communications for North Carolina
Education, Research, and Technology
Network
P.O. Box 12889
3021 Cornwallis Road
Research Triangle Park, NC 27709
Joe Ragland
+1 919 248 1404
jrr@concert.net
Area Served: North Carolina
Services: Network connections, dialup e-mail, dialup IP.

connect.com.au
29 Fitzgibbon Crescent
Caufield, Victoria 3161
AUSTRALIA
+61 3 5282239
FAX: +61 3 5285887
connect@connect.com.au
Area Served: Melbourne and Sydney, Australia

The Cyberspace Station
204 N. El Camino Real, Suite E626
Encinitas, CA 92024
+1 619 944 9498, ext. 626
help@cyber.net

Area Served: San Diego, California
Services: Dialup e-mail

DASNET
DA Systems, Inc.
1503 East Campbell Avenue
Campbell, CA 95008
+1 408 559 7434
postmaster@das.net
Area Served: California
Services: Dialup e-mail.

DataNet
Seppo Noppari
Telecom Finland
P.O. Box 228
Rautatienkatu 10
33101 Tampere
FINLAND
+358 31 243 2242
FAX: +358 31 243 2211
seppo.noppari@tele.fi
Area Served: Finland

DELPHI
General Videotex Corp.
1030 Massachusetts Ave.
Cambridge, MA 02138
800 695 4005
+1 617 491 3393
walthowe@delphi.com
Area Served: Boston, MA
Services: Dialup e-mail

DENet
The Danish Network for Research and
Education
Jan P. Sorensen
UNI-C, The Danish Computing Centre for
Research and Education
Building 305, DTH
DK-2800 Lyngby
DENMARK
Jan.P.Sorensen@uni-c.dk
+45 45 93 83 55
FAX: +45 45 93 02 20
Area Served: Denmark

DFN
DFN-Verein e. V.
Geschaeftsstelle
Pariser Strasse 44
D - 1000 Berlin 15
GERMANY
dfn-verein@dfn.dbp.de
wilhelm@dfn.dbp.de
rauschenbach@dfn.dbp.de
+49 30 88 42 99 22
FAX: +49 30 88 42 99 70
Area Served: Germany

EARN-France
Dominique Dumas
950 rue de Saint Priest
34184 Montpellier Cedex 4
FRANCE
BRUCH@FRMOP11.BITNET
BRUCH%FRMOP11.BITNET
@pucc.Princeton.EDU
+33 67 14 14 14
FAX: +33 67 52 57 63
Area Served: France

Express Access Online Communications Service
Digital Express Group, Inc.
6006 Greenbelt Road #228
Greenbelt, MD 20770
+1 301 220 2020
info@digex.com
Area Served: northern VA, Baltimore,
MD, Washington, DC
(area codes 202, 310, 410, 703)
Services: Dialup e-mail.

EZ-E-Mail
Shecora Associates, Inc.
P.O. Box 7604
Nashua, NH 03060
+1 603 672 0736
info@lemuria.sai.com
Area Served: U.S. and Canada
Services: Dialup e-mail.

Fnet
Sylvain Langlois
FNET Association
11 rue Carnot
94270 Le Kemlin-Bicetre
FRANCE
contact@fnet.fr
+33 1 45 21 02 04
FAX: +33 1 46 58 94 20
Area Served: France

FUNET
Finnish University and Research Network
Markus Sadeniemi
P.O. Box 40
SF-02101 Espoo
FINLAND
sadeniemi@funet.fi
+358 0 457 2711
FAX: +358 0 457 2302
Area Served: Finland

GARR
Gruppo Armonizzazione delle Reti per la
Ricerca
Ufficio del Ministro per lUniversita e la
Ricerca Scientifica e
Tecnologica
Lungotevere Thaon di Revel, 76

I-00196 Roma
ITALY
+39 6 390095
FAX: +39 6 392209
Area Served: Italy

Halcyon
Dataway
P.O. Box 555
Grapeview, WA 98546-0555
+1 206 426 9298
info@remote.halcyon.com
Area Served: Seattle, WA
Services: Dialup e-mail.

HoloNet
Information Access Technologies, Inc.
46 Shattuck Square
Suite 11
Berkeley, CA 94704-1152
+1 510 704 0160
FAX: +1 510 704 8019
info@holonet.net
Area Served: Berkeley, CA (area code
510)
Servics: Dialup e-mail.

HEANET
John Hayden
Chairman, HEANET Management
Committee
Higher Education Authority
Fitzwilliam Square, Dublin
IRELAND
jhayden@vax1.tcd.ie
+353 1 761545
FAX: +353 1 610492
Area Served: Ireland

IDS World Network
InteleCom Data Systems
P.O. Box 874
East Greenwich, RI 02818
+1 401 884 7856
sysadmin@ids.net
Area Served: East Greenwich and
Northern Rhode Island
Services: Dialup e-mail.

Infolan
Infonet Service Corporation
2100 East Grand Avenue
El Segundo, CA 90245
George Abe
abe@infonet.com
+1 310 335 2600
FAX: +1 310 335 2876
Area Served: International, including
U.S., Europe, Canada, Hong Kong,
Japan, Singapore, and Australia.

Institute for Global Communications (IGC)
18 De Boom Street
San Francisco, CA 94107
+1 415 442 0220
FAX: +1 415 546 1794
TELEX: 154205417
support@igc.apc.org
Area served: Worldwide
Services: Dialup e-mail; affiliated with
PeaceNet, EcoNet, and
ConflictNet; member of the Association
for Progressive Communications (APC).

ILAN
Hank Nussbacher
Israeli Academic Network Information
Center
Computer Center
Tel Aviv University
Ramat Aviv
ISRAEL
hank@vm.tau.ac.il
+972 3 6408309
Area Served: Israel

INet
University Computing Services
Wrubel Computing Center
Indiana University
750 N. State Rd. 46
Bloomington, IN 47405
Dick Ellis
+1 812 855 4240
ellis@ucs.indiana.edu
Area Served: Indiana
Services: Network connections.

ITESM
Ing. Hugo E. Garcia Torres
Director
Depto. de Telecomunicaciones y Redes
ITESM Campus Monterrey
E. Garza Sada #2501
Monterrey, N.L., C.P. 64849
MEXICO
+52 83 582 000 ext. 4130
FAX: +52 83 588 931
hugo@mtecv1.mty.itesm.mx
Area Served: Mexico

IUnet
Alessandro Berni
DIST, Universita di Genova
Via Opera Pia, 11A
16145 Genova
ITALY
+39 10 353 2747
FAX: +39 10 353 2948
ab@dist.unige.it
Area Served: Italy

JANET
Joint Academic Network
JANET Liaison Desk
c/o Rutherford Appleton Laboratory
Chilton Didcot
GB-Oxon OX11 OQX
UNITED KINGDOM
+44 235 5517
JANET-LIAISON-DESK@jnt.ac.uk
O=GB; ADMD= ; PRMD=uk.ac; O=jnt;
G=JANET-LIAISON-DESK;
Area Served: United Kingdom

JIPS
Joint Network Team
c/o Rutherford Appleton Laboratory
Chilton Didcot
Oxon OX11 0QX
United Kingdom
Dr. Bob Day
r.a.day@jnt.ac.uk
+44 235 44 5163
or contact JANET Liaison Desk
Area Served: United Kingdom

JvNCnet
Global Enterprise Service, Inc.
John von Neumann Center Network
6 von Neuman Hall
Princeton University
Princeton, NJ 08544
Sergio F. Heker
Allison Pihl
800 358 4437
+1 609 258 2400
market@jvnc.net
Area Served: U.S. and International
Services: Network connections, dialup IP.

Los Nettos
University of Southern California
Information Sciences Institute
4676 Admiralty Way
Marina del Rey, CA 90292
Ann Westine Cooper
+1 310 822 1511
los-nettos-request@isi.edu
Area Served: Los Angeles area, Southern
California
Services: Network connections.

MBnet
Director, Computing Services
University of Manitoba
603 Engineering Building
Winnipeg, Manitoba
CANADA, R3T 2N2
Attn: Gerry Miller
+1 204 474 8230
FAX: +1 204 275 5420
miller@ccm.UManitoba.ca
Area Served: Manitoba, Canada

MCI Mail
1133 19th Street, NW
7th Floor
Washington, DC 20036
800 444 6245
+1 202 833 8484
2671163@mcimail.com
3248333@mcimail.com
Are Served: U.S. and International
Services: Dialup e-mail.

MichNet
2200 Bonisteel Blvd.
Ann Arbor, MI 48109-2112
Jeff Ogden
+1 313 764 9430
info@merit.edu
Area Served: Michigan
Services: Network connections, dialup IP.

MIDnet
Midwestern States Network
29 WSEC
University of Nebraska
Lincoln, NE 68588
Dale Finkelson
+1 402 472 5032
dmf@westie.unl.edu
Area Served: Midwestern States,
including Iowa, Kansas, Oklahoma,
Arkansas, Missouri, South Dakota, and
Nebraska
Services: Network connections.

Milwaukee Internet X
Mix Communications
P.O Box 17166
Milwaukee, WI 53217
+1 414 962 8172
sysop@mixcom.com
Area Served: Milwaukee, WI
Services: Dialup e-mail.

MindVOX
Phantom Access
1562 First Avenue
Suite 351
New York, NY 10028
+1 212 988 5987
info@phantom.com
Area Served: New York City (area codes
212, 718)
Services: Dialup e-mail.

MRnet
Minnesota Regional Network
511 11th Avenue South, Box 212
Minneapolis, Minnesota 55415
Dennis Fazio
+1 612 342 2570
dfazio@mr.net
Area Served: Minnesota
Services: Network connections.

MSEN, Inc.
628 Brooks Street
Ann Arbor, MI 48103
Owen Scott Medd
+1 313 998 4562
FAX: +1 313 998 4563
info@msen.com
Area Served: U.S.
Services: Network connections, dialup IP,
dialup e-mail.

NBnet
Director, Computing Services
University of New Brunswick
Fredericton, New Brunswick
CANADA, E3B 5A3
Attn: David Macneil
+1 506 453 4573
FAX: +1 506 453 3590
DGM@unb.ca
Area Served: New Brunswick, Canada

NEARnet
New England Academic and Research
Network
BBN Systems and Technologies
10 Moulton Street
Cambridge, MA 02138
+1 617 873 8730
nearnet-staff@nic.near.net
Area Served: Maine, Vermont, New
Hampshire, Connecticut,
Massachusetts, Rhode Island
Services: Network connections, dialup IP.

Netcom Online Communication Services
P.O. Box 20774
San Jose, CA 95160
Desirree Madison-Biggs
+1 408 554 8649
info@netcom.com
Area Served: California (area codes 213,
310, 408, 415, 510, 818).
Services: Dialup e-mail, dialup IP.

netILLINOIS
University of Illinois
Computing Services Office
1304 W. Springfield
Urbana, IL 61801
Joel L. Hartmann
+1 309 677 3100
joel@bradley.bradley.edu
Area Served: Illinois
Services: Network connections.

NevadaNet
University of Nevada System
Computing Services
4505 Maryland Parkway
Las Vegas, NV 89154
Don Zitter
+1 702 784 6133

zitter@nevada.edu
Area Served: Nevada
Services: Network connections.

NLnet
Newfoundland and Labrador Network
Director, Computing and Communications
Memorial University of Newfoundland
St. John's, Newfoundland
CANADA, A1C 5S7
Attn: Wilf Bussey
+1 709 737 8329
FAX: +1 709 737 4569
wilf@kean.ucs.mun.ca
Area Served: Newfoundland and
Labrador, Canada

New Mexico Technet
4100 Osuna Boulevard, NE
Suite 103
Albuquerque, NM 87109
Lee Reynolds
+1 505 345 6555
reynolds@technet.nm.org
Area Served: Albuquerque, New Mexico
Services: Dialup e-mail.

NORDUNET
c/o SICS P.O. Box 1263
S-164 28 Kista
SWEDEN
+46 8 752 1563
FAX: +46 8 751 7230
NORDUNET@sics.se
Area Served: Norway, Denmark, Finland,
Iceland, Sweden.

NorthWestNet
Northwestern States Network
NorthWestNet
2435 233rd Place NE
Redmond, WA 98053
Eric Hood
+1 206 562 3000
ehood@nwnet.net
Area Served: Academic and research
sites in Alaska, Idaho, Montana
North Dakota, Oregon, Wyoming, and
Washington
Services: Network connections.

NSTN
Nova Scotia Technology Network
General Manager, NSTN Inc.
900 Windmill Road, Suite 107
Dartmouth, Nova Scotia
CANADA, B3B 1P7
Attn: Mike Martineau
+1 902 468 6786
FAX: +1 902 468 3679
martinea@hawk.nstn.ns.ca
Area Served: Nova Scotia, Canada

NYSERNet
New York State Education and Research
Network
111 College Place
Room 3-211
Syracuse, New York 13244
Jim Luckett
+1 315 443 4120
info@nysernet.org
Area Served: New York State and
International
Services: Network connections, dialup e-mail, dialup IP.

OARnet
Ohio Academic Research Network
Ohio Supercomputer Center
1224 Kinnear Road
Columbus, Ohio 43085
Alison Brown
+1 614 292 8100
nic@oar.net
Area Served: Ohio
Services: Network connections, dialup IP.

Old Colorado City Communications
2502 W. Colorado Avenue, #203
Colorado Springs, CO 80904
Dave Hughes
+1 719 632 4848
dave@oldcolo.com
Area Served: Colorado
Services: Dialup e-mail.

ONet
ONet Computing Services
University of Toronto
4 Bancroft Avenue, Rm 116
Toronto, Ontario
CANADA, M5S 1A1
Attn: Eugene Siciunas
+1 416 978 5058
FAX: +1 416 978 6620
eugene@vm.utcs.utoronto.ca
Area Served: Ontario, Canada
Services: Network connections.

PACCOM
Torben Nielsen
University of Hawaii
Department of ICS
2565 The Mall
Honolulu, HI 96822
U.S.A.
+1 808 949 6395
torben@hawaii.edu
Area Served: Pacific rim: Australia,
Japan, Korea, New Zealand, Hong
Kong, Hawaii.

Panix Public Access Unix
c/o Alexis Rosen

110 Riverside Drive
New York, NY 10024
alexis@panix.com
+1 212 877 4854
or
Jim Baumbach
jsb@panix.com
+1 718 965 3768
Area Served:New York City, NY (area codes 212, 718)
Services: Dialup e-mail.

Performance Systems International, Inc. (PSI)
11800 Sunrise Valley Drive
Suite 1100
Reston, VA 22091
info@psi.com
800 827 7482
+1 703 620 6651
FAX: +1 703 620 4586
Area Served: U.S. and International
Services: Network connections, dialup e-mail, dialup IP.

PIPEX
Unipalm Ltd.
216 The Science Park
Cambridge CB4 4WA
UNITED KINGDOM
Michael Howes (sales information)
Richard Nuttall (technical information)
pipex@pipex.net
+44 223 250120
FAX: +44 223 250121
Hotline Support: +44 223 250122
Area served: United Kingdom

Prince Edward Island Network
University of Prince Edward Island
Computer Services
550 University Avenue
Charlottetown, P.E.I.
CANADA, C1A 4P3
Attn: Jim Hancock
+1 902 566 0450
FAX: +1 902 566 0958
hancock@upei.ca
Area Served: Prince Edward Island, Canada

Portal Communications, Inc.
20863 Stevens Creek Blvd.
Suite 200
Cupertino, CA 95014
+1 408 973 9111
cs@cup.portal.com
info@portal.com
Area Served: Northern California (area codes 408, 415)
Services: Dialup e-mail.

PREPnet
Pennsylvania Research and Economic Partnership Network
305 South Craig Street, 2nd Floor
Pittsburgh, PA 15213-3706
Thomas W. Bajzek
+1 412 268 7870
twb+@andrew.cmu.edu
Area Served: Pennsylvania
Services: Network connections, dialup IP.

PSCNET
Pittsburgh Supercomputing Center Network
Pittsburgh Supercomputing Center
4400 5th Avenue
Pittsburgh, PA 15213
Eugene Hastings
+1 412 268 4960
pscnet-admin@psc.edu
Area Served: Eastern U.S. (Pennsylvania, Ohio, and West Virginia)
Services: Network connections.

REDID
Daniel Pimienta
Asesor Cientifico Union Latina
APTD0 2972
Sant Domingo
Republica Dominicana
pimienta!daniel@redid.org.do
+1 809 689 4973
+1 809 535 6614
FAX: +1 809 535 6646
TELEX: 1 346 0741
Area Served: Dominican Republic

RedIRIS
Secretaria RedIRIS
Fundesco
Alcala 61
28014 Madrid
SPAIN
+34 1 435 1214
FAX: +34 1 578 1773
secretaria@rediris.es
C=es;ADMD=mensatex;PRMD=iris;
O=rediris;S=secretaria;
Area Served: Spain

Relcom
Demos
6 Ovchinnikovskaya nab.
113035 Moscow
RUSSIA
postmaster@hq.demos.su
info@hq.demos.su
+7 095 231 2129
+7 095 231 6395
FAX: +7 095 233 5016
Area Served: Russia

RISCnet
InteleCom Data Systems
11 Franklin Road
East Greenwich, RI 02818
Andy Green
+1 401 885 6855
info@nic.risc.net
Area Served: Rhode Island, New England
Services: Network connections, dialup IP,
dialup e-mail.

RISQ
Reseau Interordinateurs Scientifique
Quebecois
Centre de Recherche Informatique de
Montreal (CRIM)
3744, Jean-Brillant, Suite 500
Montreal, Quebec
CANADA, H3T 1P1
Attn: Bernard Turcotte
+1 514 340 5700
FAX: +1 514 340 5777
turcotte@crim.ca
Area Served: Quebec, Canada

SASK#net
Computing Services
56 Physics
University of Saskatchewan
Saskatoon, Saskatchewan
CANADA, S7N 0W0
Dean Jones
+1 306 966 4860
FAX: +1 306 966 4938
jonesdc@admin.usask.ca
Area Served: Saskatchewan, Canada

SDSCnet
San Diego Supercomputer Center
Network
San Diego Supercomputer Center
P.O. Box 85608
San Diego, CA 92186-9784
Paul Love
+1 619 534 5043
loveep@sds.sdsc.edu
Area Served: San Diego area, Southern
California
Services: Network connections.

Seattle Online
2318 2nd Avenue, #45
Seattle, WA 98121
Bruce King
+1 206 328 2412
bruceki@online.com
Area Served: Seattle
Services: Dialup e-mail.

SESQUINET
Texas Sesquicentennial Network
Office of Networking and Computing
Systems

Rice University
Houston, TX 77251-1892
Farrell Gerbode
+1 713 527 4988
farrell@rice.edu
Area Served: Texas
Services: Network connections, dialup IP.

Sprint NSFNET ICM
Sprint NSFNET International Connections
Manager
Robert Collet
+1 703 904 2230
rcollet@icm1.icp.net
Area Served: International
Services: International network connections to NSFNET; operates under
cooperative agreement with NSF and
conforms to CCIRN guidelines.

SprintLink
Sprint
13221 Woodland Park Road
Herndon, VA 22071
Robert Doyle
+1 703 904 2167
bdoyle@icm1.icp.net
Area Served: U.S. and International
Services: Network connections,
dialup IP.

Sugar Land Unix
NeoSoft
3918 Panorama
Missouri City, TX 77459
Karl Lehenbauer
+1 713 438 8964
info@NeoSoft.com
Area Served: Houston metro area
Services: Dialup e-mail.

SUNET
Hans Wallberg
Hans.Wallberg@umdac.umu.se
or
Bjorn Eriksen
ber@sunet.se
SUNET
UMDAC
S-901 87 Umea
SWEDEN
+46 90 16 56 45
FAX: +46 90 16 67 62
Area Served: Sweden

SURAnet
Southeastern Universities Research
Association Network
1353 Computer Science Center
University of Maryland
College Park, Maryland 20742-2411
Deborah J. Nunn

+1 301 982 4600
marketing@sura.net
Area Served: Southeastern U.S.
(Alabama, Florida, Georgia, Kentucky,
Louisiana, Mississippi, North Carolina,
South Carolina, Tennessee,
Virginia, and West Virginia)
Services: Network connections.

SURFnet
P.O. Box 19035
3501 DA Utrecht
THE NETHERLANDS
+31 30310290
admin@surfnet.nl
c=nl, ADMD=00net, PRMD=SURF,
O=SURFnet, S=Admin
Area Served: The Netherlands

SWITCH
SWITCH Head Office
Limmatquai 138
CH-8001 Zurich
SWITZERLAND
+41 1 256 5454
FAX: +41 1 261 8133
postmaster@switch.ch
C=CH;ADMD=arCom;PRMD=SWITCH;
O=SWITCH;S=Postmaster;
Area Served: Switzerland

TANet
Computer Center, Ministry of Education
12th Fl, No. 106
Sec. 2, Hoping E. Road
Taipei, Taiwan
Attention: Chen Wen-Sung
nisc@twnmoe10.edu.tw
nisc@twnmoe10.bitnet
+886 2 7377010
FAX: +886 2 7377043
Area Served: Taiwan

THEnet
Texas Higher Education Network
Computation Center
University of Texas
Austin, TX 78712
William Green
+1 512 471 3241
green@utexas.edu
Area Served: Texas
Services: Network connections.

TIPnet
Technical Sales and Support
Kjell Simenstad
MegaCom AB
Kjell Simenstad
121 80 Johanneshov
Stockholm

SWEDEN
+46 8 780 5616
FAX: +46 8 686 0213
Area Served: Sweden

UKnet
UKnet Support Group
Computing Laboratory
University of Kent
Canterbury
Kent CT2 7NF
UNITED KINGDOM
Area Served: United Kingdom

UNINET Project
Manager: Mr. Vic Shaw
Foundation for Research Development
P.O. Box 2600
Pretoria 0001
SOUTH AFRICA
uninet@frd.ac.za
+27 12 841 3542
+27 12 841 2597
FAX: +27 12 804 2679
TELEX: 321312 SA
Area Served: South Africa

UNINETT
UNINETT secretariat
SINTEF Delab
N-7034 Trondheim
NORWAY
sekr@uninett.no
C=no;P=uninett;O=uninett;S=sekr;
+47 7 592980
FAX: +47 7 532586
Area Served: Norway

UUNET Canada Inc.
1 Yonge Street
Suite 1801
Toronto, Ontario
M5E 1W7
CANADA
+1 416 368 6621
FAX: +1 416 369 0515
info@uunet.ca
Area Served: Canada

UUNET Technologies, Inc.
3110 Fairview Park Drive
Suite 570
Falls Church, VA 22042
info@uunet.uu.net
800 488 6384
+1 703 204 8000
FAX: +1 703 204 8001
Area Served: U.S.
Services: Network connections, dialup e-
mail; Alternet is a product of
UUNET Technologies.

UnBol/BolNet
Prof. Clifford Paravicini
Facultad de Ingenieria Electronica
Univ. Mayor de San Andres
La Paz, Bolivia
clifford@unbol.bo
Area Served: Bolivia

VERnet
Virginia Education and Research Network
Academic Computing Center
Gilmer Hall
University of Virginia
Charlottesville, VA 22903
James Jokl
+1 804 924 0616
jaj@virginia.edu
Area Served: Virginia
Services: Network connections.

Village of Cambridge
1 Kendall Square
Building 300
Cambridge, MA 02139
+1 617 494 5226
+1 617 252 0009 (modem)
servce@village.com
Area Served: Massachusetts
Services Dialup e-mail

Westnet
Southwestern States Network
UCC
601 S. Howes, 6th Floor South
Colorado State University
Fort Collins, CO 80523
Pat Burns
+1 303 491 7260
pburns@yuma.acns.colostate.edu
Area Served: Western U.S. (Arizona, Colorado, New Mexico, Utah, Idaho, and Wyoming)
Services: Network connections.

Whole Earth 'Lectronic Link (WELL)
27 Gate Five Road
Sausalito, CA 94965
+1 415 332 4335
info@well.sf.ca.us
Area Served: San Francisco Bay area (area code 415)
Services: Dialup e-mail.

WIDE
c/o Prof. Jun Murai
KEIO University

5322 Endo, Fujisawa, 252
JAPAN
jun@wide.ad.jp
+81 466 47 5111 ext. 3330
Area Served: Japan

WiscNet
Madison Academic Computing Center
1210 W. Dayton Street
Madison, WI 53706
Tad Pinkerton
+1 608 262 8874
tad@cs.wisc.edu
Area Served: Wisconsin
Services: Network connections.

The World
Software Tool & Die
1330 Beacon Street
Brookline, MA 02146
+1 617 739 0202
office@world.std.com
Area Seved: Boston (area code 617)
Services: Dialup e-mail, USENET news, other services.

World dot Net
Internetworks, Inc.
+1 206 576 7147
info@world.net
Area Served: Oregon, Washington, Idaho
Services: Network connections.

WVNET
West Virginia Network for Educational Telecomputing
837 Chestnut Ridge Road
Morgantown, WV 26505
Harper Grimm
+1 304 293 5192
cc011041@wvnvms.wvnet.edu
Area Served: West Virginia
Services: Network connections, dialup IP.

YUNAC
Borka Jerman-Blazic, Secretary General
Jamova 39
61000 Ljubljana
YUGOSLAVIA
+38 61 159 199
FAX: +38 61 161 029
jerman-blazic@ijs.ac.mail.yu
Area Served: Slovenia, Croatia, Bosnia-Herzegovina

FYI INDEX

This file contains citations for all FYIs in *reverse* numeric order. Remember, by the time you read this, additional FYIs may have been issued. FYI citations appear in this format:

Title of FYI. Author 1.; Author 2.; Author 3. Issue date; ## p.

    (Format: PS=xxx TXT=zzz bytes) (Also RFC ##) (Obsoletes xxx;

    Obsoleted by xxx; Updates xxx; Updated by xxx)

Key to citations:

is the FYI number; ## p. is the total number of pages.

The format and byte information follows the page information in parenthesis. The format, either ASCII text (TXT) or PostScript (PS) or both, is noted, followed by an equals sign and the number of bytes for that version. (PostScript is a registered trademark of Adobe Systems Incorporated.) The example (Format: PS=xxx TXT=zzz bytes) shows that the PostScript version of the FYI is xxx bytes and the ASCII text version is zzz bytes.

The (Also RFC ####) phrase gives the equivalent RFC number for each FYI document. Each FYI is also an RFC.

"Obsoletes RFC xxx" refers to other FYIs that this one replaces; "Obsoleted by RFC xxx" refers to FYIs that have replaced this one. "Updates RFC xxx" refers to other FYIs that this one merely updates (but does not replace); "Updated by RFC xxx" refers to FYIs that have been updated by this one (but not replaced). Only immediately succeeding and/or preceding FYIs are indicated, not the entire history of each related earlier or later FYI in a related series.

Example:

1   F.Y.I. on F.Y.I.: Introduction to the F.Y.I. notes. Malkin, G.S.;
         Reynolds, J.K. 1990 March; 4 p. (Format: TXT=7867 bytes) (Also RFC
         1150)

---

18   Internet Users' Glossary. Malkin, G.S.; Parker, T.L.,eds. 1993 January; 53 p.
         (Format: TXT=104624 bytes) (Also RFC 1392)

17   The Tao of IETF: A Guide for New Attendees of the Internet Engineering
         Task Force. Malkin, G.S. 1993 January; 19 p. (Format: TXT=23569 bytes)
         (Also RFC 1391)

16   Connecting to the Internet: What connecting institutions should anticipate.
         ACM SIGUCCS Networking Task Force. 1992 August; 25 p. (Format:
         TXT=53449 bytes) (Also RFC 1359)

15   Privacy and accuracy issues in network information center databases.
         Curran, J.; Marine, A.N. 1992 August; 4 p. (Format: TXT=8858 bytes)
         (Also RFC 1355)

14   Technical overview of directory services using the X.500 protocol. Weider,
         C.; Reynolds, J.K.; Heker, S. 1992 March; 16 p. (Format TXT=35694 bytes)
         (Also RFC 1309)

13   Executive introduction to directory services using the X.500 protocol.
         Weider, C.; Reynolds, J.K. 1992 March; 4 p. (Format: TXT=9392 bytes) (Also
         RFC 1308)

12   Building a network information services infrastructure. Sitzler, D.D.; Smith,
         P.G.; Marine, A.N. 1992 February; 13 p. (Format: TXT=29135 bytes) (Also
         RFC 1302)

11   Catalog of Available X.500 Implementations. Lang, R.; Wright, R. 1991 December; 103 p. (Format: TXT=129468 bytes) (Also RFC 1292)

10   There's gold in them thar networks! or searching for treasure in all the
         wrong places. Martin, J. 1991 December; 27 p. (Format: TXT=46997 bytes)
         (Also RFC 1290)

9   Who's who in the Internet: Biographies of IAB, IESG and IRSG members.
         Malkin, G.S. 1992 May; 33 p. (Format: TXT=92119 bytes) (Also RFC 1336)
         (Obsoletes RFC 1251)

8   Site Security Handbook. Holbrook, J.P.; Reynolds, J.K.,eds. 1991 July; 101
         p. (Format: TXT=259129 bytes) (Also RFC 1244)

7   FYI on Questions and Answers: Answers to commonly asked "experienced Internet user" questions. Malkin, G.S.; Marine, A.N.; Reynolds, J.K. 1991 February; 15 p. (Format: TXT=33385 bytes) (Also RFC 1207)

6   FYI on the X window system. Scheifler, R.W. 1991 January; 3 p. (Format: TXT=3629 bytes) (Also RFC 1198)

5   Choosing a name for your computer. Libes, D. 1990 August; 8 p. (Format: TXT=18472 bytes) (Also RFC 1178)

4   FYI on questions and answers: Answers to commonly asked "new Internet user" questions. Malkin, G.S.; Marine, A.N. 1992 May; 42 p. (Format: TXT=91884 bytes) (Also RFC 1325) (Obsoletes RFC 1206)

3   FYI on where to start: A bibliography of internetworking information. Bowers, K.L.; LaQuey, T.L.; Reynolds, J.K.; Roubicek, K.; Stahl, M.K.; Yuan, A. 1990 August; 42 p. (Format: TXT=67330 bytes) (Also RFC 1175)

2   FYI on a network management tool catalog: Tools for monitoring and debugging TCP/IP internets and interconnected devices. Stine, R.H.,ed. 1990 April; 126 p. (Format: TXT=336906, PS=555225 bytes) (Also RFC 1147)

1   F.Y.I. on F.Y.I.: Introduction to the F.Y.I. notes. Malkin, G.S.; Reynolds, J.K. 1990 March; 4 p. (Format: TXT=7867 bytes) (Also RFC 1150)

IV

STD INDEX

This file contains citations for all STD RFCs in ascending numeric order. Remember, by the time you read this, additional protocols may have become STDs. For more information about STD RFCs, please refer to RFC 1311, *Introduction to the STD Notes* [24].

STD (Standard) RFC citations appear in this format:

RFC ####: Title of RFC. Author 1.; Author 2. Issue date; ## p.

> (Format: PS=xxx TXT=zzz bytes) (This STD also includes RFC ####; RFC
> ####)

Key to citations:

is the STD number. If there is no STD number to the left of a citation below, the previous STD number listed applies to that document. This is possible because the specifications of some standards are contained in more than one RFC document. You do not have the full specification of the standard if you do not have every RFC assigned the particular STD number for that standard.

RFC #### is the number of the RFC which is cited as describing all or part of the STD.

p. is the total number of pages.

The format and byte information follows the page information in parenthesis. The format, either ASCII text (TXT) or PostScript (PS) or both, is noted, followed by an equals sign and the number of bytes for that version. (PostScript is a registered trademark of Adobe Systems Incorporated.) The example (Format: PS=xxx TXT=zzz bytes) shows that the PostScript version of the RFC is xxx bytes and the ASCII text version is zzz bytes.

The (This STD also includes RFC ####; RFC ####) phrase refers to companion RFCs that are also part of the specification of the standard. This phrase will only appear for those STDs whos full specification is contained in more than one RFC.

Example:

5   RFC 791: Internet Protocol. Postel, J.B. 1981 September; 45 p. (Format: TXT=97779 bytes) (This STD also includes RFC 950; RFC 919; RFC 922; RFC 792; RFC 1112)

This document is also RFC 791. This document is not the full specification for STD 5. The full specification for STD 5 requires this document, plus RFCs 950, 919, 792, and 1112 (as indicated by the "with" information).

---

1   RFC 1360: IAB official protocol standards. Postel, J.B.,ed. 1992 September; 33 p. (Format: TXT=71860 bytes)

2   RFC 1340: Assigned Numbers. Reynolds, J.K.; Postel, J.B. 1992 July; 138 p. (Format: TXT=232974 bytes)

3   RFC 1123: Requirements for Internet hosts - application and support. Braden, R.T., ed. 1989 October; 98 p. (Format: TXT=245503 bytes) (This STD also includes RFC 1122)

        RFC 1122: Requirements for Internet hosts - communication layers. Braden, R.T., ed. 1989 October; 116 p. (Format: TXT=295992 bytes) (This STD also includes RFC 1123)

4   RFC 1009: Requirements for Internet gateways. Braden, R.T.; Postel, J.B. 1987 June; 55 p. (Format: TXT=128173 bytes)

5   RFC 791: Internet Protocol. Postel, J.B. 1981 September; 45 p. (Format: TXT=97779 bytes) (This STD also includes RFC 950; RFC 919; RFC 922; RFC 792; RFC 1112)

        RFC 950: Internet standard subnetting procedure. Mogul, J.C.; Postel, J.B. 1985 August; 18 p. (Format: TXT=39010 bytes) (This STD also includes RFC 791; RFC 919; RFC 922; RFC 792; RFC 1112)

        RFC 919: Broadcasting Internet datagrams. Mogul, J.C. 1984 October; 8 p. (Format: TXT=16838 bytes) (This STD also includes RFC 791; RFC 950; RFC 922; RFC 792; RFC 1112)

        RFC 922: Broadcasting Internet datagrams in the presence of subnets. Mogul, J.C. 1984 October; 12 p. (Format: TXT=24832 bytes) (This STD also includes RFC 791; RFC 950; RFC 919; RFC 792; RFC 1112)

        RFC 792: Internet Control Message Protocol. Postel, J.B. 1981 September; 21 p. (Format: TXT=30404 bytes) (This STD also includes RFC 791; RFC 950; RFC 919; RFC 922; RFC 1112)

RFC 1112: Host extensions for IP multicasting. Deering, S.E. 1989 August; 17 p. (Format: TXT=39904 bytes) (This STD also includes RFC 791; RFC 950; RFC 919; RFC 922; RFC 792)

6   RFC 768: User Datagram Protocol. Postel, J.B. 1980 August 28; 3 p. (Format: TXT=6069 bytes)

7   RFC 793: Transmission Control Protocol. Postel, J.B. 1981 September; 85 p. (Format: TXT=177957 bytes)

8   RFC 855: Telnet option specifications. Postel, J.B.; Reynolds, J.K. 1983 May; 4 p. (Format: TXT=6218 bytes) (This STD also includes RFC 854)

       RFC 854: Telnet Protocol specification. Postel, J.B.; Reynolds, J.K. 1983 May; 15 p. (Format: TXT=39371 bytes) (This STD also includes RFC 855)

9   RFC 959: File Transfer Protocol. Postel, J.B.; Reynolds, J.K. 1985 October; 69 p. (Format: TXT=151249 bytes)

10   RFC 821: Simple Mail Transfer Protocol. Postel, J.B. 1982 August; 58 p. (Format: TXT=124482 bytes)

11   RFC 822: Standard for the format of ARPA Internet text messages. Crocker, D. 1982 August 13; 47 p. (Format: TXT=109200 bytes) (This STD also includes RFC 1049)

       RFC 1049: Content-type header field for Internet messages. Sirbu, M.A. 1988 March; 8 p. (Format: TXT=18923 bytes) (This STD also includes RFC 822)

12   RFC 1119: Network Time Protocol (version 2) specification and implementation. Mills, D.L. 1989 September; 64 p. (Format: PS=535202 bytes)

13   RFC 1035: Domain names - implementation and specification. Mockapetris, P.V. 1987 November; 55 p. (Format: TXT=125626 bytes) (This STD also includes RFC 1034)

       RFC 1034: Domain names - concepts and facilities. Mockapetris, P.V. 1987 November; 55 p. (Format: TXT=129180 bytes) (This STD also includes RFC 1035)

14   RFC 974: Mail routing and the domain system. Partridge, C. 1986 January; 7 p. (Format: TXT=18581 bytes)

15   RFC 1157: Simple Network Management Protocol (SNMP). Case, J.D.; Fedor, M.; Schoffstall, M.L.; Davin, C. 1990 May; 36 p. (Format: TXT=74894 bytes)

16   RFC 1155: Structure and identification of management information for TCP/IP-based internets. Rose, M.T.; McCloghrie, K. 1990 May; 22 p. (Format: TXT=40927 bytes) (This STD also includes RFC 1212)

       RFC 1212: Concise MIB definitions. Rose, M.T.; McCloghrie, K.,eds. 1991 March; 19 p. (Format: TXT=43579 bytes) (This STD also includes RFC 1155)

17   RFC 1213: Management Information Base for network management of TCP/IP-based internets: MIB-II. McCloghrie, K.; Rose, M.T.,eds. 1991 March; 70 p. (Format: TXT=146080 bytes)

18   RFC 904: Exterior Gateway Protocol formal specification. Mills, D.L. 1984 April; 30 p. (Format: TXT=65226 bytes)

19   RFC 1002: Protocol standard for a NetBIOS service on a TCP/UDP transport: Detailed specifications. Internet Engineering Task Force, NetBIOS Working Group. 1987 March; 85 p. (Format: TXT=170262 bytes) (This STD also includes RFC 1001)

        RFC 1001: Protocol standard for a NetBIOS service on a TCP/UDP transport: Concepts and methods. Internet Engineering Task Force, NetBIOS Working Group. 1987 March; 68 p. (Format: TXT=158437 bytes) (This STD also includes RFC 1002)

20   RFC 862: Echo Protocol. Postel, J.B. 1983 May; 1 p. (Format: TXT=1294 bytes)

21   RFC 863: Discard Protocol. Postel, J.B. 1983 May; 1 p. (Format: TXT=1297 bytes)

22   RFC 864: Character Generator Protocol. Postel, J.B. 1983 May; 3 p. (Format: TXT=7016 bytes)

23   RFC 865: Quote of the Day Protocol. Postel, J.B. 1983 May; 1 p. (Format: TXT=1734 bytes)

24   RFC 866: Active users. Postel, J.B. 1983 May; 1 p. (Format: TXT=2087 bytes)

25   RFC 867: Daytime Protocol. Postel, J.B. 1983 May; 2 p. (Format: TXT=2405 bytes)

26   RFC 868: Time Protocol. Postel, J.B.; Harrenstien, K. 1983 May; 2 p. (Format: TXT=3140 bytes)

27   RFC 856: Telnet binary transmission. Postel, J.B.; Reynolds, J.K. 1983 May; 4 p. (Format: TXT=9192 bytes)

28   RFC 857: Telnet echo option. Postel, J.B.; Reynolds, J.K. 1983 May; 5 p. (Format: TXT=11143 bytes)

29   RFC 858: Telnet Suppress Go Ahead option. Postel, J.B.; Reynolds, J.K. 1983 May; 3 p. (Format: TXT=3825 bytes)

30   RFC 859: Telnet status option. Postel, J.B.; Reynolds, J.K. 1983 May; 3 p. (Format: TXT=4443 bytes)

31   RFC 860: Telnet timing mark option. Postel, J.B.; Reynolds, J.K. 1983 May; 4 p. (Format: TXT=8108 bytes)

32   RFC 861: Telnet extended options: List option. Postel, J.B.; Reynolds, J.K. 1983 May; 1 p. (Format: TXT=3181 bytes)

33   RFC 1350: TFTP protocol (revision 2). Sollins, K.R. 1992 July; 11 p. (Format: TXT=24599 bytes)

34   RFC 1058: Routing Information Protocol. Hedrick, C.L. 1988 June; 33 p. (Format: TXT=93285 bytes)

35   RFC 1006: ISO transport services on top of the TCP: Version 3. Rose, M.T.; Cass, D.E. 1987 May; 17 p. (Format: TXT=31935 bytes) (Obsoletes RFC 983)

RFC INDEX

Presented in this appendix is part of the version of the RFC Index that was current when this book was printed. The oldest RFC in this index is RFC 1000; it appears last on the list. The most recent is RFC 1456.

RFC citations appear in this format:

Title of RFC. Author 1.; Author 2.; Author 3. Issue date; ## p. (Format: PS=xxx TXT=zzz bytes) (Also FYI ##) (Obsoletes xxx; Obsoleted by xxx; Updates xxx; Updated by xxx)

Key to citations:

is the RFC number; ## p. is the total number of pages.

The format and byte information follows the page information in parenthesis. The format, either ASCII text (TXT) or PostScript (PS) or both, is noted, followed by an equals sign and the number of bytes for that version. (PostScript is a registered trademark of Adobe Systems Incorporated.) The example (Format: PS=xxx TXT=zzz bytes) shows that the PostScript version of the RFC is xxx bytes and the ASCII text version is zzz bytes.

The (Also FYI ##) phrase gives the equivalent FYI number if the RFC was also issued as an FYI document.

"Obsoletes xxx" refers to other RFCs that this one replaces; "Obsoleted by xxx" refers to RFCs that have replaced this one. "Updates xxx" refers to other RFCs that this one merely updates (but does not replace); "Updated by xxx" refers to RFCs that have been updated by this one (but not replaced). Only immediately succeeding and/or preceding RFCs are indicated, not the entire history of each related earlier or later RFC in a related series.

Example:

1129   Internet time synchronization: The Network Time Protocol. Mills, D.L. 1989 October; 29 p. (Format: PS=551697 bytes)

1456   Conventions for Encoding the Vietnamese Language; VISCII: Vietnamese Standard Code for Information Interchange; VIQR: Vietnamese Quoted-Readable Specification; Revision 1.1. Nguyen, C.T.; Ngo, H.D.; Bui, C.M.; Nguyen, T.V. 1993 May; 7 p. (Format: TXT=14732 bytes)

1455   Not yet issued.

1454   Comparison of Proposals for Next Version of IP. Dixon, T. 1993 May; 15 p. (Format: TXT=35046 bytes)

1453   Comment on packet video conferencing and the transport/network layers. Chimiak, W.J. 1993 April; 10 p. (Format: TXT=23563 bytes)

1452   Coexistence between version 1 and version 2 of the Internet-standard Network Management Framework. Case, J.D.; McCloghrie, K.; Rose, M.T.; Waldbusser, S. 1993 April; 17 p. (Format: TXT=32176 bytes)

1451   Manager-to-Manager Management Information Base. Case, J.D.; McCloghrie, K.; Rose, M.T.; Waldbusser, S. 1993 April; 36 p. (Format: TXT=62935 bytes)

1450   Management Information Base for version 2 of the Simple Network Management Protocol (SNMPv2). Case, J.D.; McCloghrie, K.; Rose, M.T.; Waldbusser, S. 1993 April; 27 p. (Format: TXT=42172 bytes)

1449   Transport Mappings for version 2 of the Simple Network Management Protocol (SNMPv2). Case, J.D.; McCloghrie, K.; Rose, M.T.; Waldbusser, S. 1993 April; 25 p. (Format: TXT=41161 bytes)

1448   Protocol Operations for version 2 of the Simple Network Management Protocol (SNMPv2). Case, J.D.; McCloghrie, K.; Rose, M.T.; Waldbusser, S. 1993 April; 36 p. (Format: TXT=74224 bytes)

1447   Party MIB for version 2 of the Simple Network Management Protocol (SNMPv2). McCloghrie, K.; Galvin, J.M. 1993 April; 50 p. (Format: TXT=80762 bytes)

1446   Security Protocols for version 2 of the Simple Network Management Protocol (SNMPv2). Galvin, J.M.; McCloghrie, K. 1993 April; 52 p. (Format: TXT=108733 bytes)

1445   Administrative Model for version 2 of the Simple Network Management Protocol (SNMPv2). Galvin, J.M.; McCloghrie, K. 1993 April; 47 p. (Format: TXT=99443 bytes)

1444 Conformance Statements for version 2 of the Simple Network Management Protocol (SNMPv2). Case, J.D.; McCloghrie, K.; Rose, M.T.; Waldbusser, S. 1993 April; 33 p. (Format: TXT=57744 bytes)

1443 Textual Conventions for version 2 of the Simple Network Management Protocol (SNMPv2). Case, J.D.; McCloghrie, K.; Rose, M.T.; Waldbusser, S. 1993 April; 31 p. (Format: TXT=60947 bytes)

1442 Structure of Management Information for version 2 of the Simple Network Management Protocol (SNMPv2). Case, J.D.; McCloghrie, K.; Rose, M.T.; Waldbusser, S. 1993 April; 54 p. (Format: TXT=95779 bytes)

1441 SMTP Introduction to version 2 of the Internet-standard Network Management Framework. Case, J.D.; McCloghrie, K.; Rose, M.T.; Waldbusser, S. 1993 April; 13 p. (Format: TXT=25386 bytes)

1440 Not yet issued.

1439 Uniqueness of unique identifiers. Finseth, C. 1993 March; 11 p. (Format: TXT=20477 bytes)

1438 Internet Engineering Task Force Statements of Boredom (SOBs). Chapin, A.L.; Huitema, C. 1993 April 1; 2 p. (Format: TXT=3044 bytes)

1437 Extension of MIME content-types to a new medium. Borenstein, N.; Linimon, M. 1993 April 1; 6 p. (Format: TXT=13356 bytes)

1436 Internet Gopher Protocol (a distributed document search and retrieval protocol). Anklesaria, F.; McCahill, M.; Linder, P.; Johnson, D.; Torrey, D.; Alberti, B. 1993 March; 16 p. (Format: TXT=36493 bytes)

1435 IESG advice from experience with Path MTU Discovery. Knowles, S. 1993 March; 2 p. (Format: TXT=2708 bytes)

1434 Data Link Switching: Switch-to-Switch Protocol. Dixon, R.C.; Kushi, D.M. 1993 March; 33 p. (Format: TXT=80182 bytes)

1433 Directed ARP. Garrett, J.; Hagan, J.D.; Wong, J.A. 1993 March; 18 p. (Format: TXT=41028 bytes)

1432 Recent Internet books. Quarterman, J. 1993 March; 15 p. (Format: TXT=27089 bytes)

1431 DUA metrics. Barker, P. 1993 February; 19 p. (Format: TXT=42240 bytes)

1430 Strategic plan for deploying an Internet X.500 directory service. Hardcastle-Kille, S.; Huizer, E.; Cerf, V.; Hobby, R.; Kent, S. 1993 February; 20 p. (Format: TXT=47887 bytes)

1429 Listserv Distribute Protocol. Thomas, E. 1993 February; 8 p. (Format: TXT=17759 bytes)

1428 Transition of Internet Mail from Just-Send-8 to 8bit-SMTP/MIME. Vaudreuil, G.M. 1993 February; 6 p. (Format: TXT=12064 bytes)

1427 SMTP Service Extension for Message Size Declaration. Klensin, J.; Freed, N.; Moore, K. 1993 February; 8 p. (Format: TXT=17856 bytes)

1426 SMTP Service Extension for 8bit-MIME Transport. Klensin, J.; Freed, N.; Rose, M.T.; Stefferud, E.A.; Crocker, D. 1993 February; 6 p. (Format: TXT=11661 bytes)

1425 SMTP Service Extension. Klensin, J.; Freed, N.; Rose, M.T.; Stefferud, E.A.; Crocker, D. 1993 February; 10 p. (Format: TXT=20932 bytes)

1424 Privacy Enhancement for Internet Electronic Mail: Part IV: Key Certification and Related Services. Kaliski, B.S. 1993 February; 9 p. (Format: TXT=17537 bytes)

1423 Privacy Enhancement for Internet Electronic Mail: Part III: Algorithms, Modes, and Identifiers. Balenson, D. 1993 February; 14 p. (Format: TXT=33277 bytes) (Obsoletes RFC 1115)

1422 Privacy Enhancement for Internet Electronic Mail: Part II: Certificate-Based Key Management. Kent, S.T. 1993 February; 32 p. (Format: TXT=86085 bytes) (Obsoletes RFC 1114)

1421 Privacy Enhancement for Internet Electronic Mail: Part I: Message Encryption and Authentication Procedures. Linn, J. 1993 February; 42 p. (Format: TXT=103894 bytes) (Obsoletes RFC 1113)

1420 SNMP over IPX. Bostock, S. 1993 March; 4 p. (Format: TXT=6762 bytes)

1419 SNMP over AppleTalk. Minshall, G.; Ritter, M. 1993 March; 7 p. (Format: TXT=16470 bytes)

1418 SNMP over OSI. Rose, M.T. 1993 March; 4 p. (Format: TXT=7721 bytes) (Obsoletes RFC 1161, RFC 1283)

1417 NADF Standing Documents: A Brief Overview. North American Directory Forum. 1993 February; 4 p. (Format: TXT=7270 bytes) (Obsoletes RFC 1295, RFC 1255, RFC 1218)

1416 Telnet Authentication Option. Borman, D.A.,ed. 1993 February; 7 p. (Format: TXT=13270 bytes) (Obsoletes RFC 1409)

1415 FTP-FTAM Gateway Specification. Mindel, J.L.; Slaski, R.L. 1993 January; 58 p. (Format: TXT=128261 bytes)

1414 Identification MIB. St. Johns, M.; Rose, M.T. 1993 February; 7 p. (Format: TXT=14165 bytes)

1413 Identification Protocol. St. Johns, M. 1993 February; 8 p. (Format: TXT=16291 bytes) (Obsoletes RFC 931)

1412 Telnet Authentication: SPX. Alagappan, K. 1993 January; 4 p. (Format: TXT=6952 bytes)

1411 Telnet Authentication: Kerberos Version 4. Borman, D.A.,ed. 1993 January; 4 p. (Format: TXT=7967 bytes)

1410 Not yet issued.

1409 Telnet Authentication Option. Borman, D.A.,ed. 1993 January; 7 p. (Format: TXT=13119 bytes) (Obsoleted by RFC 1416)

1408 Telnet Environment Option. Borman, D.A.,ed. 1993 January; 7 p. (Format: TXT=13936 bytes)

1407 Definitions of Managed Objects for the DS3/E3 Interface Type. Cox, T.A.; Tesink, K.,eds. 1993 January; 43 p. (Format: TXT=90682 bytes) (Obsoletes RFC 1233)

1406 Definitions of Managed Objects for the DS1 and E1 Interface Types. Baker, F.; Watt, J.,eds. 1993 January; 50 p. (Format: TXT=97559 bytes) (Obsoletes RFC 1232)

1405 Mapping between X.400 (1984/1988) and Mail-11 (DECnet mail). Allocchio, C. 1993 January; 19 p. (Format: TXT=33885 bytes)

1404 A Model for Common Operation Statistics. Stockman, B. 1993 January; 27 p. (Format: TXT=52814 bytes)

1403 BGPOSPF interaction. Varadhan, K. 1993 January; 17 p. (Format: TXT=36173 bytes) (Obsoletes RFC 1364)

1402 There's Gold in them thar Networks! or Searching for Treasure in all the Wrong Places. Martin, J. 1993 January; 39 p. (Format: TXT=71176 bytes) (Also FYI 10) (Obsoletes RFC 1290)

1401 Correspondence between the IAB and DISA on the use of DNS throughout the Internet. Chapin, A.L. 1993 January; 8 p. (Format: TXT=12528 bytes)

1400 Transition and Modernization of the Internet Registration Service. Williamson, S. 1993 March; 7 p. (Format: TXT=13008 bytes)

1399 Not yet issued.

1398 Not yet issued.

1397 Default Route Advertisement In BGP2 And BGP3 Versions of the Border Gateway Protocol. Haskin, D. 1993 January; 2 p. (Format: TXT=4124 bytes)

1396 The Process for Organization of Internet Standards Working Group (POISED). Crocker, S.D. 1993 January; 10 p. (Format: TXT=22096 bytes)

1395 BOOTP Vendor Information Extensions. Reynolds, J.K. 1993 January; 8 p. (Format: TXT=16314 bytes) (Obsoletes RFC 1084, RFC 1048; Updates RFC 951)

1394 Relationship of Telex Answerback Codes to Internet Domains. Robinson, P. 1993 January; 17 p. (Format: TXT=43776 bytes)

1393 Traceroute Using an IP Option. Malkin, G.S. 1993 January; 7 p. (Format: TXT=13140 bytes)

1392 Internet Users' Glossary. Malkin, G.S.; Parker, T.L.,eds. 1993 January; 53 p. (Format: TXT=104624 bytes) (Also FYI 18)

1391   The Tao of IETF: A Guide for New Attendees of the Internet Engineering Task Force. Malkin, G.S. 1993 January; 19 p. (Format: TXT=23569 bytes) (Also FYI 17)

1390   Transmission of IP and ARP over FDDI Networks. Katz, D. 1993 January; 11 p. (Format: TXT=22077 bytes)

1389   RIP Version 2 MIB Extension. Malkin, G.S.; Baker, F. 1993 January; 13 p. (Format: TXT=23569 bytes)

1388   RIP Version 2: Carrying Additional Information. Malkin, G.S. 1993 January; 7 p. (Format: TXT=16227 bytes) (Updates RFC 1058)

1387   RIP Version 2 Protocol Analysis. Malkin, G.S. 1993 January; 3 p. (Format: TXT=5598 bytes)

1386   The U.S. Domain. Cooper, A.; Postel, J.B. 1992 December; 31 p. (Format: TXT=62310 bytes)

1385   EIP: The Extended Internet Protocol: A framework for maintaining background compatibility. Wang, Z. 1992 November; 17 p. (Format: TXT=39166 bytes)

1384   Not yet issued.

1383   Not yet issued.

1382   SNMP MIB extensions for the X.25 packet layer. Throop, D.D.,ed. 1992 November; 69 p. (Format: TXT=153877 bytes)

1381   SNMP MIB extension for X.25 LAPB. Throop, D.D.; Baker, F. 1992 November; 33 p. (Format: TXT=71253 bytes)

1380   IESG deliberations on routing and addressing. Gross, P.G.; Almquist, P. 1992 November; 22 p. (Format: TXT=49415 bytes)

1379   Extending TCP for transactions — Concepts. Braden, R.T. 1992 November; 38 p. (Format: TXT=91353 bytes)

1378   PPP AppleTalk Control Protocol (ATCP). Parker, B. 1992 November; 16 p. (Format: TXT=28496 bytes)

1377   PPP OSI Network Layer Control Protocol (OSINLCP). Katz, D. 1992 November; 10 p. (Format: TXT=22109 bytes)

1376   PPP DECnet Phase IV Control Protocol (DNCP). Senum, S.J. 1992 November; 6 p. (Format: TXT=12448 bytes)

1375   Suggestion for new classes of IP addresses. Robinson, P. 1992 October; 7 p. (Format: TXT=16990 bytes)

1374   IP and ARP on HIPPI. Renwick, J.K.; Nicholson, A. 1992 October; 43 p. (Format: TXT=100903 bytes)

1373   Portable DUAs. Tignor, T. 1992 October; 12 p. (Format: TXT=19931 bytes)

1372   Telnet remote flow control option. Hedrick, C.L.; Borman, D. 1992 October; 6 p. (Format: TXT=11098 bytes) (Obsoletes RFC 1080)

1353   Definitions of managed objects for administration of SNMP parties. McCloghrie, K.; Davin, J.R.; Galvin, J.M. 1992 July; 26 p. (Format: TXT=59556 bytes)

1352   SNMP security protocols. Galvin, J.M.; McCloghrie, K.; Davin, J.R. 1992 July; 41 p. (Format: TXT=95732 bytes)

1351   SNMP administrative model. Davin, J.R.; Galvin, J.M.; McCloghrie, K. 1992 July; 35 p. (Format: TXT=80721 bytes)

1350   TFTP protocol (revision 2). Sollins, K.R. 1992 July; 11 p. (Format: TXT=24599 bytes) (Obsoletes RFC 783)

1349   Type of Service in the Internet protocol suite. Almquist, P. 1992 July; 28 p. (Format: TXT=68949 bytes) (Updates RFC 1248, RFC 1247, RFC 1195, RFC 1123, RFC 1122, RFC 1060, RFC 791)

1348   DNS NSAP RRs. Manning, B. 1992 July; 4 p. (Format: TXT=6871 bytes) (Updates RFC 1034, RFC 1035)

1347   TCP and UDP with Bigger Addresses (TUBA), A simple proposal for Internet addressing and routing. Callon, R.W. 1992 June; 7 p. (Format: TXT=26562, PS=42398 bytes)

1346   Resource allocation, control, and accounting for the use of network resources. Jones, P. 1992 June; 6 p. (Format: TXT=13084 bytes)

1345   Character mnemonics and character sets. Simonsen, K. 1992 June; 103 p. (Format: TXT=249737 bytes)

1344   Implications of MIME for Internet mail gateways. Borenstein, N. 1992 June; 8 p. (Format: TXT=25872, PS=51812 bytes)

1343   User agent configuration mechanism for multimedia mail format information. Borenstein, N. 1992 June; 10 p. (Format: TXT=29295, PS=59978 bytes)

1342   Representation of non-ASCII text in Internet message headers. Moore, K. 1992 June; 7 p. (Format: TXT=15845 bytes)

1341   MIME (Multipurpose Internet Mail Extensions): Mechanisms for specifying and describing the format of Internet message bodies. Borenstein, N.; Freed, N. 1992 June; 69 p. (Format: TXT=211117, PS=347082 bytes)

1340   Assigned Numbers. Reynolds, J.K.; Postel, J.B. 1992 July; 138 p. (Format: TXT=232974 bytes) (Obsoletes RFC 1060)

1339   Remote mail checking protocol. Dorner, S.; Resnick, P. 1992 June; 5 p. (Format: TXT=13115 bytes)

1338   Supernetting: An address assignment and aggregation strategy. Fuller, V.; Li, T.; Yu, J.Y.; Varadhan, K. 1992 June; 20 p. (Format: TXT=47975 bytes)

1337   TIME-WAIT assassination hazards in TCP. Braden, R.T. 1992 May; 11 p. (Format: TXT=22887 bytes)

1336   Who's who in the Internet: Biographies of IAB, IESG and IRSG members. Malkin, G.S. 1992 May; 33 p. (Format: TXT=92119 bytes) (Also FYI 9) (Obsoletes RFC 1251)

1335   Two-tier address structure for the Internet: A solution to the problem of address space exhaustion. Wang, Z.; Crowcroft, J. 1992 May; 7 p. (Format: TXT=15418 bytes)

1334   Not yet issued.

1333   PPP link quality monitoring. Simpson, W.A. 1992 May; 15 p. (Format: TXT=29965 bytes)

1332   PPP Internet Protocol Control Protocol (IPCP). McGregor, G. 1992 May; 12 p. (Format: TXT=17613 bytes) (Obsoletes RFC 1172)

1331   Point-to-Point Protocol (PPP) for the transmission of multi-protocol datagrams over point-to-point links. Simpson, W.A. 1992 May; 66 p. (Format: TXT=129892 bytes) (Obsoletes RFC 1171, RFC 1172)

1330   Recommendations for the phase I deployment of OSI Directory Services (X.500) and OSI Message Handling Services (X.400) within the ESnet community. ESnet Site Coordinating Committee, X.500/X.400 Task Force. 1992 May; 87 p. (Format: TXT=192925 bytes)

1329   Thoughts on address resolution for dual MAC FDDI networks. Kuehn, P. 1992 May; 28 p. (Format: TXT=58150 bytes)

1328   X.400 1988 to 1984 downgrading. Hardcastle-Kille, S.E. 1992 May; 5 p. (Format: TXT=10006 bytes)

1327   Mapping between X.400(1988)/ISO 10021 and RFC 822. Hardcastle-Kille, S.E. 1992 May; 113 p. (Format: TXT=228598 bytes) (Obsoletes RFC 1148, RFC 1138, RFC 1026, RFC 987; Updates RFC 822)

1326   Mutual encapsulation considered dangerous. Tsuchiya, P.F. 1992 May; 5 p. (Format: TXT=11241 bytes)

1325   FYI on questions and answers: Answers to commonly asked "new Internet user" questions. Malkin, G.S.; Marine, A.N. 1992 May; 42 p. (Format: TXT=91884 bytes) (Also FYI 4) (Obsoletes RFC 1206)

1324   Discussion on computer network conferencing. Reed, D. 1992 May; 11 p. (Format: TXT=24988 bytes)

1323   TCP extensions for high performance. Jacobson, V.; Braden, R.T.; Borman, D.A. 1992 May; 37 p. (Format: TXT=84558 bytes) (Obsoletes RFC 1072, RFC 1185)

1322   Unified approach to inter-domain routing. Estrin, D.; Rekhter, Y.; Hotz, S. 1992 May; 38 p. (Format: TXT=96934 bytes)

1321   MD5 Message-Digest algorithm. Rivest, R.L. 1992 April; 21 p. (Format: TXT=35222 bytes)

1320   MD4 Message-Digest algorithm. Rivest, R.L. 1992 April; 20 p. (Format: TXT=32407 bytes) (Obsoletes RFC 1186)

1319   MD2 Message-Digest algorithm. Kaliski, B.S. 1992 April; 17 p. (Format: TXT=25661 bytes) (Updates RFC 1115)

1318   Definitions of managed objects for parallel-printer-like hardware devices. Stewart, B.,ed. 1992 April; 11 p. (Format: TXT=19570 bytes)

1317   Definitions of managed objects for RS-232-like hardware devices. Stewart, B.,ed. 1992 April; 17 p. (Format: TXT=30442 bytes)

1316   Definitions of managed objects for character stream devices. Stewart, B.,ed. 1992 April; 17 p. (Format: TXT=35143 bytes)

1315   Management Information Base for frame relay DTEs. Brown, C.; Baker, F.; Carvalho, C. 1992 April; 19 p. (Format: TXT=33825 bytes)

1314   File format for the exchange of images in the Internet. Katz, A.R.; Cohen, D. 1992 April; 23 p. (Format: TXT=54072 bytes)

1313   Today's programming for KRFC AM 1313 Internet talk radio. Partridge, C. 1992 April 1; 3 p. (Format: TXT=5444 bytes)

1312   Message Send Protocol 2. Nelson, R.; Arnold, G. 1992 April; 8 p. (Format: TXT=18037 bytes) (Obsoletes RFC 1159)

1311   Introduction to the STD notes. Postel, J.B.,ed. 1992 March; 5 p. (Format: TXT=11308 bytes)

1310   Internet standards process. Chapin, A.L. 1992 March; 23 p. (Format: TXT=54738 bytes)

1309   Technical overview of directory services using the X.500 protocol. Weider, C.; Reynolds, J.K.; Heker, S. 1992 March; 16 p. (Format: TXT=35694 bytes) (Also FYI 14)

1308   Executive introduction to directory services using the X.500 protocol. Weider, C.; Reynolds, J.K. 1992 March; 4 p. (Format: TXT=9392 bytes) (Also FYI 13)

1307   Dynamically switched link control protocol. Nicholson, A.; Young, J. 1992 March; 13 p. (Format: TXT=24145 bytes)

1306   Experiences supporting by-request circuit-switched T3 networks. Nicholson, A.; Young, J. 1992 March; 10 p. (Format: TXT=25788 bytes)

1305   Network Time Protocol (Version 3): Specification, implementation, and analysis. Mills, D.L. 1992 March; 113 p. (Format: TXT=307085, tar.Z=815759 bytes) (Obsoletes RFC 1119)

1304   Definitions of managed objects for the SIP interface type. Cox, T.A.; Tesink, K.,eds. 1992 February; 25 p. (Format: TXT=5241 bytes)

1303   Convention for describing SNMP-based agents. McCloghrie, K.; Rose, M.T. 1992 February; 12 p. (Format: TXT=22915 bytes)

1302   Building a network information services infrastructure. Sitzler, D.D.; Smith, P.G.; Marine, A.N. 1992 February; 13 p. (Format: TXT=29135 bytes) (Also FYI 12)

1301   Multicast Transport Protocol. Armstrong, S.M.; Freier, A.O.; Marzullo, K.A. 1992 February; 38 p. (Format: TXT=91976 bytes)

1300   Remembrances of things past. Greenfield, S.R. 1992 February; 4 p. (Format: TXT=4963 bytes)

1299   Not yet issued.

1298   SNMP over IPX. Wormley, R.B.; Bostock, S. 1992 February; 5 p. (Format: TXT=7878 bytes)

1297   NOC integrated trouble ticket system: Functional specification wish list ("NOC TT requirements"). Johnson, D.S. 1992 January; 12 p. (Format: TXT=32964 bytes)

1296   Internet Growth (1981-1991). Lottor, M. 1992 January; 9 p. (Format: TXT=20103 bytes)

1295   User bill of rights for entries and listing in the public directory. North American Directory Forum. 1992 January; 2 p. (Format: TXT=3502 bytes)

1294   Multiprotocol interconnect over Frame Relay. Bradley, T.; Brown, C.; Malis, A.G. 1992 January; 28 p. (Format: TXT=54992 bytes)

1293   Inverse Address Resolution Protocol. Bradley, T.; Brown, C. 1992 January; 6 p. (Format: TXT=11368 bytes)

1292   Catalog of Available X.500 Implementations. Lang, R.; Wright, R. 1991 December; 103 p. (Format: TXT=129468 bytes) (Also FYI 11)

1291   Mid-Level networks: Potential technical services. Aggarwal, V. 1991 December; 10 p. (Format: TXT=24314, PS=218918 bytes)

1290   There's Gold in them thar Networks! or Searching for Treasure in all the Wrong Places. Martin, J. 1991 December; 27 p. (Format: TXT=46997 bytes) (Also FYI 10)

1289   DECnet phase IV MIB extensions. Saperia, J. 1991 December; 64 p. (Format: TXT=122272 bytes)

1288   Finger User Information Protocol. Zimmerman, D.P. 1991 December; 12 p. (Format: TXT=25161 bytes) (Obsoletes RFC 1196)

1287   Towards the future Internet architecture. Clark, D.D.; Chapin, L.A.; Cerf, V.G.; Braden, R.T.; Hobby, R. 1991 December; 29 p. (Format: TXT=59812 bytes)

1286   Definitions of managed objects for bridges. Decker, E.; Langille, P.; Rijsinghani, A.; McCloghrie, K. 1991 December; 40 p. (Format: TXT=79104 bytes)

1285 FDDI Management Information Base. Case, J.D. 1992 January; 46 p. (Format: TXT=99747 bytes)

1284 Definitions of managed objects for the Ethernet-like interface types. Cook, J.,ed. 1991 December; 21 p. (Format: TXT=43225 bytes)

1283 SNMP over OSI. Rose, M.T. 1991 December; 8 p. (Format: TXT=16814 bytes) (Obsoletes RFC 1161)

1282 BSD rlogin. Kantor, B. 1991 December; 5 p. (Format: TXT=10704 bytes) (Obsoletes RFC 1258)

1281 Guidelines for the secure operations of the Internet. Pethia, R.D.; Crocker, S.D.; Fraser, B.Y. 1991 November; 10 p. (Format: TXT=22618 bytes)

1280 IAB official protocol standards. Postel, J.B.,ed. 1992 March; 32 p. (Format: TXT=70458 bytes) (Obsoletes RFC 1250; Obsoleted by RFC 1360)

1279 X.500 and domains. Hardcastle-Kille, S.E. 1991 November; 13 p. (Format: TXT=26669, PS=170029 bytes)

1278 String encoding of presentation address. Hardcastle-Kille, S.E. 1991 November; 5 p. (Format: TXT=10256, PS=128696 bytes)

1277 Encoding network addresses to support operations over non-OSI lower layers. Hardcastle-Kille, S.E. 1991 November; 10 p. (Format: TXT=22254 , PS=176169 bytes)

1276 Replication and distributed operations extensions to provide an Internet directory using X.500. Hardcastle-Kille, S.E. 1991 November; 17 p. (Format: TXT=33731, PS=217170 bytes)

1275 Replication requirements to provide an Internet directory using X.500. Hardcastle-Kille, S.E. 1991 November; 2 p. (Format: TXT=4616, PS=83736 bytes)

1274 COSINE and Internet X.500 schema. Hardcastle-Kille, S.E.; Barker, P. 1991 November; 60 p. (Format: TXT=92827 bytes)

1273 Measurement study of changes in service-level reachability in the global TCP/IP Internet: Goals, experimental design, implementation, and policy considerations. Schwartz, M.F. 1991 November; 8 p. (Format: TXT=19949 bytes)

1272 Internet accounting: Background. Mills, C.; Hirsh, D.; Ruth, G.R. 1991 November; 19 p. (Format: TXT=46562 bytes)

1271 Remote network monitoring Management Information Base. Waldbusser, S. 1991 November; 81 p. (Format: TXT=184111 bytes)

1270 SNMP communications services. Kastenholz, F.,ed. 1991 October; 11 p. (Format: TXT=26167 bytes)

1269 Definitions of managed objects for the Border Gateway Protocol: Version 3. Willis, S.; Burruss, J.W. 1991 October; 13 p. (Format: TXT=25717 bytes)

1268 Application of the Border Gateway Protocol in the Internet. Rekhter, Y.; Gross, P.,eds. 1991 October; 13 p. (Format: TXT=31102 bytes) (Obsoletes RFC 1164)

1267 Border Gateway Protocol 3 (BGP-3). Lougheed, K.; Rekhter, Y. 1991 October; 35 p. (Format: TXT=80724 bytes) (Obsoletes RFC 1163)

1266 Experience with the BGP protocol. Rekhter, Y.,ed. 1991 October; 9 p. (Format: TXT=21938 bytes)

1265 BGP protocol analysis. Rekhter, Y.,ed. 1991 October; 8 p. (Format: TXT=20728 bytes)

1264 Internet Engineering Task Force internet routing protocol standardization criteria. Hinden, R.M. 1991 October; 8 p. (Format: TXT=17016 bytes)

1263 TCP extensions considered harmful. O'Malley, S.; Peterson, L.L. 1991 October; 19 p. (Format: TXT=54078 bytes)

1262 Guidelines for Internet measurement activities. Cerf, V.G.,ed. 1991 October; 3 p. (Format: TXT=6381 bytes)

1261 Transiton of NIC services. Williamson, S.; Nobile, L. 1991 September; 3 p. (Format: TXT=4488 bytes)

1260 Not yet issued.

1259 Building the open road: The NREN as test-bed for the national public network. Kapor, M. 1991 September; 23 p. (Format: TXT=62944 bytes)

1258 BSD Rlogin. Kantor, B. 1991 September; 5 p. (Format: TXT=10763 bytes) (Obsoleted by RFC 1282)

1257 Isochronous applications do not require jitter-controlled networks. Partridge, C. 1991 September; 5 p. (Format: TXT=11075 bytes)

1256 ICMP router discovery messages. Deering, S.E.,ed. 1991 September; 19 p. (Format: TXT=44628 bytes)

1255 Naming scheme for c=U.S. North American Directory Forum. 1991 September; 25 p. (Format: TXT=53783 bytes) (Obsoletes RFC 1218)

1254 Gateway congestion control survey. Mankin, A.; Ramakrishnan, K.K., eds. 1991 August; 25 p. (Format: TXT=69793 bytes)

1253 OSPF version 2: Management Information Base. Baker, F.; Coltun, R. 1991 August; 42 p. (Format: TXT=77232 bytes) (Obsoletes RFC 1252)

1252 OSPF version 2: Management Information Base. Baker, F.; Coltun, R. 1991 August; 42 p. (Format: TXT=77250 bytes) (Obsoletes RFC 1248; Obsoleted by RFC 1253)

1251 Who's who in the internet: Biographies of IAB, IESG and IRSG members. Malkin, G.S. 1991 August; 26 p. (Format: TXT=72721 bytes) (Also FYI 9) (Obsoleted by RFC 1336)

1250   IAB official protocol standards. Postel, J.B.,ed. 1991 August; 28 p. (Format: TXT=65279 bytes) (Obsoletes RFC 1200; Obsoleted by RFC 1280)

1249   DIXIE protocol specification. Howes, T.; Smith, M.; Beecher, B. 1991 August; 10 p. (Format: TXT=20693 bytes)

1248   OSPF version 2: Management Information Base. Baker, F.; Coltun, R. 1991 July; 42 p. (Format: TXT=77126 bytes) (Obsoleted by RFC 1252; Updated by RFC 1349)

1247   OSPF version 2. Moy, J. 1991 July; 189 p. (Format: PS=1063028, TXT=443917 bytes) (Obsoletes RFC 1131; Updated by RFC 1349)

1246   Experience with the OSPF protocol. Moy, J.,ed. 1991 July; 31 p. (Format: PS=146913, TXT=72180 bytes)

1245   OSPF protocol analysis. Moy, J.,ed. 1991 July; 12 p. (Format: PS=64094, TXT=27492 bytes)

1244   Site Security Handbook. Holbrook, J.P.; Reynolds, J.K.,eds. 1991 July; 101 p. (Format: TXT=259129 bytes) (Also FYI 8)

1243   Appletalk Management Information Base. Waldbusser, S.,ed. 1991 July; 29 p. (Format: TXT=61985 bytes)

1242   Benchmarking terminology for network interconnection devices. Bradner, S.,ed. 1991 July; 12 p. (Format: TXT=22817 bytes)

1241   Scheme for an internet encapsulation protocol: Version 1. Woodburn, R.A.; Mills, D.L. 1991 July; 17 p. (Format: TXT=42468, PS=128921 bytes)

1240   OSI connectionless transport services on top of UDP: Version 1. Shue, C.; Haggerty, W.; Dobbins, K. 1991 June; 8 p. (Format: TXT=18140 bytes)

1239   Reassignment of experimental MIBs to standard MIBs. Reynolds, J.K. 1991 June; 2 p. (Format: TXT=3656 bytes) (Updates RFC 1229, RFC 1230, RFC 1231, RFC 1232, RFC 1233)

1238   CLNS MIB for use with Connectionless Network Protocol (ISO 8473) and End System to Intermediate System (ISO 9542). Satz, G. 1991 June; 32 p. (Format: TXT=65159 bytes) (Obsoletes RFC 1162)

1237   Guidelines for OSI NSAP allocation in the internet. Collela, R.; Gardner, E.P.; Callon, R.W. 1991 July; 38 p. (Format: PS=162808, TXT=119962 bytes)

1236   IP to X.121 address mapping for DDN. Morales, L.F., Jr.; Hasse, P.R. 1991 June; 7 p. (Format: TXT=12626 bytes)

1235   Coherent File Distribution Protocol. Ioannidis, J.; Maguire, G.Q., Jr. 1991 June; 12 p. (Format: TXT=29345 bytes)

1234   Tunneling IPX traffic through IP networks. Provan, D. 1991 June; 6 p. (Format: TXT=12333 bytes)

1233   Definitions of managed objects for the DS3 Interface type. Cox, T.A.; Tesink, K.,eds. 1991 May; 23 p. (Format: TXT=49559 bytes) (Updated by RFC 1239)

1232   Definitions of managed objects for the DS1 Interface type. Baker, F.; Kolb, C.P.,eds. 1991 May; 28 p. (Format: TXT=60757 bytes) (Updated by RFC 1239)

1231   IEEE 802.5 Token Ring MIB. McCloghrie, K.; Fox, R.; Decker, E. 1991 May; 23 p. (Format: TXT=53542 bytes) (Updated by RFC 1239)

1230   IEEE 802.4 Token Bus MIB. McCloghrie, K.; Fox, R. 1991 May; 23 p. (Format: TXT=53100 bytes) (Updated by RFC 1239)

1229   Extensions to the generic-interface MIB. McCloghrie, K.,ed. 1991 May; 16 p. (Format: TXT=36022 bytes) (Updated by RFC 1239)

1228   SNMP-DPI: Simple Network Management Protocol Distributed Program Interface. Carpenter, G.; Wijnen, B. 1991 May; 50 p. (Format: TXT=96972 bytes)

1227   SNMP MUX protocol and MIB. Rose, M.T. 1991 May; 13 p. (Format: TXT=25868 bytes)

1226   Internet protocol encapsulation of AX.25 frames. Kantor, B. 1991 May; 2 p. (Format: TXT=2573 bytes)

1225   Post Office Protocol: Version 3. Rose, M.T. 1991 May; 16 p. (Format: TXT=37340 bytes) (Obsoletes RFC 1081)

1224   Techniques for managing asynchronously generated alerts. Steinberg, L. 1991 May; 22 p. (Format: TXT=54303 bytes)

1223   OSI CLNS and LLC1 protocols on Network Systems HYPERchannel. Halpern, J.M. 1991 May; 12 p. (Format: TXT=29601 bytes)

1222   Advancing the NSFNET routing architecture. Braun, H.W.; Rekhter, Y. 1991 May; 6 p. (Format: TXT=15067 bytes)

1221   Host Access Protocol (HAP) specification: Version 2. Edmond, W. 1991 April; 68 p. (Format: TXT=156550 bytes) (Updates RFC 907)

1220   Point-to-Point Protocol extensions for bridging. Baker, F.,ed. 1991 April; 18 p. (Format: TXT=38165 bytes)

1219   On the assignment of subnet numbers. Tsuchiya, P.F. 1991 April; 13 p. (Format: TXT=30609 bytes)

1218   Naming scheme for c=U.S. North American Directory Forum. 1991 April; 23 p. (Format: TXT=42698 bytes)

1217   Memo from the Consortium for Slow Commotion Research (CSCR). Cerf, V.G. 1991 April 1; 5 p. (Format: TXT=11079 bytes)

1216   Gigabit network economics and paradigm shifts. Richard, P.; Kynikos, P. 1991 April 1; 4 p. (Format: TXT=8130 bytes)

1215   Convention for defining traps for use with the SNMP. Rose, M.T.,ed. 1991 March; 9 p. (Format: TXT=19336 bytes)

1214   OSI internet management: Management Information Base. LaBarre, L.,ed. 1991 April; 83 p. (Format: TXT=172564 bytes)

1213   Management Information Base for network management of TCP/IP-based internets: MIB-II. McCloghrie, K.; Rose, M.T.,eds. 1991 March; 70 p. (Format: TXT=146080 bytes) (Obsoletes RFC 1158)

1212   Concise MIB definitions. Rose, M.T.; McCloghrie, K.,eds. 1991 March; 19 p. (Format: TXT=43579 bytes)

1211   Problems with the maintenance of large mailing lists. Westine, A.; Postel, J.B. 1991 March; 54 p. (Format: TXT=96167 bytes)

1210   Network and infrastructure user requirements for transatlantic research collaboration: Brussels, July 16-18, and Washington July 24-25, 1990. Cerf, V.G.; Kirstein, P.T.; Randell, B.,eds. 1991 March; 36 p. (Format: TXT=79048 bytes)

1209   Transmission of IP datagrams over the SMDS Service. Piscitello, D.M.; Lawrence, J. 1991 March; 11 p. (Format: TXT=25280 bytes)

1208   Glossary of networking terms. Jacobsen, O.J.; Lynch, D.C. 1991 March; 18 p. (Format: TXT=41156 bytes)

1207   FYI on Questions and Answers: Answers to commonly asked "experienced Internet user" questions. Malkin, G.S.; Marine, A.N.; Reynolds, J.K. 1991 February; 15 p. (Format: TXT=33385 bytes) (Also FYI 7)

1206   FYI on Questions and Answers: Answers to commonly asked "new Internet user" questions. Malkin, G.S.; Marine, A.N. 1991 February; 32 p. (Format: TXT=72479 bytes) (Also FYI 4) (Obsoletes RFC 1177; Obsoleted by RFC 1325)

1205   5250 Telnet interface. Chmielewski, P. 1991 February; 12 p. (Format: TXT=27179 bytes)

1204   Message Posting Protocol (MPP). Yeh, S.; Lee, D. 1991 February; 6 p. (Format: TXT=11371 bytes)

1203   Interactive Mail Access Protocol: Version 3. Rice, J. 1991 February; 49 p. (Format: TXT=123325 bytes) (Obsoletes RFC 1064)

1202   Directory Assistance service. Rose, M.T. 1991 February; 11 p. (Format: TXT=21645 bytes)

1201   Transmitting IP traffic over ARCNET networks. Provan, D. 1991 February; 7 p. (Format: TXT=16959 bytes) (Obsoletes RFC 1051)

1200   IAB official protocol standards. Defense Advanced Research Projects Agency, Internet Activities Board. 1991 April; 31 p. (Format: TXT=67069 bytes) (Obsoletes RFC 1140; Obsoleted by RFC 1250)

1199   Request for Comments Summary: RFC Numbers 1100-1199. Reynolds, J.K. 1991 December; 22 p. (Format: TXT=46443 bytes)

1198 FYI on the X window system. Scheifler, R.W. 1991 January; 3 p. (Format: TXT=3629 bytes) (Also FYI 6)

1197 Using ODA for translating multimedia information. Sherman, M. 1990 December; 2 p. (Format: TXT=3620 bytes)

1196 Finger User Information Protocol. Zimmerman, D.P. 1990 December; 12 p. (Format: TXT=24799 bytes) (Obsoletes RFC 1194; Obsoleted by RFC 1288)

1195 Use of OSI IS-IS for routing in TCP/IP and dual environments. Callon, R.W. 1990 December; 65 p. (Format: PS=381799, TXT=192628 bytes) (Updated by RFC 1349)

1194 Finger User Information Protocol. Zimmerman, D.P. 1990 November; 12 p. (Format: TXT=24626 bytes) (Obsoletes RFC 742; Obsoleted by RFC 1196)

1193 Client requirements for real-time communication services. Ferrari, D. 1990 November; 24 p. (Format: TXT=61540 bytes)

1192 Commercialization of the Internet summary report. Kahin, B.,ed. 1990 November; 13 p. (Format: TXT=35253 bytes)

1191 Path MTU discovery. Mogul, J.C.; Deering, S.E. 1990 November; 19 p. (Format: TXT=47936 bytes) (Obsoletes RFC 1063)

1190 Experimental Internet Stream Protocol: Version 2 (ST-II). Topolcic, C.,ed. 1990 October; 148 p. (Format: TXT=386909 bytes) (Obsoletes IEN 119)

1189 Common Management Information Services and Protocols for the Internet (CMOT and CMIP). Warrier, U.S.; Besaw, L.; LaBarre, L.; Handspicker, B.D. 1990 October; 15 p. (Format: TXT=32928 bytes) (Obsoletes RFC 1095)

1188 Proposed standard for the transmission of IP datagrams over FDDI networks. Katz, D. 1990 October; 11 p. (Format: TXT=22424 bytes) (Obsoletes RFC 1103)

1187 Bulk table retrieval with the SNMP. Rose, M.T.; McCloghrie, K.; Davin, J.R. 1990 October; 12 p. (Format: TXT=27220 bytes)

1186 MD4 message digest algorithm. Rivest, R.L. 1990 October; 18 p. (Format: TXT=35391 bytes) (Obsoleted by RFC 1320)

1185 TCP extension for high-speed paths. Jacobson, V.; Braden, R.T.; Zhang, L. 1990 October; 21 p. (Format: TXT=49508 bytes) (Obsoleted by RFC 1323)

1184 Telnet Linemode option. Borman, D.A.,ed. 1990 October; 23 p. (Format: TXT=53085 bytes) (Obsoletes RFC 1116)

1183 New DNS RR definitions. Everhart, C.F.; Mamakos, L.A.; Ullmann, R.; Mockapetris, P.V. 1990 October; 11 p. (Format: TXT=23788 bytes) (Updates RFC 1034, RFC 1035)

1182 Not yet issued.

1181   RIPE terms of reference. Blokzijl, R. 1990 September; 2 p. (Format: TXT=2523 bytes)

1180   TCP/IP tutorial. Socolofsky, T.J.; Kale, C.J. 1991 January; 28 p. (Format: TXT=65494 bytes)

1179   Line printer daemon protocol. McLaughlin, L. 1990 August; 14 p. (Format: TXT=24324 bytes)

1178   Choosing a name for your computer. Libes, D. 1990 August; 8 p. (Format: TXT=18472 bytes) (Also FYI 5)

1177   FYI on Questions and Answers: Answers to commonly asked "new internet user" questions. Malkin, G.S.; Marine, A.N.; Reynolds, J.K. 1990 August; 24 p. (Format: TXT=52852 bytes) (Also FYI 4) (Obsoleted by RFC 1206)

1176   Interactive Mail Access Protocol: Version 2. Crispin, M.R. 1990 August; 30 p. (Format: TXT=67330 bytes) (Obsoletes RFC 1064)

1175   FYI on where to start: A bibliography of internetworking information. Bowers, K.L.; LaQuey, T.L.; Reynolds, J.K.; Roubicek, K.; Stahl, M.K.; Yuan, A. 1990 August; 42 p. (Format: TXT=67330 bytes) (Also FYI 3)

1174   IAB recommended policy on distributing internet identifier assignment and IAB recommended policy change to internet "connected" status. Cerf, V.G. 1990 August; 9 p. (Format: TXT=21321 bytes)

1173   Responsibilities of host and network managers: A summary of the "oral tradition" of the Internet. VanBokkelen, J. 1990 August; 5 p. (Format: TXT=12527 bytes)

1172   Point-to-Point Protocol (PPP) initial configuration options. Perkins, D.; Hobby, R. 1990 July; 38 p. (Format: TXT=76132 bytes) (Obsoleted by RFC 1331, RFC 1332)

1171   Point-to-Point Protocol (PPP) for the transmission of multi-protocol datagrams over Point-to-Point links. Perkins, D. 1990 July; 48 p. (Format: TXT=92321 bytes) (Obsoletes RFC 1134; Obsoleted by RFC 1331)

1170   Public key standards and licenses. Fougner, R.B. 1991 January; 2 p. (Format: TXT=3144 bytes)

1169   Explaining the role of GOSIP. Cerf, V.G.; Mills, K.L. 1990 August; 15 p. (Format: TXT=30255 bytes)

1168   Intermail and Commercial Mail Relay services. Westine, A.; DeSchon, A.L.; Postel, J.B.; Ward, C.E. 1990 July; 23 p. (Format: PS=149816 bytes)

1167   Thoughts on the National Research and Education Network. Cerf, V.G. 1990 July; 8 p. (Format: TXT=20682 bytes)

1166   Internet numbers. Kirkpatrick, S.; Stahl, M.K.; Recker, M. 1990 July; 182 p. (Format: TXT=566778 bytes) (Obsoletes RFC 1117, RFC 1062, RFC 1020)

1165 Network Time Protocol (NTP) over the OSI Remote Operations Service. Crowcroft, J.; Onions, J.P. 1990 June; 10 p. (Format: TXT=18277 bytes)

1164 Application of the Border Gateway Protocol in the Internet. Honig, J.C.; Katz, D.; Mathis, M.; Rekhter, Y.; Yu, J.Y. 1990 June; 23 p. (Format: TXT=56278 bytes) (Obsoleted by RFC 1268)

1163 Border Gateway Protocol (BGP). Lougheed, K.; Rekhter, Y. 1990 June; 29 p. (Format: TXT=69404 bytes) (Obsoletes RFC 1105; Obsoleted by RFC 1267)

1162 Connectionless Network Protocol (ISO 8473) and End System to Intermediate System (ISO 9542) Management Information Base. Satz, G. 1990 June; 70 p. (Format: TXT=109893 bytes) (Obsoleted by RFC 1238)

1161 SNMP over OSI. Rose, M.T. 1990 June; 8 p. (Format: TXT=16036 bytes) (Obsoleted by RFC 1283)

1160 Internet Activities Board. Cerf, V. 1990 May; 11 p. (Format: TXT=28182 bytes) (Obsoletes RFC 1120)

1159 Message Send Protocol. Nelson, R. 1990 June; 2 p. (Format: TXT=3957 bytes) (Obsoleted by RFC 1312)

1158 Management Information Base for network management of TCP/IP-based internets: MIB-II. Rose, M.T.,ed. 1990 May; 133 p. (Format: TXT=212152 bytes) (Obsoleted by RFC 1213)

1157 Simple Network Management Protocol (SNMP). Case, J.D.; Fedor, M.; Schoffstall, M.L.; Davin, C. 1990 May; 36 p. (Format: TXT=74894 bytes) (Obsoletes RFC 1098)

1156 Management Information Base for network management of TCP/IP-based internets. McCloghrie, K.; Rose, M.T. 1990 May; 91 p. (Format: TXT=138781 bytes) (Obsoletes RFC 1066)

1155 Structure and identification of management information for TCP/IP-based internets. Rose, M.T.; McCloghrie, K. 1990 May; 22 p. (Format: TXT=40927 bytes) (Obsoletes RFC 1065)

1154 Encoding header field for internet messages. Robinson, D.; Ullmann, R. 1990 April; 7 p. (Format: TXT=12214 bytes)

1153 Digest message format. Wancho, F.J. 1990 April; 4 p. (Format: TXT=6632 bytes)

1152 Workshop report: Internet research steering group workshop on very-high-speed networks. Partridge, C. 1990 April; 23 p. (Format: TXT=64003 bytes)

1151 Version 2 of the Reliable Data Protocol (RDP). Partridge, C.; Hinden, R.M. 1990 April; 4 p. (Format: TXT=8293 bytes) (Updates RFC 908)

1150 F.Y.I. on F.Y.I.: Introduction to the F.Y.I. notes. Malkin, G.S.; Reynolds, J.K. 1990 March; 4 p. (Format: TXT=7867 bytes) (Also FYI 1)

1149   Standard for the transmission of IP datagrams on avian carriers. Waitzman, D. 1990 April 1; 2 p. (Format: TXT=3329 bytes)

1148   Mapping between X.400(1988) / ISO 10021 and RFC 822. Hardcastle-Kille, S.E. 1990 March; 94 p. (Format: TXT=194292 bytes) (Obsoleted by RFC 1327; Updates RFC 1138)

1147   FYI on a network management tool catalog: Tools for monitoring and de-bugging TCP/IP Internets and interconnected devices. Stine, R.H.,ed. 1990 April; 126 p. (Format: TXT=336906, PS=555225 bytes) (Also FYI 2)

1146   TCP alternate checksum options. Zweig, J.; Partridge, C. 1990 March; 5 p. (Format: TXT=10955 bytes) (Obsoletes RFC 1145)

1145   TCP alternate checksum options. Zweig, J.; Partridge, C. 1990 February; 5 p. (Format: TXT=11052 bytes) (Obsoleted by RFC 1146)

1144   Compressing TCP/IP headers for low-speed serial links. Jacobson, V. 1990 February; 43 p. (Format: TXT=120959, PS=534729 bytes)

1143   Q method of implementing Telnet option negotiation. Bernstein, D.J. 1990 February; 10 p. (Format: TXT=23331 bytes)

1142   OSI IS-IS Intra-domain routing protocol. Oran, D.,ed. 1990 February; 157 p. (Format: PS=1204297, TXT=425379 bytes)

1141   Incremental updating of the Internet checksum. Mallory, T.; Kullberg, A. 1990 January; 2 p. (Format: TXT=3587 bytes) (Updates RFC 1071)

1140   IAB official protocol standards. Defense Advanced Research Projects Agency, Internet Activities Board. 1990 May; 27 p. (Format: TXT=60501 bytes) (Obsoletes RFC 1130; Obsoleted by RFC 1200)

1139   Echo function for ISO 8473. Hagens, R.A. 1990 January; 6 p. (Format: TXT=14229 bytes)

1138   Mapping between X.400(1988) / ISO 10021 and RFC 822. Hardcastle-Kille, S.E. 1989 December; 92 p. (Format: TXT=191029 bytes) (Obsoleted by RFC 1327; Updates RFC 1026; Updated by RFC 1148)

1137   Mapping between full RFC 822 and RFC 822 with restricted encoding. Hardcastle-Kille, S.E. 1989 December; 3 p. (Format: TXT=6436 bytes) (Updates RFC 976)

1136   Administrative Domains and Routing Domains: A model for routing in the Internet. Hares, S.; Katz, D. 1989 December; 10 p. (Format: TXT=22158 bytes)

1135   Helminthiasis of the Internet. Reynolds, J.K. 1989 December; 33 p. (Format: TXT=77033 bytes)

1134   Point-to-Point Protocol (PPP): A proposal for multi-protocol transmission of datagrams over Point-to-Point links. Perkins, D. 1989 November; 38 p. (Format: TXT=87352 bytes) (Obsoleted by RFC 1171)

1133 Routing between the NSFNET and the DDN.Yu, J.Y.; Braun, H.W. 1989 November; 10 p. (Format: TXT=23169 bytes)

1132 Standard for the transmission of 802.2 packets over IPX networks. McLaughlin, L.J. 1989 November; 4 p. (Format: TXT=8128 bytes)

1131 OSPF specification. Moy, J. 1989 October; 107 p. (Format: PS=857280 bytes) (Obsoleted by RFC 1247)

1130 IAB official protocol standards. Defense Advanced Research Projects Agency, Internet Activities Board. 1989 October; 17 p. (Format: TXT=33858 bytes) (Obsoletes RFC 1100; Obsoleted by RFC 1140)

1129 Internet time synchronization: The Network Time Protocol. Mills, D.L. 1989 October; 29 p. (Format: PS=551697 bytes)

1128 Measured performance of the Network Time Protocol in the Internet system. Mills, D.L. 1989 October; 20 p. (Format: PS=633742 bytes)

1127 Perspective on the Host Requirements RFCs. Braden, R.T. 1989 October; 20 p. (Format: TXT=41267 bytes)

1126 Goals and functional requirements for inter-autonomous system routing. Little, M. 1989 October; 25 p. (Format: TXT=62725 bytes)

1125 Policy requirements for inter-Administrative Domain routing. Estrin, D. 1989 November; 18 p. (Format: TXT=55248, PS=282123 bytes)

1124 Policy issues in interconnecting networks. Leiner, B.M. 1989 September; 54 p. (Format: PS=315692 bytes)

1123 Requirements for Internet hosts - application and support. Braden, R.T.,ed. 1989 October; 98 p. (Format: TXT=245503 bytes) (Updated by RFC 1349)

1122 Requirements for Internet hosts - communication layers. Braden, R.T., ed. 1989 October; 116 p. (Format: TXT=295992 bytes) (Updated by RFC 1349)

1121 Act one - the poems. Postel, J.B.; Kleinrock, L.; Cerf, V.G.; Boehm, B. 1989 September; 6 p. (Format: TXT=10644 bytes)

1120 Internet Activities Board. Cerf, V. 1989 September; 11 p. (Format: TXT=26123 bytes) (Obsoleted by RFC 1160)

1119 Network Time Protocol (version 2) specification and implementation. Mills, D.L. 1989 September; 64 p. (Format: PS=535202 bytes) (Obsoletes RFC 1059, RFC 958; Obsoleted by RFC 1305)

1118 Hitchhikers guide to the Internet. Krol, E. 1989 September; 24 p. (Format: TXT=62757 bytes)

1117 Internet numbers. Romano, S.; Stahl, M.K.; Recker, M. 1989 August; 109 p. (Format: TXT=324666 bytes) (Obsoletes RFC 1062, RFC 1020, RFC 997; Obsoleted by RFC 1166)

1116 Telnet Linemode option. Borman, D.A.,ed. 1989 August; 21 p. (Format: TXT=47473 bytes) (Obsoleted by RFC 1184)

1115   Privacy enhancement for Internet electronic mail: Part III - algorithms, modes, and identifiers [Draft]. Linn, J. 1989 August; 8 p. (Format: TXT=18226 bytes) (Updated by RFC 1319)

1114   Privacy enhancement for Internet electronic mail: Part II - certificate-based key management [Draft]. Kent, S.T.; Linn, J. 1989 August; 25 p. (Format: TXT=69661 bytes)

1113   Privacy enhancement for Internet electronic mail: Part I - message encipherment and authentication procedures [Draft]. Linn, J. 1989 August; 34 p. (Format: TXT=89293 bytes) (Obsoletes RFC 989, RFC 1040)

1112   Host extensions for IP multicasting. Deering, S.E. 1989 August; 17 p. (Format: TXT=39904 bytes) (Obsoletes RFC 988, RFC 1054)

1111   Request for comments on Request for Comments: Instructions to RFC authors. Postel, J.B. 1989 August; 6 p. (Format: TXT=11793 bytes) (Obsoletes RFC 825)

1110   Problem with the TCP big window option. McKenzie, A.M. 1989 August; 3 p. (Format: TXT=5778 bytes)

1109   Report of the second Ad Hoc Network Management Review Group. Cerf, V.G. 1989 August; 8 p. (Format: TXT=20642 bytes)

1108   U.S. Department of Defense security options for the Internet Protocol. Kent, S.T. 1991 November; 17 p. (Format: TXT=41791 bytes) (Obsoletes RFC 1038)

1107   Plan for Internet directory services. Sollins, K.R. 1989 July; 19 p. (Format: TXT=51773 bytes)

1106   TCP big window and NAK options. Fox, R. 1989 June; 13 p. (Format: TXT=37105 bytes)

1105   Border Gateway Protocol (BGP). Lougheed, K.; Rekhter, Y. 1989 June; 17 p. (Format: TXT=37644 bytes) (Obsoleted by RFC 1163)

1104   Models of policy-based routing. Braun, H.W. 1989 June; 10 p. (Format: TXT=25468 bytes)

1103   Proposed standard for the transmission of IP datagrams over FDDI Networks. Katz, D. 1989 June; 9 p. (Format: TXT=19439 bytes) (Obsoleted by RFC 1188)

1102   Policy routing in Internet protocols. Clark, D.D. 1989 May; 22 p. (Format: TXT=59664 bytes)

1101   DNS encoding of network names and other types. Mockapetris, P.V. 1989 April; 14 p. (Format: TXT=28677 bytes) (Updates RFC 1034, RFC 1035)

1100   IAB official protocol standards. Defense Advanced Research Projects Agency, Internet Activities Board. 1989 April; 14 p. (Format: TXT=30101 bytes) (Obsoletes RFC 1083; Obsoleted by RFC 1130)

1099 Request for comments summary: RFC numbers 1000-1099. Reynolds, J.K. 1991 December; 22 p. (Format: TXT=49108 bytes)

1098 Simple Network Management Protocol (SNMP). Case, J.D.; Fedor, M.; Schoffstall, M.L.; Davin, C. 1989 April; 34 p. (Format: TXT=71563 bytes) (Obsoletes RFC 1067; Obsoleted by RFC 1157)

1097 Telnet subliminal-message option. Miller, B. 1989 April 1; 3 p. (Format: TXT=5490 bytes)

1096 Telnet X display location option. Marcy, G.A. 1989 March; 3 p. (Format: TXT=4634 bytes)

1095 Common Management Information Services and Protocol over TCP/IP (CMOT). Warrier, U.S.; Besaw, L. 1989 April; 67 p. (Format: TXT=157506 bytes) (Obsoleted by RFC 1189)

1094 NFS: Network File System Protocol specification. Sun Microsystems, Inc. 1989 March; 27 p. (Format: TXT=51454 bytes)

1093 NSFNET routing architecture. Braun, H.W. 1989 February; 9 p. (Format: TXT=20629 bytes)

1092 EGP and policy based routing in the new NSFNET backbone. Rekhter, J. 1989 February; 5 p. (Format: TXT=11865 bytes)

1091 Telnet terminal-type option. VanBokkelen, J. 1989 February; 7 p. (Format: TXT=13439 bytes) (Obsoletes RFC 930)

1090 SMTP on X.25. Ullmann, R. 1989 February; 4 p. (Format: TXT=6141 bytes)

1089 SNMP over Ethernet. Schoffstall, M.L.; Davin, C.; Fedor, M.; Case, J.D. 1989 February; 3 p. (Format: TXT=4458 bytes)

1088 Standard for the transmission of IP datagrams over NetBIOS networks. McLaughlin, L.J. 1989 February; 3 p. (Format: TXT=5749 bytes)

1087 Ethics and the Internet. Defense Advanced Research Projects Agency, Internet Activities Board. 1989 January; 2 p. (Format: TXT=4582 bytes)

1086 ISO-TP0 bridge between TCP and X.25. Onions, J.P.; Rose, M.T. 1988 December; 9 p. (Format: TXT=19934 bytes)

1085 ISO presentation services on top of TCP/IP based internets. Rose, M.T. 1988 December; 32 p. (Format: TXT=64643 bytes)

1084 BOOTP vendor information extensions. Reynolds, J.K. 1988 December; 8 p. (Format: TXT=16327 bytes) (Obsoletes RFC 1048)

1083 IAB official protocol standards. Defense Advanced Research Projects Agency, Internet Activities Board. 1988 December; 12 p. (Format: TXT=27128 bytes) (Obsoleted by RFC 1100)

1082 Post Office Protocol: Version 3: Extended service offerings. Rose, M.T. 1988 November; 11 p. (Format: TXT=25423 bytes)

1081   Post Office Protocol: Version 3. Rose, M.T. 1988 November; 16 p. (Format: TXT=37009 bytes) (Obsoleted by RFC 1225)

1080   Telnet remote flow control option. Hedrick, C.L. 1988 November; 4 p. (Format: TXT=6688 bytes)

1079   Telnet terminal speed option. Hedrick, C.L. 1988 December; 3 p. (Format: TXT=4942 bytes)

1078   TCP port service Multiplexer (TCPMUX). Lottor, M. 1988 November; 2 p. (Format: TXT=3248 bytes)

1077   Critical issues in high bandwidth networking. Leiner, B.M.,ed. 1988 November; 46 p. (Format: TXT=116464 bytes)

1076   HEMS monitoring and control language. Trewitt, G.; Partridge, C. 1988 November; 42 p. (Format: TXT=98774 bytes) (Obsoletes RFC 1023)

1075   Distance Vector Multicast Routing Protocol. Waitzman, D.; Partridge, C.; Deering, S.E. 1988 November; 24 p. (Format: TXT=54731 bytes)

1074   NSFNET backbone SPF-based Interior Gateway Protocol. Rekhter, J. 1988 October; 5 p. (Format: TXT=10872 bytes)

1073   Telnet window size option. Waitzman, D. 1988 October; 4 p. (Format: TXT=7639 bytes)

1072   TCP extensions for long-delay paths. Jacobson, V.; Braden, R.T. 1988 October; 16 p. (Format: TXT=36000 bytes) (Obsoleted by RFC 1323)

1071   Computing the Internet checksum. Braden, R.T.; Borman, D.A.; Partridge, C. 1988 September; 24 p. (Format: TXT=54941 bytes) (Updated by RFC 1141)

1070   Use of the Internet as a subnetwork for experimentation with the OSI network layer. Hagens, R.A.; Hall, N.E.; Rose, M.T. 1989 February; 17 p. (Format: TXT=37354 bytes)

1069   Guidelines for the use of Internet-IP addresses in the ISO Connectionless-Mode Network Protocol. Callon, R.W.; Braun, H.W. 1989 February; 10 p. (Format: TXT=24268 bytes) (Obsoletes RFC 986)

1068   Background File Transfer Program (BFTP). DeSchon, A.L.; Braden, R.T. 1988 August; 27 p. (Format: TXT=51004 bytes)

1067   Simple Network Management Protocol. Case, J.D.; Fedor, M.; Schoffstall, M.L.; Davin, J.R. 1988 August; 33 p. (Format: TXT=69592 bytes) (Obsoleted by RFC 1098)

1066   Management Information Base for network management of TCP/IP-based internets. McCloghrie, K.; Rose, M.T. 1988 August; 90 p. (Format: TXT=135177 bytes) (Obsoleted by RFC 1156)

1065   Structure and identification of management information for TCP/IP-based internets. McCloghrie, K.; Rose, M.T. 1988 August; 21 p. (Format: TXT=38858 bytes) (Obsoleted by RFC 1155)

1064   Interactive Mail Access Protocol: Version 2. Crispin, M.R. 1988 July; 26 p. (Format: TXT=57813 bytes) (Obsoleted by RFC 1176, RFC 1203)

1063   IP MTU discovery options. Mogul, J.C.; Kent, C.A.; Partridge, C.; McCloghrie, K. 1988 July; 11 p. (Format: TXT=27121 bytes) (Obsoleted by RFC 1191)

1062   Internet numbers. Romano, S.; Stahl, M.K.; Recker, M. 1988 August; 65 p. (Format: TXT=198729 bytes) (Obsoletes RFC 1020; Obsoleted by RFC 1117)

1061   Not yet issued.

1060   Assigned numbers. Reynolds, J.K.; Postel, J.B. 1990 March; 86 p. (Format: TXT=177923 bytes) (Obsoletes RFC 1010; Obsoleted by RFC 1340; Updated by RFC 1349)

1059   Network Time Protocol (version 1) specification and implementation. Mills, D.L. 1988 July; 58 p. (Format: TXT=140890 bytes) (Obsoleted by RFC 1119)

1058   Routing Information Protocol. Hedrick, C.L. 1988 June; 33 p. (Format: TXT=93285 bytes)

1057   RPC: Remote Procedure Call Protocol specification: Version 2. Sun Microsystems, Inc. 1988 June; 25 p. (Format: TXT=52462 bytes) (Obsoletes RFC 1050)

1056   PCMAIL: A distributed mail system for personal computers. Lambert, M.L. 1988 June; 38 p. (Format: TXT=85368 bytes) (Obsoletes RFC 993)

1055   Nonstandard for transmission of IP datagrams over serial lines: SLIP. Romkey, J.L. 1988 June; 6 p. (Format: TXT=12911 bytes)

1054   Host extensions for IP multicasting. Deering, S.E. 1988 May; 19 p. (Format: TXT=45465 bytes) (Obsoletes RFC 988; Obsoleted by RFC 1112)

1053   Telnet X.3 PAD option. Levy, S.; Jacobson, T. 1988 April; 21 p. (Format: TXT=48952 bytes)

1052   IAB recommendations for the development of Internet network management standards. Cerf, V.G. 1988 April; 14 p. (Format: TXT=30569 bytes)

1051   Standard for the transmission of IP datagrams and ARP packets over ARCNET networks. Prindeville, P.A. 1988 March; 4 p. (Format: TXT=7779 bytes) (Obsoleted by RFC 1201)

1050   RPC: Remote Procedure Call Protocol specification. Sun Microsystems, Inc. 1988 April; 24 p. (Format: TXT=51540 bytes) (Obsoleted by RFC 1057)

1049   Content-type header field for Internet messages. Sirbu, M.A. 1988 March; 8 p. (Format: TXT=18923 bytes)

1048　BOOTP vendor information extensions. Prindeville, P.A. 1988 February; 7 p. (Format: TXT=15423 bytes) (Obsoleted by RFC 1084)

1047　Duplicate messages and SMTP. Partridge, C. 1988 February; 3 p. (Format: TXT=5888 bytes)

1046　Queuing algorithm to provide type-of-service for IP links. Prue, W.; Postel, J.B. 1988 February; 11 p. (Format: TXT=30106 bytes)

1045　VMTP: Versatile Message Transaction Protocol: Protocol specification. Cheriton, D.R. 1988 February; 123 p. (Format: TXT=272058 bytes)

1044　Internet Protocol on Network System's HYPERchannel: Protocol specification. Hardwick, K.; Lekashman, J. 1988 February; 43 p. (Format: TXT=103241 bytes)

1043　Telnet Data Entry Terminal option: DODIIS implementation. Yasuda, A.; Thompson, T. 1988 February; 26 p. (Format: TXT=59478 bytes) (Updates RFC 732)

1042　Standard for the transmission of IP datagrams over IEEE 802 networks. Postel, J.B.; Reynolds, J.K. 1988 February; 15 p. (Format: TXT=35201 bytes) (Obsoletes RFC 948)

1041　Telnet 3270 regime option. Rekhter, Y. 1988 January; 6 p. (Format: TXT=11608 bytes)

1040　Privacy enhancement for Internet electronic mail: Part I: Message encipherment and authentication procedures. Linn, J. 1988 January; 29 p. (Format: TXT=76276 bytes) (Obsoletes RFC 989; Obsoleted by RFC 1113)

1039　DoD statement on Open Systems Interconnection protocols. Latham, D. 1988 January; 3 p. (Format: TXT=6194 bytes) (Obsoletes RFC 945)

1038　Draft revised IP security option. St. Johns, M. 1988 January; 7 p. (Format: TXT=15879 bytes) (Obsoleted by RFC 1108)

1037　NFILE - a file access protocol. Greenberg, B.; Keene, S. 1987 December; 86 p. (Format: TXT=197312 bytes)

1036　Standard for interchange of USENET messages. Horton, M.R.; Adams, R. 1987 December; 19 p. (Format: TXT=46891 bytes) (Obsoletes RFC 850)

1035　Domain names - implementation and specification. Mockapetris, P.V. 1987 November; 55 p. (Format: TXT=125626 bytes) (Obsoletes RFC 973, RFC 882, RFC 883; Updated by RFC 1101, RFC 1183, RFC 1348)

1034　Domain names - concepts and facilities. Mockapetris, P.V. 1987 November; 55 p. (Format: TXT=129180 bytes) (Obsoletes RFC 973, RFC 882, RFC 883; Updated by RFC 1101, RFC 1183, RFC 1348)

1033　Domain administrators operations guide. Lottor, M. 1987 November; 22 p. (Format: TXT=37263 bytes)

1032 Domain administrators guide. Stahl, M.K. 1987 November; 14 p. (Format: TXT=29454 bytes)

1031 MILNET name domain transition. Lazear, W.D. 1987 November; 10 p. (Format: TXT=20137 bytes)

1030 On testing the NETBLT Protocol over divers networks. Lambert, M.L. 1987 November; 16 p. (Format: TXT=40964 bytes)

1029 More fault tolerant approach to address resolution for a Multi-LAN system of Ethernets. Parr, G. 1988 May; 17 p. (Format: TXT=44019 bytes)

1028 Simple Gateway Monitoring Protocol. Davin, J.R.; Case, J.D.; Fedor, M.; Schoffstall, M.L. 1987 November; 38 p. (Format: TXT=82440 bytes)

1027 Using ARP to implement transparent subnet gateways. Carl-Mitchell, S.; Quarterman, J.S. 1987 October; 8 p. (Format: TXT=21297 bytes)

1026 Addendum to RFC 987: (Mapping between X.400 and RFC 822). Hardcastle-Kille, S.E. 1987 September; 4 p. (Format: TXT=7117 bytes) (Obsoleted by RFC 1327; Updates RFC 987; Updated by RFC 1138)

1025 TCP and IP bake off. Postel, J.B. 1987 September; 6 p. (Format: TXT=11648 bytes)

1024 HEMS variable definitions. Partridge, C.; Trewitt, G. 1987 October; 74 p. (Format: TXT=126536 bytes)

1023 HEMS monitoring and control language. Trewitt, G.; Partridge, C. 1987 October; 17 p. (Format: TXT=40992 bytes) (Obsoleted by RFC 1076)

1022 High-level Entity Management Protocol (HEMP). Partridge, C.; Trewitt, G. 1987 October; 12 p. (Format: TXT=25348 bytes)

1021 High-level Entity Management System (HEMS). Partridge, C.; Trewitt, G. 1987 October; 5 p. (Format: TXT=12993 bytes)

1020 Internet numbers. Romano, S.; Stahl, M.K. 1987 November; 51 p. (Format: TXT=146864 bytes) (Obsoletes RFC 997; Obsoleted by RFC 1062, RFC 1117)

1019 Report of the Workshop on Environments for Computational Mathematics. Arnon, D. 1987 September; 8 p. (Format: TXT=21151 bytes)

1018 Some comments on SQuID. McKenzie, A.M. 1987 August; 3 p. (Format: TXT=7931 bytes)

1017 Network requirements for scientific research: Internet task force on scientific computing. Leiner, B.M. 1987 August; 19 p. (Format: TXT=49512 bytes)

1016 Something a host could do with source quench: The Source Quench Introduced Delay (SQuID). Prue, W.; Postel, J.B. 1987 July; 18 p. (Format: TXT=47922 bytes)

1015 Implementation plan for interagency research Internet. Leiner, B.M. 1987 July; 24 p. (Format: TXT=63159 bytes)

1014   XDR: External Data Representation standard. Sun Microsystems, Inc. 1987 June; 20 p. (Format: TXT=39316 bytes)

1013   X Window System Protocol, version 11: Alpha update April 1987. Scheifler, R.W. 1987 June; 101 p. (Format: TXT=244905 bytes)

1012   Bibliography of Request For Comments 1 through 999. Reynolds, J.K.; Postel, J.B. 1987 June; 64 p. (Format: TXT=129194 bytes)

1011   Official Internet protocols. Reynolds, J.K.; Postel, J.B. 1987 May; 52 p. (Format: TXT=74593 bytes) (Obsoletes RFC 991)

1010   Assigned numbers. Reynolds, J.K.; Postel, J.B. 1987 May; 44 p. (Format: TXT=78179 bytes) (Obsoletes RFC 990; Obsoleted by RFC 1060)

1009   Requirements for Internet gateways. Braden, R.T.; Postel, J.B. 1987 June; 55 p. (Format: TXT=128173 bytes) (Obsoletes RFC 985)

1008   Implementation guide for the ISO Transport Protocol. McCoy, W. 1987 June; 73 p. (Format: TXT=204664 bytes)

1007   Military supplement to the ISO Transport Protocol. McCoy, W. 1987 June; 23 p. (Format: TXT=51280 bytes)

1006   ISO transport services on top of the TCP: Version 3. Rose, M.T.; Cass, D.E. 1987 May; 17 p. (Format: TXT=31935 bytes) (Obsoletes RFC 983)

1005   ARPANET AHIP-E Host Access Protocol (enhanced AHIP). Khanna, A.; Malis, A.G. 1987 May; 31 p. (Format: TXT=69957 bytes)

1004   Distributed-protocol authentication scheme. Mills, D.L. 1987 April; 8 p. (Format: TXT=21402 bytes)

1003   Issues in defining an equations representation standard. Katz, A.R. 1987 March; 7 p. (Format: TXT=19816 bytes)

1002   Protocol standard for a NetBIOS service on a TCP/UDP transport: Detailed specifications. Defense Advanced Research Projects Agency, Internet Activities Board, End-to-End Services Task Force, NetBIOS Working Group. 1987 March; 85 p. (Format: TXT=170262 bytes)

1001   Protocol standard for a NetBIOS service on a TCP/UDP transport: Concepts and methods. Defense Advanced Research Projects Agency, Internet Activities Board, End-to-End Services Task Force, NetBIOS Working Group. 1987 March; 68 p. (Format: TXT=158437 bytes)

1000   Request For Comments reference guide. Reynolds, J.K.; Postel, J.B. 1987 August; 149 p. (Format: TXT=323960 bytes) (Obsoletes RFC 999)

VI

ISI's RFC RETRIEVAL INFORMATION

This appendix includes the full text of the file in-notes/rfc-retrieval.txt available for anonymous FTP from host ISI.EDU. The information is current as of February 1992. The file may also be obtained by sending a message to *rfc-info@isi.edu*, with *help: ways_to_get_rfcs* in the body of the message.

This appendix contains more complete information regarding retrieval from each site than was noted in Section 8.1.6, especially concerning the various commands for retrieving RFCs via the different mail servers.

Where and how to get new RFCs

RFCs may be obtained via e-mail or anonymous FTP from many RFC Repositories. The Primary Repositories will have the RFC available when it is first announced, as will many Secondary Repositories. Some Secondary Repositories may take a few days to make available the most recent RFCs.

Primary Repositories:

RFCs can be obtained via anonymous FTP from *ds.internic.net, nic.ddn.mil, ftp.nisc.sri.com, nis.nsf.net, nisc.jvnc.net, venera.isi.edu, wuarchive.wustl.edu,* and *src.doc.ic.ac.uk.*

1. ds.internic.net

RFCs may be obtained from ds.internic.net via FTP, WAIS, and electronic mail. Through FTP, RFCs are stored as *rfc/rfcnnnn.txt* or *rfc/rfcnnnn.ps* where *nnnn* is the RFC number. Login as anonymous and provide your e-mail address as the password. Through WAIS, you may use either your local WAIS client or telnet to *ds.internic.net* and login as *wais* (no password required) to access a WAIS client. Help information and a tutorial for using WAIS are available online. The WAIS database to search is *rfcs*.

Directory and Database Services also provides a mail server interface. Send a mail message to mailserv@ds.internic.net and include any of the following commands in the message body: **document-by-name rfcnnnn** where *nnnn* is the RFC number. The text version is sent. **file /ftp/rfc/ rfcnnnn.yyy** where *nnnn* is the RFC number and *yyy* is txt or ps. **help** to get information on how to use the mailserver.

The InterNIC Directory and Database Services Collection of Resource Listings, Internet Documents such as RFCs, FYIs, STDs, and Internet Drafts, and Publically Accessible Databases are also now available via Gopher. All their collections are WAIS indexed and can be searched from the Gopher menu. To access the InterNIC Gopher Servers, please connect to **internic.net port 70.** Contact: *admin@ds.internic.net*

2. nic.ddn.mil

RFCs can be obtained via FTP from **nic.ddn.mil** with the pathname *rfc/rfcnnnn.txt* (where *nnnn* refers to the number of the RFC). Login with FTP username *anonymous* and password *guest*. Contact: *scottw@nic.ddn.mil*

3. ftp.nisc.sri.com

RFCs can be obtained via anonymous FTP from **ftp.nisc.sri.com** with the pathname *rfc/rfcnnnn.txt* or *rfc/rfcnnnn.ps* (where *nnnn* refers to the number of the RFC). Login with FTP username *anonymous* and password *guest*. To obtain the RFC Index, use the pathname *rfc/rfc-index.txt*.

SRI also provides an automatic mail service for those sites which cannot use FTP. Address the request to *mail-server@nisc.sri.com* and in the body of the message indicate the RFC to be sent: *send rfcNNNN.txt* or *send rfcNNNN.ps* where *NNNN* is the RFC number. Multiple requests may be included in the same message by listing the send commands on separate lines. To request the RFC Index, the command should read: *send rfc-index*. Contact: *rfc-update@nisc.sri.com*

4. nis.nsf.net

To obtain RFCs from nis.nsf.net via anonymous FTP, login with username *anonymous* and password *guest*; then connect to the RFC directory (cd RFC). The file name is of the form *RFCnnnn.TXT-1* (where *nnnn* refers to the number of the RFC).

The NIS also provides an automatic mail service for those sits which cannot use FTP. Address the request to *nis-info@nis.nsf.net* and leave the subject field of the message blank. The first line of the text of the message must be *SEND RFCnnnn.TXT-1*, where *nnnn* is replaced by the RFC number. Contact: *jo_ann_ward@um.cc.umich.edu*

5. nisc.jvnc.net

RFCs can also be obtained via anonymous FTP from *nisc.jvnc.net*, with the pathname *rfc/RFCnnnn.TXT.v* (where *nnnn* refers to the number of the RFC and *v* refers to the version number of the RFC).

JvNCnet also provides a mail service for those sites which cannot use FTP. Address the request to *sendrfc@jvnc.net* and in the subject field of the message indicate the RFC number, as in Subject: *RFCnnnn* where *nnnn* is the RFC number. Please note that RFCs whose numbers are less than 1000 need not place a 0. (For example, RFC932 is fine.) No text in the body of the message is needed. Contact: *becker@nisc.jvnc.net*

6. venera.isi.edu

RFCs can be obtained via anonymous FTP from *venera.isi.edu*, with the pathname *in-notes/rfcnnnn.txt* (where *nnnn* refers to the number of the RFC). Login with FTP username *anonymous* and password *guest*.

RFCs can also be obtained via electronic mail from *venera.isi.edu* by using the RFC-INFO service. Address the request to *rfc-info@isi.edu* with a message body of:

```
                    Retrieve: RFC
                    Doc-ID: RFCnnnn
```

(where *nnnn* refers to the number of the RFC (always use 4 digits - the DOC-ID of RFC-822 is RFC0822)). The *rfc-info@isi.edu* server provides other ways of selecting RFCs based on keywords and such; for more information send a message to *rfc-info@isi.edu* with the message body *help: help*. Contact: *rfc-manager@isi.edu*

7. wuarchive.wustl.edu

RFCs can also be obtained via anonymous FTP from *wuarchive.wustl.edu* with the pathname *info/rfc/rfcnnnn.txt.Z* (where *nnnn* refers to the number of the RFC and *Z* indicates that the document is in compressed form). At *wuarchive.wustl.edu* the RFCs are in an archive file system and various archives can be mounted as part of an NFS file system. Please contact Chris Myers (*chris@wugate.wustl.edu*) if you want to mount this file system in your NFS. Contact: *chris@wugate.wustl.edu*

8. src.doc.ic.ac.uk

RFCs can be obtained via anonymous FTP from *src.doc.ic.ac.uk* with the pathname *rfc/rfcnnnn.txt.Z* or *rfc/rfcnnnn.ps.Z* (where *nnnn* refers to the number of the RFC). Login with FTP username *anonymous* and password *<your-email-address>*. To obtain the RFC Index, use the pathname *rfc/rfc-index.txt.Z*. (The trailing *.Z* indicates that the document is in compressed form.)

The host *src.doc.ic.ac.uk* also provides an automatic mail service for those sites in the U.K. which cannot use FTP. Address the request to *info-server@doc.ic.ac.uk* with a Subject: line of wanted and a message body of:

```
request sources
topic path rfc/rfcnnnn.txt.Z
request end
```

(where *nnnn* refers to the number of the RFC.) Multiple requests may be included in the same message by giving multiple topic path commands on separate lines. To request the RFC Index, the command should read: *topic path rfc/rfc-index.txt.Z*. The archive is also available using NIFTP and the ISO FTAM system. Contact: *ukuug-soft@doc.ic.ac.uk*

9. ftp.concert.net

To obtain RFCs from ftp.concert.net via anonymous FTP, login with username *anonymous* and your internet e-mail address as password. The RFCs can be found in the directory /rfc, with file names of the form: *rfcNNNN.txt* or *rfcNNNN.ps* where *NNNN* refers to the RFC number. This repository is also accessible via WAIS and the Internet Gopher. Contact: *rfc-mgr@concert.net*

Secondary repositories:

Sweden

Host:	sunic.sunet.se
Directory:	rfc
Host:	chalmers.se
Directory:	rfc

Germany

Site:	University of Dortmund
Host:	walhalla.informatik.uni-dortmund.de
Directory:	pub/documentation/rfc
Notes:	RFCs in compressed format

France

Site:	Institut National de la Recherche en Informatique et Automatique (INRIA)
Address:	info-server@inria.fr
Notes:	RFCs are available via e-mail to the address. Info Server manager is Mire Yamajako (yamajako@inria.fr).

Netherlands

Site:	EUnet
Host:	mcsun.eu.net
Directory:	rfc
Notes:	RFCs in compressed format.

Finland

Site:	FUNET
Host:	funet.fi
Directory:	rfc
Notes:	RFCs in compressed format. Also provides e-mail access by sending mail to *archive-server@funet.fi.*

Norway

Host:	ugle.unit.no
Directory:	pub/rfc

Denmark

Site:	University of Copenhagen
Host:	ftp.diku.dk (freja.diku.dk)
Directory:	rfc

Australia and Pacific Rim

Site:	munnari
Contact:	Robert Elz <kre@cs.mu.OZ.AU>
Host:	munnari.oz.au
Directory:	rfc
	RFCs in compressed format rfcNNNN.Z
	postscript RFCs rfcNNNN.ps.Z

United States

Site: cerfnet
Contact: help@cerf.net
Host: nic.cerf.net
Directory: netinfo/rfc

Requests for special distribution of RFCs should be addressed to either the author of the RFC in question or to *nic@nic.ddn.mil*.

Submissions for Requests for Comments should be sent to *postel@isi.edu*. Please consult RFC 1111, Instructions to RFC Authors, for further information.

Requests to be added to or deleted from this distribution list should be sent to *rfc-request@nic.ddn.mil*.

Changes to this file *rfc-retrieval.txt* should be sent to Joyce K. Reynolds (*jkrey@isi.edu*).

VII

RFC Sets

The Table of Contents for the *Internet Technology Handbook* is presented here, followed by the contents of the first two Updates to the Handbook. The Handbook gathers the most pertinent RFCs, organizes them into related categories, and presents them with introductory text to explain their significance. The Handbook is more than 6,000 pages in six volumes.

However, you may be interested in obtaining RFCs singly. This Table of Contents can help you identify just those RFCs that pertain to a particular topic of interest. It is provided as an aid in easing the confusion someone new to networking may feel when faced with more than 1,350 RFC documents to choose from! This is not a complete list of the RFCs. A complete list of the RFCs is available as the *RFC Index*.

VOLUME 1

RFC 1201   Transmitting IP traffic over ARCNET networks
RFC 1209   Transmission of IP datagrams over the SMDS Service
RFC 1171   Point-to-Point Protocol for the transmission of multi-protocol datagrams over Point-to-Point links
RFC 1172   Point-to-Point Protocol (PPP) initial configuration options

SECTION 5. INTERNET LAYER PROTOCOLS

5.1. Internet Layer Protocols
RFC 791   Internet Protocol
RFC 792   Internet Control Message Protocol
RFC 1190   Experimental Internet Stream Protocol: Version 2 (ST-II)
RFC 1226   Internet protocol encapsulation of AX.25 frames.

5.2. Functions and Algorithms
RFC 815   IP datagram reassembly algorithms
RFC 1191   Path MTU discovery
RFC 1071   Computing the Internet checksum
RFC 1141   Incremental updating of the Internet checksum

5.3. Subnetting
RFC 950   Internet standard subnetting procedure
RFC 1219   On the assignment of subnet numbers

5.4. Broadcasting and Multicasting
RFC 919   Broadcasting Internet datagrams
RFC 922   Broadcasting Internet datagrams in the presence of subnets
RFC 947   Multi-network broadcasting within the Internet
RFC 1112   Host extensions for IP multicasting

5.5. OSI Coexistence
RFC 1069   Guidelines for the use of Internet-IP addresses in the ISO Connectionless-Mode Network Protocol
RFC 1070   Use of the Internet as a subnetwork for experimentation with the OSI network layer
RFC 1236   IP to X.121 address mapping for DDN
RFC 1223   OSI CLNS and LLC1 protocols on Network Systems HYPERchannel
RFC 1237   Guidelines for OSI NSAP allocation in the Internet

VOLUME 3

SECTION 6. ROUTING

6.1. Architecture and Requirements
RFC 975   Autonomous confederations
RFC 1136   Administrative Domains and Routing Domains: A model for routing in the Internet
RFC 1102   Policy routing in Internet protocols
RFC 1124   Policy issues in interconnecting networks
RFC 1009   Requirements for Internet gateways
RFC 1126   Goals and functional requirements for inter-autonomous system routing
RFC 1222   Advancing the NSFNET routing architecture

6.2. Intra-Domain (Interior) Gateway Protocols
RFC 1058   Routing Information Protocol
RFC 1074   NSFNET backbone SPF-based Interior Gateway Protocol
RFC 1247   OSPF version 2
RFC 1245   OSPF protocol analysis
RFC 1246   Experience with the OSPF protocol
RFC 1027   Using ARP to implement transparent subnet gateways
RFC 1195   Use of OSI IS-IS for routing in TCP/IP and dual environments

6.3. Inter-Domain (Exterior) Gateway Protocols

RFC 827   Exterior Gateway Protocol (EGP)
RFC 904   Exterior Gateway Protocol formal specification
RFC 888   STUB Exterior Gateway Protocol
RFC 911   EGP Gateway under Berkeley UNIX 4.2
RFC 1092   EGP and policy based routing in the new NSFNET backbone
RFC 1133   Routing between the NSFNET and the DDN
RFC 1163   Border Gateway Protocol (BGP)
RFC 1164   Application of the Border Gateway Protocol in the Internet

SECTION 7. TRANSPORT LAYER PROTOCOLS

7.1. Internet Transport Layer Protocols

RFC 793   Transmission Control Protocol
RFC 768   User Datagram Protocol
RFC 938   Internet Reliable Transaction Protocol functional and interface specification
RFC 1045   VMTP: Versatile Message Transaction Protocol: Protocol specification
RFC 908   Reliable Data Protocol
RFC 1151   Version 2 of the Reliable Data Protocol (RDP)

7.2. TCP Functions

RFC 813   Window and acknowlegement strategy in TCP
RFC 1146   TCP alternate checksum options
RFC 1072   TCP extensions for long-delay paths

7.3. Performance and Implementation

RFC 816   Fault isolation and recovery
RFC 896   Congestion control in IP/TCP internetworks
RFC 970   On packet switches with infinite storage
RFC 1144   Compressing TCP/IP headers for low-speed serial links
RFC 1242   Benchmarking terminology for network interconnection devices

7.4. OSI Coexistence

RFC 1006   ISO transport services on top of the TCP: Version 3
RFC 1007   Military supplement to the ISO Transport Protocol
RFC 1008   Implementation guide for the ISO Transport Protocol
RFC 1240   OSI connectionless transport services on top of UDP: Version 1

VOLUME 4

SECTION 8. MONITORING AND MANAGEMENT

8.1. Network Management Policy

RFC 1052   IAB recommendations for the development of Internet network management standards
RFC 1109   Report of the second Ad Hoc Network Management Review Group

8.2. Architectural and Protocol Features

RFC 1155   Structure and identification of management information for TCP/IP-based internets
RFC 1157   Simple Network Management Protocol (SNMP)
RFC 1089   SNMP over Ethernet
RFC 1161   SNMP over OSI
RFC 1187   Bulk table retrieval with the SNMP
RFC 1215   Convention for defining traps for use with the SNMP
RFC 1228   SNMP-DPI: Simple Network Management Protocol Distributed Program Interface
RFC 1189   Common Management Information Services and Protocols for the Internet (CMOT and CMIP)

8.3. Management Information Bases
RFC 1156   Management Information Base for network management of TCP/IP-based internets
RFC 1213   Management Information Base for network management of TCP/IP-based internets: MIB-II
RFC 1214   OSI internet management: Management Information Base
RFC 1212   Concise MIB definitions
RFC 1229   Extensions to the generic-interface MIB
RFC 1239   Reassignment of experimental MIBs to standard MIBs
RFC 1227   SNMP MUX protocol and MIB
RFC 1230   IEEE 802.4 Token Bus MIB
RFC 1231   IEEE 802.5 Token Ring MIB
RFC 1232   Definitions of managed objects for the DS1 Interface type
RFC 1233   Definitions of managed objects for the DS3 Interface type
RFC 1238   CLNS MIB for use with Connectionless Network Protocol (ISO 8473) and End System to Intermediate System (ISO 9542)
RFC 1243   Appletalk Management Information Base
RFC 1253   OSPF version 2: Management Information Base

8.4. Network Management Operations
RFC 1147   FYI on a network management tool catalog: Tools for monitoring and debugging TCP/IP internets and interconnected devices
RFC 1173   Responsibilities of host and network managers: A summary of the oral tradition of the Internet
RFC 1224   Techniques for managing asynchronously generated alerts

VOLUME 5

SECTION 9. UTILITY PROTOCOLS

9.1. Presentation Services
RFC 1085   ISO presentation services on top of TCP/IP based internets
RFC 854   Telnet Protocol specification
RFC 855   Telnet option specifications
RFC 856   Telnet binary transmission
RFC 857   Telnet echo option
RFC 858   Telnet Suppress Go Ahead option
RFC 859   Telnet status option
RFC 860   Telnet timing mark option
RFC 861   Telnet extended options: List option
RFC 1184   Telnet Linemode option
RFC 1205   5250 Telnet interface
RFC 734   SUPDUP Protocol
RFC 747   Recent extensions to the SUPDUP Protocol
RFC 749   Telnet SUPDUP-Output option

9.2. Directory Services
RFC 1196   Finger User Information Protocol
RFC 866   Active users
RFC 887   Resource Location Protocol
RFC 954   NICNAME/WHOIS
RFC 814   Name, addresses, ports, and routes
RFC 952   DoD Internet host table specification
RFC 953   Hostname Server
RFC 1031   MILNET name domain transition
RFC 1032   Domain administrators guide
RFC 1033   Domain administrators operations guide
RFC 1034   Domain names - concepts and facilities
RFC 1035   Domain names - implementation and specification
RFC 1101   DNS encoding of network names and other types

RFC 1107   Plan for Internet directory services
RFC 1202   Directory Assistance service
RFC 1218   Naming scheme for c=US

9.3. Time Protocols
RFC 867   Daytime Protocol
RFC 868   Time Protocol
RFC 1119   Network Time Protocol (version 2) specification and implementation
RFC 1129   Internet time synchronization: The Network Time Protocol
RFC 1165   Network Time Protocol (NTP) over the OSI Remote Operations Service

9.4. Remote Procedure Calls
RFC 1057   RPC: Remote Procedure Call Protocol specification: Version 2

9.5. Network Access Protocols
RFC 1001   Protocol standard for a NetBIOS service on a TCP/UDP transport: Concepts and methods
RFC 1002   Protocol standard for a NetBIOS service on a TCP/UDP transport: Detailed specifications

9.6. File Transfer Protocols
RFC 913   Simple File Transfer Protocol
RFC 959   File Transfer Protocol
RFC 783   TFTP Protocol (revision 2)
RFC 998   NETBLT: A bulk data transfer protocol
RFC 1235   Coherent File Distribution Protocol

9.7. File Access Protocols
RFC 1037   NFILE - a file access protocol
RFC 1094   NFS: Network File System Protocol specification

9.8. Miscellaneous Utilities
RFC 862   Echo Protocol
RFC 863   Discard Protocol
RFC 864   Character Generator Protocol
RFC 865   Quote of the Day Protocol
RFC 1139   Echo function for ISO 8473

VOLUME 6

SECTION 10. APPLICATION PROTOCOLS

10.1. Electronic Mail
RFC 821   Simple Mail Transfer Protocol
RFC 822   Standard for the format of ARPA Internet text messages
RFC 934   Proposed standard for message encapsulation
RFC 1153   Digest message format
RFC 886   Proposed standard for message header munging
RFC 1049   Content-type header field for Internet messages
RFC 1154   Encoding header field for internet messages
RFC 987   Mapping between X.400 and RFC 822
RFC 1026   Addendum to RFC 987: (Mapping between X.400 and RFC 822)
RFC 1137   Mapping between full RFC 822 and RFC 822 with restricted encoding
RFC 1148   Mapping between X.400(1988) / ISO 10021 and RFC 822
RFC 1113   Privacy enhancement for Internet electronic mail: Part I - message encipherment and authentication procedures
RFC 1114   Privacy enhancement for Internet electronic mail: Part II - certificate-based key management
RFC 1115   Privacy enhancement for Internet electronic mail: Part III - algorithms, modes, and identifiers

RFC 1047   Duplicate messages and SMTP
RFC 974   Mail routing and the domain system
RFC 1168   Intermail and Commercial Mail Relay services
RFC 1056   PCMAIL: A distributed mail system for personal computers
RFC 1176   Interactive Mail Access Protocol: Version 2
RFC 1203   Interactive Mail Access Protocol: Version 3
RFC 1225   Post Office Protocol: Version 3
RFC 1082   Post Office Protocol: Version 3: Extended service offerings
RFC 977   Network News Transfer Protocol
RFC 1204   Message Posting Protocol (MPP)
RFC 1159   Message Send Protocol

10.2. Security
RFC 1135   Helminthiasis of the Internet
RFC 931   Authentication server
RFC 1004   Distributed-protocol authentication scheme
RFC 1186   MD4 message digest algorithm
RFC 1244   Site Security Handbook

10.3. Miscelleneous Applications
RFC 1198   FYI on the X window system
RFC 1197   Using ODA for translating multimedia information
RFC 1179   Line printer daemon protocol

INTERNET TECHNOLOGY HANDBOOK
MAY 1992 UPDATE
Table of Contents
The May Update to the *Internet Technology Handbook* contains 661 pages.
SECTION 1. INTRODUCTION
SECTION 2. ADDITIONAL RFCS
RFC 1310   Internet standards process
RFC 1311   Introduction to the STD notes
RFC 1108   U.S. Department of Defense security options for the Internet Protocol
RFC 1281   Guidelines for the secure operations of the Internet

SECTION 3. REPLACEMENT RFCS
RFC 1325   FYI on questions and answers: Answers to commonly asked new Internet user
           questions
RFC 1280   IAB official protocol standards
RFC 1331   Point-to-Point Protocol (PPP) for the transmission of multi-protocol datagrams over
           point-to-point links
RFC 1332   PPP Internet Protocol Control Protocol (IPCP)
RFC 1267   Border Gateway Protocol 3 (BGP-3)
RFC 1268   Application of the Border Gateway Protocol in the Internet
RFC 1323   TCP exensions for high performance
RFC 1283   SNMP over OSI
RFC 1255   Naming scheme for c=US
RFC 1288   Finger User Information Protocol
RFC 1305   Network Time Protocol (Version 3): Specification, implementation, and analysis
RFC 1312   Message Send Protocol 2
RFC 1320   MD4 Message-Digest algorithm
RFC 1327   Mapping between X.400(1988)/ISO 10021 and RFC 822

SECTION 4. SUMMARIES OF OTHER RFCS
APPENDIX A. STD Index
APPENDIX B. Updated RFC Index
APPENDIX C. Acronym List

INTERNET TECHNOLOGY HANDBOOK
AUGUST 1992 UPDATE
Table of Contents
The August Update to the *Internet Technology Handbook* contains 231 pages.
SECTION 1. INTRODUCTION
SECTION 2. ADDITIONAL RFCS
RFC 1358   Charter of the Internet Architecture Board (IAB)

SECTION 3. REPLACEMENT RFCS
RFC 1340   Assigned Numbers
RFC 1356   Multiprotocol Interconnect on X.25 and ISDN in the Packet Mode
RFC 1349   Type of Service in the Internet Protocol Suite
RFC 1350   TFTP Protocol (Revision 2)

SECTION 4. SUMMARIES OF OTHER RFCS
APPENDIX A. STD Index
APPENDIX B. Updated RFC Index
APPENDIX C. Acronym List

INTERNATIONAL CONNECTIVITY

SRI thanks Larry Landweber for this information regarding countries that have some form of network connectivity. The most recent version of this list appears regularly in the *Internet Society News* (see Section 12.5).

Copies of various International Connectivity tables are available by anonymous FTP from *ftp.cs.wisc.edu* in the *connectivity_table* directory. Contacts for various countries and postscript versions of world/regional maps showing network connections will also be available in this directory in the near future.

Total number of entities with international network connectivity: 109 Note that some entities have more than one type of connectivity.

Description	<5	>5	Total
BITNET	20	29	49
Internet		46	46
UUCP	40	49	89
FIDONET	15	52	67
OSI	9	17	26

Table VIII-1: Entities with International Connectivity

Table VIII-2: International Network Connectivity

Bitnet	Internet	UUCP	Fidonet	OSI	Abr	Country
-	-	-	-	-	AF	Afghanistan
-	-	-	-	-	AL	Albania
-	-	-	-	-	DZ	Algeria
-	-	-	-	-	AS	American Samoa
-	-	-	-	-	AD	Andorra
-	-	-	-	-	AO	Angora
-	-	-	-	-	AI	Anguilla
-	*	-	-	-	AQ	Antartica
-	-	*	-	-	AG	Antigua and Barbuda
B	I	U	F	-	AR	Argentina
-	-	u	-	-	AM	Armenia
-	-	-	-	-	AW	Aruba
-	I	U	F	-	AU	Australia
B	I	U	F	O	AT	Austria
-	-	*	-	-	AZ	Azerbaijan
-	-	-	-	-	BS	Bahamas
B	I	U	F	o	BH	Bahrain
-	-	-	-	-	BD	Bangladesh
-	-	*	-	-	BB	Barbados
B	I	U	F	O	BE	Belgium
-	-	*	-	-	BZ	Belize
-	-	-	-	-	BJ	Benin
-	-	-	-	-	BM	Bermuda
-	-	-	-	-	BT	Bhutan
-	-	u	-	-	BO	Bolivia
-	-	-	f	-	BW	Botswana
-	-	-	-	-	BV	Bouvet Island
B	I	U	F	O	BR	Brazil
-	-	-	-	-	BN	Brunei Darussalam
-	*	U	F	-	BG	Bulgaria
-	-	u	-	-	BF	Burkina Faso
-	-	-	-	-	BI	Burundi
-	-	U	F	-	BY	Byelorussian SSR
-	-	*	-	-	KH	Cambodia
-	-	-	-	-	CM	Camaroon
B	I	U	F	O	CA	Canada
-	-	-	-	-	CV	Cape Verde
-	-	-	-	-	KY	Cayman Islands
-	-	-	-	-	CF	Central African Rep.
-	-	-	-	-	TD	Chad
-	-	-	-	-	IO	Chagos Islands
B	I	U	f	-	CL	Chile
-	-	u	-	O	CN	China
-	-	-	-	-	CX	Christmas Island
-	-	*	-	-	CI	Cote d'Ivoire
-	-	-	-	-	CC	Cocos Keeling Islands
b	-	u	-	-	CO	Colombia
-	-	-	-	-	KM	Comoros
-	-	*	-	-	CG	Congo
-	-	-	-	-	CK	Cook Islands
b	*	u	-	-	CR	Costa Rica
b	-	-	f	o	??	Croatia
-	-	u	-	-	CU	Cuba
b	-	U	-	-	CY	Cyprus
B	I	U	F	-	CS	Czechoslovakia
b	I	U	F	o	DK	Denmark
-	-	-	-	-	DJ	Djibouti
-	-	*	-	-	DM	Dominica
-	-	u	-	-	DO	Dominican Republic
-	-	-	-	-	TP	East Timor
b	-	u	-	-	EC	Ecuador
b	-	u	j	-	EG	Egypt
-	-	-	-	-	SV	El Salvador
-	-	U	F	-	GQ	Equatorial Guinea
-	*	U	F	-	EE	Estonia
-	-	-	f	-	ET	Ethiopia
-	-	-	-	-	FK	Falkland Islands
-	-	-	-	-	FO	Faroe Islands
-	-	u	-	-	FJ	Fiji
B	I	U	F	o	FI	Finland
B	I	U	F	O	FR	France
-	-	u	-	-	PF	French Polynesia
-	-	-	-	-	TF	French Southern Terr.
-	-	-	-	-	GA	Gabon
-	-	-	-	-	GM	Gambia
-	-	-	-	-	GG	Georgia
B	I	U	F	O	DE	Germany
-	-	-	j	-	GH	Ghana
-	-	-	-	-	GI	Gibraltar
B	I	U	F	o	GR	Greece
-	-	-	f	-	GL	Greenland
-	-	u	-	-	GD	Grenada
-	-	u	-	-	GP	Guadeloupe
-	-	u	-	-	GU	Guam
-	-	u	-	-	GT	Guatemala
-	-	u	-	-	GF	Guiana
-	-	-	-	-	GN	Guinea
-	-	-	-	-	GW	Guinea-Bissau
-	-	-	-	-	GY	Guyana
-	-	-	-	-	HT	Haiti
-	-	-	-	-	HM	Heard and McDonald Is.
-	-	u	-	-	HN	Honduras
B	I	-	F	-	HK	Hong Kong
b	I	U	F	-	HU	Hungary
-	I	U	f	-	IS	Iceland
b	I	U	-	-	IN	India
-	-	u	-	-	ID	Indonesia
-	-	-	-	-	IR	Iran
-	-	-	-	-	IQ	Iraq
B	I	U	F	o	IE	Ireland
B	I	U	F	-	IL	Israel
B	I	U	F	O	IT	Italy
-	-	u	-	-	JM	Jamaica
B	I	U	F	-	JP	Japan
-	-	-	-	-	JO	Jordan
-	-	-	-	-	KK	Kazakhstan
-	-	f	-	-	KE	Kenya
-	-	-	-	-	KI	Kiribati
-	-	-	-	-	KP	Korea
B	I	U	F	-	KR	Korea
-	-	-	-	-	KW	Kuwait
-	-	-	-	-	KG	Kyrgyzstan
-	-	-	-	-	LA	Lao People's Dem. Rep.
-	-	U	F	-	LV	Latvia
-	-	-	-	-	LB	Lebanon
-	-	-	-	-	LS	Lesotho
-	-	-	-	-	LR	Liberia
-	-	-	-	-	LY	Libya
-	-	-	-	-	LI	Liechtenstein
-	-	u	F	o	LT	Lithuania
b	-	u	F	o	LU	Luxembourg
-	-	-	F	-	MO	Macau
-	-	-	-	-	MG	Madagascar
-	-	-	-	-	MW	Malawi
b	-	u	F	-	MY	Malaysia
-	-	-	-	-	MV	Maldives

Bitnet	Internet	UUCP	Fidonet	OSI	Abr	Country
-	-	u	-	-	ML	Mali
-	-	-	-	-	MT	Malta
-	-	-	-	-	MH	Marshall Islands
-	-	u	-	-	MQ	Martinique
-	-	-	-	-	MR	Mauritania
-	-	-	j	-	MU	Mauritius
B	I	u	f	-	MX	Mexico
-	-	-	-	-	FM	Micronesia
-	-	-	F	-	MD	Moldova
-	-	-	-	-	MC	Monaco
-	-	-	-	-	MN	Mongolia
-	-	-	-	-	MS	Montserrat
-	-	-	-	-	MA	Morocco
-	-	-	-	-	MZ	Mozambique
-	-	-	-	-	MM	Myanmar
-	-	u	-	-	NA	Namibia
-	-	-	-	-	NR	Nauru
-	-	-	-	-	NP	Nepal
B	I	U	F	O	NL	Netherlands
-	-	-	-	-	AN	Netherlands Antilles
-	-	-	-	-	NT	Neutral Zone
-	-	u	-	-	NC	New Caledonia & Depend.
-	I	u	f	-	NZ	New Zealand
-	-	u	-	-	NI	Nicaragua
-	-	u	-	-	NE	Niger
-	-	-	-	-	NG	Nigeria
-	-	-	-	-	NU	Niue Island
-	-	-	-	-	NF	Norfolk Island
-	-	-	-	-	MP	Northern Mariana Islands
B	I	U	F	O	NO	Norway
-	-	-	-	-	OM	Oman
-	-	u	-	-	PK	Pakistan
-	-	-	-	-	PW	Palau
*	-	-	-	-	PA	Panama
-	-	u	-	-	PG	Papua New Guinea
-	-	u	-	-	PY	Paraguay
-	-	U	-	-	PE	Peru
-	-	u	F	-	PH	Philippines
-	-	-	-	-	PN	Pitcairn Island
b	I	U	F	-	PL	Poland
b	I	U	F	O	PT	Portugal
B	I	U	F	-	PR	Puerto Rico
-	-	-	-	-	QA	Qatar
-	-	-	-	-	RE	Reunion
-	*	-	-	-	RO	Romania
b	-	U	F	-	RU	Russia
-	-	-	-	-	RW	Rwanda
-	-	-	-	-	SH	Saint Helena
-	-	*	-	-	KN	Saint Kitts and Nevis
-	-	*	-	-	LC	Saint Lucia
-	-	-	-	-	PM	Saint Pierre and Miquelon
-	-	-	-	-	VC	Saint Vincent and the Grenadines
-	-	-	-	-	SM	San Marino
-	-	-	-	-	ST	Sao Tome and Principe
B	-	-	-	-	SA	Saudi Arabia
-	-	u	j	-	SN	Senegal
-	-	u	-	-	SC	Seychelles
-	-	-	-	-	SL	Sierra Leone
b	I	u	F	-	SG	Singapore
b	-	-	F	O	SI	Slovenia
-	-	-	-	-	SB	Solomon Islands
-	-	-	-	-	SO	Somalia
-	I	U	F	o	ZA	South Africa
-	-	-	-	-	ES	Spain

Bitnet	Internet	UUCP	Fidonet	OSI	Abr	Country
B	I	U	F	O	LK	Sri Lanka
-	-	u	-	-	SD	Sudan
-	-	-	-	-	SR	Suriname
-	-	-	-	-	SJ	Svalbard & Jan Mayen Is.
-	-	-	-	-	SZ	Swaziland
-	-	-	-	-	SE	Sweden
B	I	U	F	o	CH	Switzerland
B	I	U	F	O	SY	Syria
-	-	-	-	-	TW	Taiwan, Province of China
B	I	u	F	-	TJ	Tajikistan
-	-	u	-	-	TZ	Tanzania
-	-	-	j	-	TH	Thailand
-	-	-	F	-	TG	Togo
-	-	u	-	-	TK	Tokelau Islands
-	-	-	-	-	TO	Tonga
-	-	-	-	-	TT	Trinidad and Tobago
-	-	u	-	-	TN	Tunisia
b	I	u	j	-	TR	Turkey
-	-	-	-	-	TM	Turkmenistan
-	-	-	-	-	TC	Turks and Caicos Islands
-	-	-	-	-	TV	Tuvalu
-	-	u	-	-	UG	Uganda
-	-	-	-	-	UA	Ukraine
-	-	U	F	-	AE	United Arab Emirates
-	-	-	-	-	GB	United Kingdom
b	I	U	F	O	US	United States
B	I	U	F	O	UM	U. S. Minor Outlying Islands
-	-	-	-	-	UY	Uruguay
-	-	U	f	-	UZ	Uzbekistan
-	-	U	-	-	VU	Vanuatu
-	-	u	-	-	VA	Vatican City State
-	-	-	-	-	VE	Venezuela
-	I	U	-	-	VN	Vietnam
-	-	-	-	-	VG	Virgin Islands, British
-	-	-	-	-	VI	Virgin Islands, U.S.
-	*	-	-	-	WF	Wallis and Futuna Islands
-	-	-	-	-	EH	Western Sahara
-	-	-	-	-	WS	Western Samoa
-	-	-	-	-	YE	Yemen
-	-	-	-	-	YU	Yugoslavia
b	I	U	f	-	ZR	Zaire
-	-	-	-	-	ZM	Zambia
-	-	-	f	-	ZW	Zimbabwe
-	-	u	f	-		

BITNET	Entities with international BITNET links. BITNET is used generically to refer to BITNET plus similar networks around the world (e.g., EARN, NETNORTH, GULFNET, etc.). **b**: minimal, < 5 domestic sites **B**: widespread, >= 5 domestic sites
INTERNET	Entities with international IP links. **I**: = operational
UUCP	Entities with domestic UUCP sites which are connected to the Global Multiprotocol Open Internet.) **u**: minimal, < 5 domestic sites **U**: widespread, >= 5 domestic sites
FIDONET	Entities with international FIDONET links. **f**: minimal, < 5 domestic sites **F**: widespread, >= 5 domestic sites
OSI	Entities with networks offering X.400 services and which are connected to the Global Multiprotocol Open Internet. **o**: minimal, < 5 domestic sites **O**: widespread, >= 5 domestic sites

Possible e-mail connections to Angola, Gambia, Ghana, Malawi, Mongolia Reunion, and Tanzania have not been verified and hence are not included in the table or in the above totals.

The Antartica Internet connection appears to be intermittently online. There are Internet hosts in Guam but they do not respond to ping and hence are not included.

Please send corrections, information, and/or comments to:

Larry Landweber
Computer Sciences Dept.
University of Wisconsin - Madison
1210 W. Dayton St.
Madison, WI 53706
lhl@cs.wisc.edu
FAX +1 608 265 2635

Include details, e.g., on connection, sites, contacts, protocols, etc.

GOSIP DOCUMENT INFORMATION

GOSIP DOCUMENT INFORMATION

This information was compiled and made available by the National Institute of Standards and Technology (NIST).

August, 1991

Below is the information needed to obtain the U.S. GOSIP, NIST/OSI Implementors Workshop (OIW) documents, Government Network Management Profile (GNMP) documentation, GOSIP Users Guide, and GOSIP testing documentation. All prices quoted are in U.S. dollars and represent the most up-to-date information available at this time; for further pricing information and ordering details, contact the seller (all addresses and tele- phone numbers are found at the end of this bulletin).

Note: WordPerfect 5.1 files must be transferred in binary mode. A LaserWriter printer definition was used in creating the PostScript files. A commonly available set of fonts (for example, Helvetica 10-pt) must be available on your local printer for your local output to be correctly displayed. This applies to all WordPerfect 5.1 and PostScript files re-trievable on-line as indicated below.

GOSIP

GOSIP Version 1.

GOSIP Version 1 (Federal Information Processing Standard 146) was published in August 1988. It became mandatory in applicable federal procurements in August 1990.

Addenda to Version 1 of GOSIP have been published in the Federal Register and are included in Version 2 of GOSIP. Users should obtain Version 2.

GOSIP Version 2.

Version 2 became a Federal Information Processing Standard (FIPS) on April 3, 1991, and will be mandatory in federal procurements initiated eighteen months after that date, for the new functionality contained in Version 2. The Version 1 mandate continues to be in effect. Version 2 of GOSIP supersedes Version 1 of GOSIP. Version 2 of GOSIP makes clear what protocols apply to the GOSIP Version 1 mandate and what protocols are new for Version 2.

NIST Point of Contact:

hardcopy:
      Jerry Mulvenna

on-line:
      NTIS Sales Dept., FIPS 146-1, Price $17.00

      available through anonymous ftp from *osi.ncsl.nist.gov* (129.6.55.1) as
      ./pub/gosip/gosip_v2.txt   —ascii
      ./pub/gosip/gosip_v2.ps   —PostScript
      ./pub/gosip/gosip_v2.ps.Z   —PostScript Compressed
      ./pub/gosip/gosip_v2.w51   —WordPerfect 5.1

Note: Pictures are not included in the files given above.

NIST Workshop for Implementors of OSI Documents

The output of the NIST Workshop for Implementors of OSI (OIW) is a pair of aligned documents, one representing Stable Implementation Agreements (SIA), the other containing Working Implementation Agreements (WIA) that have not yet gone into the stable document. Material is in either one or the other of these documents, but not both, and the documents have the same index structure.

The SIA is reproduced in its entirety at the beginning of each calendar year, with an incremented version number. Replacement page sets are distributed subsequently three times during each year (after each Workshop), reflecting errata to the stable material, as well as new functionality declared stable. In this way an up-to-date document is maintained.

The WIA is reproduced in its entirety after each Workshop (held in March, June, September, and December). OIW attendees automatically receive the WIA, as well as the replacement pages to the SIA. The remaining 1991 meeting dates are September 9-13 and December 9-13. The 1992 meeting dates are: March 9-13, June 8-12, September 21-25, and December 14-18. All of the 1992 meetings are currently planned to be at NIST.

SIA documentation is available from the U.S. Government Printing Office (GPO), National Technical Information Service (NTIS), and the IEEE Computer Society. SIA documentation is also online, as described below.

Effective April 1991, WIA documentation is in draft form and not sold to the public. It will be distributed to Workshop attendees as usual. WIA documentation is also online, as described below.

NIST Points of Contact for the OIW:

Tim Boland   —management information
Chair, OIW

Brenda Gray   —administrative information
OIW Registrar

SIA, Version 4.

Version 4, Edition 1 of the SIA, Special Publication 500-183, has been published by NIST, and was distributed to Workshop attendees in March 1991. SIA, V4E1 is currently available from the U.S. Government Printing Office, and is expected to be available from the National Technical Information Service and the IEEE Computer Society. Version 4 supersedes Version 3. Version 4 contains all of the functionality (including errata) contained in Version 3, plus additional functionality.

NIST Point of Contact:

Tim Boland

hardcopy:

U.S. Government Printing Office
GPO Stock Number: 903-015-00000-4
Price: $59.00 (base document plus updates) - domestic
$73.75 (base document plus updates) - foreign
NTIS (base document)
Order Number: PB 91-171967
Price: $74.00 (paper); $21.50 (microfiche)
IEEE Computer Society Press
CSP# 2350
Price: $75.00, $60.00 (Member)

on-line:

available through anonymous ftp from osi.ncsl.nist.gov (129.6.55.1) as
./pub/oiw/agreements/XS-9106.stb —ascii (stable)
./pub/oiw/agreements/Xs-9106.w51—WordPerfect 5.1 (stable)
./pub/oiw/agreements/XW-9106.wk—ascii (working)
./pub/oiw/agreements/Xw-9106.w51—WordPerfect 5.1 (working)

Note: For the entire stable document, reference *stable-out.all.Z* for the ASCII file, and *Stable_w51.all.Z* for the WordPerfect 5.1 file. Helvetica fonts ranging in size from 8-pt through 30-pt were used in the preparation of the OIW files. In the above,

X is part number (1 to 23), where a part describes a particular piece of OSI functionality, and corresponds to a chapter of a book. To access each piece of the book, retrieve filenames with syntax described above. *9106* refers to the month (June) and year (1991) of the agreements that are on-line. For the entire working document, reference *work-out.all.Z* for the ASCII file, and *Work_w51.All.Z* for the WordPerfect 5.1 file. The *.Z* mentioned above indicates compressed mode.

GOSIP Users Guide

GOSIP Users Guide for GOSIP Version 2

The companion Users Guide for GOSIP Version 2 assists Federal agencies in planning for and procuring OSI. It provides tutorial information on OSI protocols as well as information on OSI registration, GOSIP technical evaluation, and GOSIP transition strategies. This document is currently available from the NIST ADP Standards Processing Coordinator (see end of list) and should be used instead of the GOSIP Version 1 Users Guide.

NIST Point of Contact:

Tim Boland

hardcopy:

NIST Standards Processing Coordinator (ADP) (see addresses at end)

on-line:

available through anonymous ftp from osi.ncsl.nist.gov (129.6.55.1) as
./pub/gug/X.txt   —ascii
./pub/gug/chs.all   —ascii (entire doc)
./pub/gug/chs.all.Z   —ascii (entire doc) compressed

Note: In the above, *X* denotes the part of the book being requested; it is either a chapter number (for example, ch10) or appendix (for example, appa). Figures given in the hardcopy are not provided on-line.

GOSIP testing

On August 15, 1990, NIST announced a testing program for GOSIP, FIPS 146. The program consists of two parts: 1) GOSIP Conformance Testing conducted by commercial laboratories accredited through the National Voluntary Laboratory Accreditation Program (NVLAP) and 2) multi-vendor interoperability testing conducted under the auspices of industry interoperability testing and registration services. This program is supported by a set of documents and registers that are available on-line.

NIST Point of Contact:

JP Favreau

hardcopy:

Standards Processing Coordinator (ADP) (see addresses at end)

on-line:

available through anonymous ftp from osi.ncsl.nist.gov (129.6.55.1) as
./pub/gosip.v1/X   —ascii

Note: In the above, *X* indcates any one of the following ASCII files:

MOT-Assessment.handbook

GOSIP Means of Testing Assessment handbook

NVLAP.handbook

NVLAP Handbook, Operational Requirements for the Laboratory Accreditation Program of Computer Applications

Testing for GOSIP Conformance Testing: Requirements for
Accreditation

regist-criteria.handbook

GOSIP registration criteria

testing-FIPS.draft

Final Draft for the future FIPS Guideline, GOSIP Conformance and Interoperation Testing and Registration

ats.reg   Register for GOSIP V1 Abstract Test Suites

product.reg

Register for GOSIP V1 Compliant Products

int-ats.reg

Register for GOSIP V1 Interoperability Test Suites

int-service.reg

Register for GOSIP V1 Interoperability Test Services

lab.reg   Register for GOSIP V1 NVLAP Accredited Laboratories

mot.reg   Register for GOSIP V1 Means of Testing

GNMP

Version 1 of the Government Network Management Profile (GNMP)
is being progressed as a Federal Information Processing Standard
(FIPS) for System and Network Management. The technical specification of V.1 GNMP is now available both on-line and in hardcopy.

NIST Point of Contact:

Fran Nielsen

hardcopy:

NIST Standards Processing Coordinator (ADP)

on-line:

available through anonymous ftp from osi.ncsl.nist.gov (129.6.55.1) as
./pub/gnmp/gnmp.ascii   —ascii
./pub/gnmp/gnmp.ps   —PostScript
./pub/gnmp/gnmp.ps.Z   —PostScript Compressed

NOTE: PostScript figures are in the files in the same subdirectory as
figN.ps where N = 1,2,.....,10

MHS Evaluation Guidelines

This document assists users in evaluating performance and functional characteristics of MHS implementations to determine which system is best for them.

NIST Point of Contact:

> Steve Trus

hardcopy:

> NTIS Sales Dept., Order # PB 90-269598
> Price: $23.00

on-line:

> available through anonymous ftp from osi.ncsl.nist.gov (129.6.55.1) as
> ./pub/eval_guide/mhs.doc.ps —PostScript
> ./pub/eval_guide/mhs.doc.ps.Z —PostScript Compressed

Note: Pictures are not included in the copy provided on-line.

Addresses/Telephone Numbers

> Jerry Mulvenna
> Technology, B217
> Gaithersburg, MD 20899
> (301) 975-3631
> mulvenna@osi.ncsl.nist.gov
>
> Tim Boland   —management information (OIW)
> Chairman, OIW
> Technology, B217
> Gaithersburg, MD 20899
> (301) 975-3608
> boland@ecf.ncsl.nist.gov
>
> Jean-Philippe Favreau
> Technology, B 141
> Gaithersburg, MD 20899
> (301) 975-3634
> favreau@osi.ncsl.nist.gov
>
> Brenda Gray   —administrative information (OIW)
> OIW Registrar
> Technology, B217
> Gaithersburg, MD 20899
> (301) 975-3664
>
> Fran Nielsen
> Technology, B-214
> Gaithersburg, MD 20899
> (301) 975-3669
> nielsen@osi.ncsl.nist.gov

Steve Trus
Technology, B-225
Gaithersburg, MD 20899
(301) 975-3617
trus@osi.ncsl.nist.gov

National Technical Information Service (NTIS)
U.S. Department of Commerce
5285 Port Royal Road
Springfield, VA 22161
(703)487-4650, FTS—737-4650

IEEE Computer Society Press
Order Department
10662 Los Vaqueros Circle
Los Alamitos, CA 90720
1-800-272-6657

U.S. Government Printing Office
Washington, DC 20402
(202) 783-3238

Standards Processing Coordinator (ADP)
National Institute of Standards and Technology
Technology Building, Room B-64
Gaithersburg, MD 20899
(301) 975-2816

INDEX